Bauman's Challenge

Also by Mark Davis
FREEDOM AND CONSUMERISM: A Critique of Zygmunt Bauman's Sociology

Also by Keith Tester
ANIMALS AND SOCIETY: The Humanity of Animal Rights
BAUMAN BEFORE POSTMODERNITY: Invitation, Conversations and Annotated Bibliography 1953–1989 (*co-authored*)
BAUMAN BEYOND POSTMODERNITY: Conversations, Critiques and Annotated Bibliography 1989–2005 (*co-authored*)
CIVIL SOCIETY
COMPASSION, MORALITY AND THE MEDIA
CONVERSATIONS WITH ZYGMUNT BAUMAN
ERIC ROHMER: Film as Theology
HUMANITARIANISM AND MODERN CULTURE
MEDIA, CULTURE AND MORALITY
MORAL CULTURE
THE FLANEUR (*edited*)
THE SOCIAL THOUGHT OF ZYGMUNT BAUMAN
THE INHUMAN CONDITION
THE LIFE AND TIMES OF POST-MODERNITY
THE TWO SOVEREIGNS: Social Contradictions of European Modernity

Bauman's Challenge

Sociological Issues for the 21st Century

Edited by

Mark Davis
University of Leeds, UK

and

Keith Tester
University of Hull, UK

palgrave
macmillan

First published 2010 by
PALGRAVE MACMILLAN

Palgrave Macmillan in the UK is an imprint of Macmillan Publishers Limited, registered in England, company number 785998, of Houndmills, Basingstoke, Hampshire RG21 6XS.

Palgrave Macmillan in the US is a division of St Martin's Press LLC, 175 Fifth Avenue, New York, NY 10010.

Palgrave Macmillan is the global academic imprint of the above companies and has companies and representatives throughout the world.

Palgrave® and Macmillan® are registered trademarks in the United States, the United Kingdom, Europe and other countries

ISBN 978-0-230-22134-5 hardback

This book is printed on paper suitable for recycling and made from fully managed and sustained forest sources. Logging, pulping and manufacturing processes are expected to conform to the environmental regulations of the country of origin.

A catalogue record for this book is available from the British Library.

A catalog record for this book is available from the Library of Congress.

10 9 8 7 6 5 4 3 2 1
19 18 17 16 15 14 13 12 11 10

Printed and bound in Great Britain by
CPI Antony Rowe, Chippenham and Eastbourne

Contents

Acknowledgements

The editors are grateful to all the contributors for the enthusiasm, goodwill and commitment with which they participated in this project. Collectively and individually they have all responded beyond our hopes to Bauman's challenge.

Mark Davis and Keith Tester dedicate this book with love, admiration and respect to the memory of Janina Bauman, 18 August 1926–29 December 2009.

Notes on Contributors

Zygmunt Bauman is Emeritus Professor of Sociology at the University of Leeds, UK. He is a globally prominent sociologist who has published numerous landmark works in an acclaimed career spanning over 40 years. Among his numerous publications, the most significant are *Legislators and Interpreters* (1987); *Modernity & the Holocaust* (1989), for which he was awarded the Amalfi Prize and the Adorno Prize; *Postmodern Ethics* (1993); *In Search of Politics* (1999); *Liquid Modernity* (2000); and *Society Under Siege* (2002). His most recent work includes *Liquid Life* (2005), *Liquid Fear* (2006), *Consuming Life* (2007) and *The Art of Life* (2008).

Peter Beilharz is Professor of Sociology and Director of the Thesis Eleven Centre for Cultural Sociology at La Trobe University, Australia. He has written and edited 23 books, six of them on Zygmunt Bauman. His most recent is *Socialism and Modernity* (University of Minnesota Press, 2009). He is presently writing studies of Australian modernity and working on collaborative books on Jean Martin, the founding mother of Australian sociology and on the history of rock music in Australia.

Tony Blackshaw teaches social and cultural studies in sport and leisure at Sheffield Hallam University. He is author of *Key Concepts in Community Studies* (Sage, 2009), *Zygmunt Bauman* (Routledge, 2005) and *Leisure Life: Myth, Masculinity and Modernity* (Routledge, 2003). He is also the co-author of *The Sage Dictionary of Leisure Studies* (Sage, 2009) and *New Perspectives on Sport and 'Deviance': Consumption, Performativity and Social Control* (Routledge, 2004). His current projects involve a forthcoming book on Leisure (Routledge) and a study on the life and oral history at Leeds, which is making an attempt to follow in the footsteps of Richard Hoggart.

Tom Campbell is a final year doctoral candidate at the school of Sociology and Social Policy, University of Leeds, UK. His thesis is concerned with writing a genealogy of dyslexia, where dyslexia is considered as an event in the history of reading. He is joint-editor of the book *Disability Studies: Emerging Insights and Perspectives* (The Disability Press, 2008) and has contributed the chapter 'Towards a Sociology of Impairment?' to that collection. His wider work also considers the relationships between ontologies of resistance and ethics.

Mark Davis is Lecturer in Sociology and Director of the Bauman Institute at the University of Leeds, UK. He is author of *Freedom and Consumerism: A Critique of Zygmunt Bauman's Sociology* (Ashgate, 2008) and has written on various aspects of Bauman's sociology. His ongoing research interests are focused upon the social and political consequences of consumerism, in particular how freedom and choice can be reconciled with the challenge of creating fairer, more sustainable and more stable societies around the world. He is currently working as an advisor to the Council of Europe on creating a 'Europe of Shared and Social Responsibilities' (DGIII/DCS 2009: 13).

Mark Featherstone is Senior Lecturer in Sociology at Keele University, UK. He works in the area of utopias and dystopias and has recently published a research monograph, *Tocqueville's Virus: Utopia and Dystopia in Western Social and Political Thought* (Routledge, 2007), on this subject. He is currently writing the second volume of this study, *Planet Utopia: Utopia, Dystopia, and Globalisation,* which is also scheduled to be published by Routledge.

Kieran Flanagan is Reader in Sociology at the University of Bristol, UK. His first book was *Sociology in Liturgy: Re-Presentations of the Holy* (1991). With Peter C. Jupp he has edited *Postmodernity, Sociology and Religion* (1996), *Virtue Ethics and Sociology: Issues of Modernity and Religion* (2001) and *A Sociology of Spirituality* (2007). Recently, he has written essays on conversion and on naming and the place of religious belief in the relationships between sociology and theology. His latest book is *Sociology in Theology: Reflexivity and Belief* (2007). His current projects are on Charles Taylor, and his forthcoming book is titled *Sociology at Prayer: Utterances in the Wilderness.*

Stjepan G. Mestrovic is Professor of Sociology at Texas A&M University, USA. He is the author of over 15 books in the area of social theory, including *The Coming Fin de Siecle: An Application of Durkheim's Sociology to Modernity and Postmodernity* (1991), *Durkheim and Postmodern Culture* (1992), *The Barbarian Temperament: Towards a Postmodern Critical Theory* (1993) and *Postemotional Society* (1997). He is also a distinguished expert in matters of war crimes and genocide and has recently published *The Trials of Abu Ghraib: An Expert Witness Account of Shame and Honor* (2007) and *Rules of Engagement? A Social Anatomy of an American War Crime – Operation Iron Triangle, Iraq* (2008).

John O'Neill is Distinguished Research Professor of Sociology at York University, Toronto, Canada. He is a Member of the Centre for

Comparative Literature at the University of Toronto and a Fellow of the Royal Society of Canada. He was Senior Scholar at the Laidlaw Foundation 1993–4, working on the Children at Risk Programme. He is co-editor of the *International Quarterly*, *Philosophy of the Social Sciences* and *The Journal of Classical Sociology*. He is author of *Incorporating Cultural Theory: Maternity at the Millennium* (2002), *The Poverty of Postmodernism* (1995) and *Critical Conventions: Interpretation in the Literary Arts and Sciences* (1992). Currently, he is working on the political economy of child suffering, welfare state theory and civic practice.

William Outhwaite studied at the Universities of Oxford and Sussex, where he taught for many years. He is now Professor of Sociology at Newcastle University. He is author of *Habermas: A Critical Introduction* (Polity Press, 1994) and editor of *The Blackwell Dictionary of Twentieth-Century Social Thought* (Blackwell, 1993). His recent publications include *Social Theory and Postcommunism* (Blackwell, 2005, with Larry Ray), *The Future of Society* (Blackwell, 2006) and *European Society* (Polity, 2008). He is currently working on social and political change in Europe since 1989, supported by a Leverhulme Major Research Fellowship.

Abby Peterson is Professor of Sociology at the University of Gothenburg, Sweden. She has published extensively within the field of political and cultural sociology and is the author of *Contemporary Political Protest: Essays on Political Militancy* (Ashgate, 2001), joint-editor of *The Policing of Transnational Protest* (Ashgate, 2006, with Donatella della Porta and Herbert Reiter) and co-editor of the journal *Acta Sociologica*. She is presently directing research on protest mobilization in Europe and on policing organized crime in Sweden.

Paul A. Taylor is Senior Lecturer in Communications Theory at the University of Leeds, UK. His ongoing research interests are focused upon critical theories of mass culture. Founding editor of the *International Journal of Žižek Studies* and Editorial Board member of the *International Journal of Baudrillard Studies*, his recent and forthcoming monographs include *Digital Matters: The Culture and Theory of the Matrix* (Routledge, 2005), *Critical Theories of Mass Culture: Then and Now* (Open University Press, 2008) and *Žižek and the Media* (forthcoming).

Keith Tester is Professor of Sociology at the University of Hull. He is an Honorary Member of the Thesis Eleven Centre for Cultural Sociology at La Trobe University, Australia, and a Fellow of the Royal Society of Arts. He is on the editorial boards of *The Journal of Classical Sociology*, *Journal of Human Rights* and *Thesis Eleven*. His main research interests are the entwinement of culture and morality; the heritage of critical theory, especially the social thought of Zygmunt Bauman; as well as questions of film and theology. His major publications include *Media, Culture and Morality* (Routledge, 1994), *Moral Culture* (Sage, 1997), *Conversations with Zygmunt Bauman* (Polity, 2001) and *The Social Thought of Zygmunt Bauman* (Palgrave Macmillan, 2004). His recent publications are *Eric Rohmer: Film as Theology* (Palgrave Macmillan, 2008) and *Humanitarianism and Modern Culture* (Penn State University Press, 2010).

Chris Till is a doctoral candidate in the School of Social Policy and Sociology at the University of Leeds, UK. His thesis is on the emergence of male anorexia nervosa in psychiatric literature. He is co-editor of the book *Disability Studies: Emerging Insights and Perspectives* (The Disability Press, 2008) and has contributed the chapter 'Male Anorexia Nervosa: Risk, Subjectivity and Disability' to that collection.

Editors' Introduction

Mark Davis and Keith Tester

What challenges do we face at the start of the 21st century? Amidst a global economic recession and the growing importance of adaptation to climate change, individual men and women are also increasingly uncertain of how simply to go about the business of their everyday lives. The consumer model of the life-project – such a seemingly dominant and legitimate pattern for each of us to follow, or to aspire to, until very recently – is now seen as overly one-dimensional and increasingly targeted for blame as answers are sought to larger natural and social problems. Within this broader context, a number of core social problems have led to the very foundations of our global societies being reconsidered and re-examined. Whether it is as an ongoing re-evaluation of Enlightenment values such as freedom, truth, justice and reason, or as a robust analysis of ideological thought in the hope of a progressive politics of the future, sociology is made to the measure of such a world; the ambitious critique of everyday life that the discipline offers is perfectly placed to provide an invaluable commentary on precisely those social processes that are shaping our individual lives in the global societies of the 21st century.

One of the most prominent global sociologists of our times is Zygmunt Bauman. His work continues to narrate the existential and experiential aspects of what it means to be human in the uncertain times of an era that he has described in his later writings as 'liquid modern'. As the 'conclusion' to this collection, Bauman himself outlines what he sees as the 'triple challenge' that faces men and women at the start of the 21st century – the urgent need to reunite power with politics, to rethink our understanding of notions of risk and uncertainty and to seek genuinely global solutions to global problems – each of which are challenges that require a uniquely *sociological* insight, in order to grasp fully the complex social, political, cultural and economic aspects of our emerging global age.

This unique and original collection by internationally renowned scholars and emergent talent within the discipline uses critical engagements with Bauman's sociology to identify and better understand those diverse challenges that face globalized human societies at the start of the 21st century, including the future of Europe, at a time when political power appears evermore fragmented; global social exclusion; ethics and morality in the face of epistemological and ontological uncertainty wrought by the challenge of relativism; the changing role of religion and theology in social life; the increasing bureaucratization and micro-management of everyday life and the challenge this presents to genuine critical thinking; and the enduring significance of sociology as a discipline that continues to address these challenges in evermore dynamic and insightful ways. Throughout each of the original contributions included here, the concern is to go beyond mere exegesis on Bauman and, instead, to show the multifarious and manifest uses to which his work might be put and the contemporary issues that it reveals.

Each contribution to the collection was prepared separately and is thus self-contained, although there is much to be gained from reading each of the chapters in relation to others, as salient ideas and issues are considered anew and in different ways by different authors. It is our opinion as editors that a detailed synopsis of the individual chapters is unnecessary here, as the quality and accessibility of each of them means that they work extremely well in their own right and we do not see it as our role to guide the reader in how the collection should be read. That is to say, the collection flows in such a way that it can be read linearly – moving roughly sequentially through those related issues and concerns noted above – but it is also illuminating to approach the collection in a more circuitous way. That is, in following Bauman's own epistemological principle that knowledge is circular rather than linear, and that we do not move from vulnerable to less vulnerable forms of knowledge, we believe that the collection also works more as a prism, shedding light both on aspects of Bauman's sociology and also on those sociological challenges that face each of us at the start of the 21st century.

1
Bauman's Europe; Europe's Bauman

William Outhwaite

Zygmunt Bauman is of course an extraordinary theorist,[1] but I shall discuss here some of the ways in which he may be seen to exemplify a number of typical sites or predicaments.

First, and most parochially, he is one of the clusters of immigrants who fundamentally shaped British sociology and social theory in the second half of the 20th century. They include Stanislaw Andreski, Gi Baldamus, Zevedei Barbu, Julius Carlebach, Percy Cohen, Ralf Dahrendorf, Norbert Elias, Ernest Gellner, Stuart Hall, Karl Mannheim, Ilya Neustadt, Karl Popper, John Rex, Teodor Shanin, Alfred Sohn-Rethel, and Sami Zubaida. Bauman's age puts him among the younger members of this list, but he settled in the UK much later than most of the others and his rise to prominence also came later, in the late 1970s and 1980s, at a time when a more 'continental' style of social theory was becoming more dominant.[2]

Secondly, he is part of a specifically Polish cohort which includes the sociologist Maria Hirszowicz, the philosopher Leszek Kołakowski and the economist Włodzimierz Brus, who were driven out of Poland at the same time and on the same counter-Socratic grounds that they had corrupted students and encouraged their oppositional activity. To this cohort one could add, from an earlier wave of emigration, Czesław Miłosz (1911–2004), who lived in France and the US but whose work was very influential in the UK as well, and Stanislaw Andreski (1919–2007), who founded Sociology at Reading, where Hirszowicz also taught. Thirdly, like Brus, Hirszowicz and Kołakowski, though unlike Andreski, Bauman is part of an ex-communist cohort, joining in Britain an ex–communist left which has been exceptionally important in the country's intellectual life.[3]

Of the contemporary European social theorists with whom Bauman might be compared, the most obvious are perhaps Bourdieu, Derrida, Eco, Foucault, Giddens, Habermas and Žižek. Despite the untimely death of three of them, all continue to be central to social and cultural theory in the early 21st century, as well as holding or having held significant roles as public intellectuals.[4] Each is or was firmly grounded in their native or, in Bauman's case, adopted country, while having a major presence in the rest of Europe.

Bauman has probably been the most reluctant to embrace the role of public intellectual, which accrued largely as a result of his accelerating output of stunningly original and stimulating work in social theory and partly also because of the transformation of Eastern Europe and Russia from the late 1980s onwards. He received the Amalfi European Prize in 1990 and the Adorno Prize in 1998. He is emeritus professor both at Leeds and at Warsaw, and to date has honorary degrees from Vilnius, Prague, London, Bristol and New York.

The comprehensive bibliography in Kilminster and Varcoe (1996) illustrates, at least from the supply side, some main lines of the reception of his work. Initially he writes, not surprisingly, mostly in Polish for a Polish audience (with the exception of some short publications in Israel and the US), though focusing substantially on the United States and Britain, where he studied working-class history in the second half of the 1950s. A brief flurry of publications in Czechoslovakia coincides with the Prague Spring, after which (apart from an article in Yugoslavia) the scene shifts to the West (where the 1989 revolutions and their aftermath later inspire a similar flow of occasional publications).

An earlier Polish work appears in 1971 in Italian translation, setting a pattern for more or less simultaneous publication of his work which may say as much about the openness of Italian publishing as about Bauman's reputation in that country, high though of course it is. Italy certainly makes a sharp contrast with France, where there appears to be no book in the period covered and only articles in 1967 and 1970 in the Marxist *L' Homme et la Société*, followed by another only in 1992, in Michel Maffesoli's cosmopolitanly oriented journal *Sociétés*. A German translation of *Modernity and the Holocaust* appeared with a three-year lag in 1992 (embellished with the supratitle *Dialektik der Ordnung*), followed by regular translations of subsequent works.[5] In Sweden, *Modernity and the Holocaust* was translated immediately and this also initiated regular translations there and in Denmark. *Towards a Critical Sociology* had been published in Brazil in 1977, and *Culture as Praxis* in Serbian in 1984.

The first Polish translation, of *Modernity and Ambivalence*, was in 1991, the year of its British and US publication.

France was, then, until recently the exception to this rising trend, although Bauman follows the French scene closely, engages substantially with French social thought and is as comfortable in French as in any of his other languages. For some reason, then, Bauman did not benefit from the *ouverture* of French publishers to translations of foreign works which seems to have begun sometime in the mid-1980s. Catherine Portevin, in her introduction to an interview with Bauman in Télérama.fr no. 2039, following the French publication of *Legislators and Interpreters* as *La Décadence des intellectuels*, wrote that 'his thought is still little known in France, where it is often badly translated and published in scraps without any chronological logic'.[6] It is apparently only in the middle of the present decade that Bauman's intellectual presence in France began to catch up with that of elsewhere in Europe.

Turning to the sociological and related journals, the *Polish Sociological Review* (formerly *Bulletin*) and *Czech Sociological Review* have each produced special issues on Bauman (in 2006), as have *Theory, Culture and Society* in the UK (1998) and *Revista Anthropos* in Barcelona (2005). In France, there have been shorter discussions and an interview in *L'Esprit* (Chardel, 2005; Desaunay, Foessel and Padis, 2005) and *La Pensée* (Tosel, 2006). His principal interpreters are in the UK (Dennis Smith and Keith Tester, more recently Anthony Elliott, Tony Blackshaw and Mark Davis),[7] Australia (Peter Beilharz) and Denmark (Michael Hviid Jacobsen). In Germany, Jens Kastner and Thomas Kron wrote their doctoral theses on Bauman (Kastner, 2000; Kron, 2001). Kron edited a book on him with Matthias Junge, now in its second edition and including contributions from a wide range of German authors as well as some of the usual suspects from the English-language literature (Junge and Kron, 2002; 2007); Junge has since published a monograph on him (2006).

So much for Europe's Bauman. Bauman's Europe was shaped, then, in a much sharper way than for a Western European, by its partition after World War II. What he wrote of the Bulgarian–French theorist Tzvetan Todorov, that he was 'well placed [to address the question of European values] thanks to a biography that spanned both sides of what some people see as Europe's outer frontier', is also true, *mutatis mutandis*, of himself.[8] A duality which for Western sociologists was a resource for theory construction, whether of industrial society (with or without convergence) or totalitarianism which was a permanent lived reality in the East, between, as Yevtushenko ironically put it, 'the city of no and the city of yes'.[9]

Bauman's early work in English has been well discussed by Dennis Smith (1999: chapter 5), and James Satterwhite (1992) puts it and related Polish-language work in its regional context.[10] After he left Poland, as Smith (1999: 71) again notes, the tone is rather of someone showing you round a house where they previously lived, pointing out its drawbacks but also its strengths. Bauman's article of 1971 was printed along with a friendly critique from Kołakowski, arguing that he was too pessimistic about the prospects for radical change.

> Is the demand for freedom the affair of a handful of intellectuals and are these societies insensitive to political slavery or at least ready to accept it? If we tried to answer this question by asking what percentage of the population is for the time being committed to the active struggle for political freedom, the figures would not be impressive, to be sure. But this way of inquiry would be unreliable, to put it mildly, as an attempt to discover historical trends.
>
> (Kołakowski, 1971: 56)

And contrary to Bauman's developmentalist assumption that the consolidation of the economic and social transformation in post-war Poland conduces to stability, Kołakowski argues that 'the less this population feels to be violently torn out of its "natural" condition, the more adapted to industrial life, the more educated, the more open to the variety of life, the greater its ability to develop a class consciousness and to resist exploitation' (Kołakowski, 1971: 58). A decade later, of course, the rise of Solidarity gave Kołakowski the last laugh – which is not of course to say that Bauman was wrong in his account, which he substantially modified in the 1980s (Smith, 1999: chapter 7).

1989 led, not surprisingly, to a number of retrospective pieces on the causes of the revolutions. After this, Bauman's work turned more to themes which were less geographically focused – the axis of differentiation, where there was one, being sometimes between Europe and North America and sometimes between the global North and South. His book on the Holocaust, which I discuss below, does of course have a precise geographical referent, though here again he is concerned with general implications as much as the specifics of what happened in central and eastern Europe.

When he turned specifically to the theme of Europe, in a short book which grew out of an invited lecture, he offers a fairly familiar narrative of the integration process before focusing on the more worrying dynamic of exclusion which increasingly accompanies it. There is also however a darker theme, again linking Stalinist rule by terror with capitalist insecurity, *Unsicherheit* or 'précarité'.[11] The capitalist version has been a major concern of Bauman's recent work, notably in *Society Under Siege*. It is easy to see why it would. It is a dominant feature of much social analysis, notably by Beck and Sennett, as well as several of the French theorists on whom Bauman draws substantially. But it also points to a theory of domination which can be traced perhaps to some of his earlier analysis, of Stalinism and of the Holocaust, as well as to his personal experience as a cog in the repressive apparatus and, for a much longer period, as its victim.

This theme can be found in his early work, rounded off in 1982 by *Memories of Class*. Ian Varcoe and Richard Kilminster, in their superb 'Addendum' to the Festschrift which they edited in 1996, note this aspect of factory regulations documented by the Hammonds. Bauman is struck by the Foucauldian implications of these pointless regulations: 'full domination over workers' bodies' (Bauman, 1982: 63).[12] Kilminster and Varcoe (1982: 220–21) go on to relate this to Bauman's analysis of the 'means testing' of welfare claimants and of his book on the Holocaust. Without going into the details of their discussion here, or of the massive debates around Bauman's analysis of the Holocaust, it is perhaps worth pointing to a feature of pre-Holocaust anti-Semitic policy which jumps out from memoirs such as those by Karl Löwith and Viktor Klemperer: the fine distinctions the Nazis drew not just between 'full' and fractional Jews but between the partial and temporary immunities from persecution conferred by military service in World War I and even certain types of resulting disablement. Specialists may disagree on how far such processes of classification and exclusion contributed to making the Holocaust possible, but no one would deny that they played some role, as did the underlying alleged distinction between Jew and non-Jew (Bauman, 1998).

Hans Joas, in his discussion of *Modernity and the Holocaust* and its German reception, also points to this theme and situates it in the context of Bauman's work as a whole. 'When we read what he has to say about postmodernity we may be seduced into characterizing him as an optimist. But when we study his analysis of modernity we may actually be frightened to see how much he describes it as a narration of terror' (Joas, 1998: 51). Joas goes on to refer to a significant contribution by Bauman to a conference on 'modernity and barbarism'. Bauman has of course since moved on from the simple antithesis of modern and postmodern, and he would probably accept something more like Peter Wagner's more nuanced account of the duality of modernity, but the underlying theme remains potent. In *Society Under Siege* he focuses on contemporary management strategies as he had done earlier on Victorian factory regulations. The uncertain life expectancy of contemporary institutions is not a mere by-product of capitalist concentration or globalization. As Richard Sennett, Daniel Cohen and others have shown, it is explicitly pursued as a management strategy of control, and fuelled by incentives. In Sennett's analysis, writes Bauman, 'perfectly viable businesses are gutted or abandoned, capable employees are set adrift rather than rewarded, simply because the organization must prove to the market that it is capable of change'. At an individual level, what is required is a kind of entrepreneurship, flexibility and networking, rather than the traditional white-collar employee's bureaucratically and hierarchically framed loyalty. Employees, as Cohen puts it, have to 'demonstrate to the company that they have done their job well'. In practice, this will tend to mean meeting artificially set targets both for 'performance' and for more tenuous interpersonal qualities of cooperativeness: 'it is now the subjectivity of the worker which is at issue.' Something like this is now seen also in education: school and university students are increasingly graded not only on their performance on increasingly denatured assessment exercises but on qualities such as 'co-operativeness' or 'ability to work in a group' – even when the task in view is something as solitary as the writing of a PhD thesis in the humanities. Such generalization of a compulsory *Sittlichkeit* of politeness is, as Bauman would no doubt agree, the death of any genuine morality of the kind for which he has argued at length.

This degradation of working life is of course mirrored and sometimes replaced, in Bauman's analysis, by the alienation of consumption. An early version of this critique, in *Memories of Class*, brings out this parallelism: deprived young people

> belong to the first generation about to be squeezed finally out of the role of producers and goaded into a status determined by consumption alone; the first generation not to undergo the body-and-mind drill administered by the factory-located disciplining powers, but trained solely in the new consumer discipline, aimed at eliciting proper responses to proper offers. The consumer orientation, first developed as a by-product, and an outlet, of the industrial pattern of control, has been finally prised from the original stem and transformed into a self-sustained and self-perpetuating form of life. This transformation certainly calls for a new type of power, in many respects sharply different from the disciplining power, specializing in the bodily drill, which made possible the advent of industrial society.
>
> (p. 179)

The centrality of the theme of suffering, and particularly what Lévinas calls 'useless suffering' to Bauman's work has recently been well brought out by Michael Hviid Jacobsen and Sophia Marshman (2008). As they note (p. 15), his focus is on the suffering of social collectivities rather than of individuals. It is also arguably more on the *production* than on the experience of suffering: the structural conditions which generate it, often via the disabling of human sympathy in the minds of the perpetrators of suffering. In his very illuminating *Conversations* with Keith Tester, he refers to this process as 'disempowering the moral sense' (Bauman and Tester, 2001: 132).[13]

The theme of suffering, of course, goes along with those of fear and insecurity in an unholy trinity. We have largely got rid of the sort of pervasive state terror which characterized Stalinism and to some extent the post-Stalinist regimes. In return we have *précarité* in employment and in our personal lives, the final apotheosis of Beck's 'risk society' in its environmental dimension as well as others, and now a financial catastrophe affecting or likely to affect, pretty much, the entire globe.[14] The mismatch between what we ought to worry about (climate change, starvation etc.) and what we do worry about (the off-chance of a terrorist getting on a plane with a concealed weapon)[15] is probably as great as it had been since we ceased to worry about the fate of our immortal souls (as, of course, some people still do). Bauman (2004: 82) puts it very well:

> The security we fear for, about which we are told and encouraged and groomed to be fearful, while being promised by the powers-that-be that it will be granted, is no longer the kind of security Roosevelt or Beveridge had in mind. It is not the security of our place in society, of personal dignity, of honour of workmanship, self-respect, human understanding and humane treatment, but instead a security of the body and personal belongings. It is not security from those who refuse us jobs or deny our humanity when we are in a job, from those who take away our self-respect, and humiliate or dishonour us – but a security against trespassers on our property and strangers at the doorway, prowlers and beggars in the streets, sexual offenders at home and outside, poisoners of wells and hijackers of planes.

How might an analysis of this kind be brought more specifically to bear on Europe as a region of globality? The answer must be in part historical. It was in Europe, though soon afterwards in North America, that factory production became common, and it was Europe which gave the world totalitarianism in its Stalinist and fascist forms. The normalization of bodies and minds has been pushed further in modern Europe than elsewhere. And yet Europe still displays a diversity of belief and a degree of secularization which stands out on a world scale.[16] France, where the term 'pensée unique' was coined, is one of the main sites of intellectual resistance to neoliberal orthodoxy, even if the French managers studied by Cohen are not so different from Sennett's North Americans. In a rather upbeat passage in his first 'conversation' with Keith Tester (Bauman and Tester, 201: 31), Bauman says,

> Europe is the pluralist culture *avant la lettre*. In that lay its strength, and perhaps even its uniqueness ... we may say that that Europe could be seen as a greenhouse of universal humanity because of its amazing aptitude for communicating across the cultural (or any other) divides.

Here, as elsewhere, Bauman's focus is properly on European modernity, or now, in his terms, liquid modernity, rather than on regional specificities. There is however a sense in which Europe does stand out for the particular way in which European cosmopolitanism (a term which he says he dislikes, presumably for its overtones of self-congratulation), coexists with an inward-looking attitude for which the outside world is some sort of threat. Bauman, like Balibar, Kristeva, Todorov and many other theorists,[17] is particularly concerned with Europe's treatment of residents of non-European origin or descent. Another source of anxiety would be Europe's long-standing indifference to the harmful effects of the Common Agricultural Policy on producers in less developed countries. A third might be the well-meaning bumbling of some of the European Union's poorly coordinated diplomatic initiatives. To say that the EU's record is better in these areas than that of the United States (especially under the Bush II administration) may be true but is beside the point, since the EU sets itself, and is measured against, higher standards than a mere national state. For the EU, the standards themselves are permanently up for question, along with so much else of its operations. The erosion of social policy too, to which Bauman has rightly directed much of his attention and which is illustrated by the quotation above, is more dramatic in a region which since the time of Bismarck (!) has prided itself on its achievements in this area.

It is clear that Bauman roams intellectually, and to substantial extent also physically, around Europe. An hour or two on the Internet yields a whole raft of interviews with Europe-wide and in some cases pan-European media in which he surveys its political and social condition with acute observations. On the whole though, he is interested in commonalities and examples which illustrate general developmental trends, rather than detailed and systematic differences between its component states and regions. As he writes of corporatism in *Memories of Class*, in a chapter which ranges back to Walras as well as across the capitalist Europe of the 1980s, the diversity of policies and institutions conceal the general corporatist trend. 'It is all too easy to overlook the forest behind the trees and to take policy proclamations for reversals of history' (p. 159). Earlier, as he established himself in the West, he refused the role of 'area specialist' or 'sovietologist' (Bauman and Tester, 2006: 273) and commented on affairs in the communist world only in relation to specific events such as the rise of Solidarity (Bauman, 1980; 1992).[18]

As he notes in another interview (Jacobsen and Tester, 2005, reprinted in Tester and Jacobsen, 2006: 269) many of his earlier criticisms of Poland and communism turned out to apply to the West as well:

> When working on [an essay on the sociological profession – Bauman, 19] I thought ... that I was trying to resolve a thoroughly local and hopefully temporary, Polish (or the 'socialist camp's') dilemma, which arose from the authoritarian nature of the political regime and from its bid to manage everything and eliminate the un-manageable ... I just did not realise at the time that the local Polish experience was but an extreme and particularly festering specimen of a contention that in the plight of sociology was neither incidental nor local.

Europe, which has clutched to its bosom the slogan of soft power, for reasons which are all too obvious, is centrally concerned by the way in which political power has fragmented under modern conditions. In an interview in 2005 with German Radio, reprinted in the magazine *Freitag*, Bauman suggests that power has migrated:

- upwards, to a global space dominated by multinational enterprises, leaving governments the choice between 'the destruction of the economy and the destruction of the society'
- sideways, through 'deregulation' which deprives national states of many of the powers they previously enjoyed
- downwards, as cost-cutting governments demand that citizens take more action to guard themselves against risks.

There is, again, nothing specifically European about these processes except that the legitimacy of European states has substantially relied on the provision of economic security and the idea that this is a legitimate focus of politics. 'The budding European federation is now facing the task of repeating the feat accomplished by the nation state of early modernity: the task of bringing together power and politics presently separated and navigating in different directions' (Bauman, 2004: 131).

This process of political alienation, as analysed by a host of thinkers from Marx (1844) to Régis Debray (1981) leads, not surprisingly, to estrangement *from* politics. As Vivien Schmidt (2006) and others have shown, the European Union is stuck in what I have elsewhere called a non-decision trap (Outhwaite, 2010), in which the democratic deficit at the Union level reinforces that in the national states. An exception, if there is one, might be found in Western countries like Italy and in a number of new members from the East, where the European level is seen as a counter to local problems, but the evidence in the latter case is rather disappointing so far.

Bauman's sociology, like his public interventions, is not, as *Spiegel* once wrote of Luhmann, 'above the clouds'. It is grounded, not so much in empirical *data*, as in striking *examples* selected with a keen eye to the telling illustration of a theme which might otherwise seem speculative. He is not so much a sociologist *of* Europe as a European sociologist with a worldwide reputation. And, as he would no doubt say, what do they know of Europe, who only Europe know?

Notes

1. Peter Wagner puts it well in his endorsement to Peter Beilharz's *Bauman Reader* (2001): 'a European intellectual of the old style who is entirely up to the exigencies of our time'.
2. Dennis Smith (1999) perceptively discusses this aspect of Bauman's career.
3. Not of course without some uncomfortable moments, such as E. P. Thompson's savage critique discussed by Keith Tester (2006).
4. Such roles may be sought out deliberately or, more usually, by the result of invitations. These may be nationally based, as when the BBC invites Giddens to deliver a lecture series; internationally, as when the German Book Trade invites the Polish/British Bauman to receive its Prize; or when the Polish paper *Polityka* invites Michnik and Habermas to a debate published there and in *Die Zeit* (Habermas and Michnik 1993); or transnationally/European as in the case of the Charlemagne Prize or contributions to pan-European media such as *Eurozine*. Interventions will most often be national but may be transnational in their origin and/or destination, as in the joint declaration by Habermas and Derrida (2003). For a tentative discussion of the internationalization or Europeanization of such activities see Outhwaite (2008).

5. Hans Joas (1998: 49) discusses the enormous impact of this book in Germany, which had only recently been through the *Historikerstreit*: 'you might imagine what it meant to Germans when a Jewish sociologist from Poland and Britain was understood to say that the Holocaust is not absolutely incomparable and not due to the particularities of German history. Such a voice could not be ignored – it truly had to be taken seriously because it is not possible in this case to derive the ideas from ideological intentions to whitewash the guilt and responsibility of the German people.'
6. Cf. Le Guay (2007).
7. Richard Kilminster and Ian Varcoe also deserve a mention for their superb Festschrift and their own very substantial contributions in it.
8. Although no one could seriously deny that Bulgaria and, a fortiori, Poland, are part of Europe, the important point is the fact of division.
9. Yevgeny Yevtushenko, '**Между городом нет и городом да**'. As Bauman says of the Western discussion of the carnevalesque 1968, 'It struck me right away that when Warsaw students took to the streets, no one laughed' (Tester and Jacobsen, 2006: 274).
10. In an autobiographical memoir, another Polish sociologist, Piotr Sztompka (2008; 191–2), recalls that the two books of the 1960s which most influenced him as a student were Ossowski's on the peculiarities of the social sciences (Ossowski, 1962) and one by Bauman: '*An Outline of the Marxist theory of Society* (1964) was the title, and that was where the Marxism ended. Instead, the astute student could find a quite adept discussion of the works of Parsons, Merton, Lundberg, Lazarsfeld, Lasswell, and Mills. All this was adorned with some lip service give to a number of Soviet thinkers, the required dosage of "political correctness" at the time.'
11. The German and French terms are not added just for decoration. The former, has multiple senses shading into Angst, while the latter has formed a major focus of public debate in France, linked to the earlier theme of the *nouveaux pauvres*, a term which has not caught on in Britain to quite the same extent, though it probably will now in the aftermath of the credit crash and recession.
12. This ties in, of course, with his general tendency to focus on social order as 'the common denominator of other modern undertakings: industrialism, capitalism, democracy ... The longing for human-made order lubricated the wheels of the three "society-centred" modern pursuits' (Bauman and Tester, 2001: 78; see also Beilharz, 2006).
13. In an earlier conversation (p. 25) he speaks of learning from Marx his 'disgust for all forms of socially produced injustice, the urge to debunk the lies in which the social responsibility for human misery tends to be wrapped and thus removed from view, and the urge to smell a rat whenever a clamp on human freedom is contemplated or justified'.
14. It was not surprising that the most recent congress of the German Sociological Association (2008) took as its theme 'unsichere Zeiten'.
15. See for example Bauman (2005).
16. As I write these lines, the news is that some London buses will carry for a time the message: 'God probably doesn't exist, so why not stop worrying and enjoy your life'. And as Bauman notes (Bauman and Tester, 2001: 29), 'Europe never invented a concept of anti-European activity'.

17. Not to mention, of course, the large number of specialists in this area, such as Yasemin Soysal and Tariq Modood in the UK.
18. Interestingly, Agnes Heller (1978: 157–8) took a similar line on leaving Hungary for Australia, in an interview with *Telos*.

> 'My persistent advocacy of leftist radicalism and radical Marxist philosophy necessitated a relativization of Eastern Europe, insofar as I identify more with the concerns and endeavours of leftist radicals of the Western world. For them, Eastern Europe is an inevitable warning. Leszek Kołakowski has made a different choice; he remains deeply committed to Eastern Europe.
>
> The greatest concern of Eastern Europe was and remains the liberation of civil society and the guaranteeing of civil liberties. I never intended to cast doubt on the justification of those goals, although they had already been superseded by new theoretical considerations. To identify with Eastern Europe would have meant either the acceptance of a liberal or even conservative way of thought, or the complete renunciation of philosophy.

Compare with Satterwhite (1992: 118 and n. 121).

References

Bauman, Z. (1980), *Intimations of Postmodernity*. London: Routledge.
Bauman, Z. (1992), *Intimations of Postmodernity*. London: Routledge.
Bauman, Z. (1982), *Memories of Class: The Pre-History and After-Life of Class*. London: Routledge and Kegan Paul.
Bauman, Z. (1998), 'Allosemitism: Premodern, Modern, Postmodern', in Bryan Cheyette and Laura Marcus (eds), *Modernity, Culture and 'the Jew'*. Cambridge: Polity, 143–56.
Bauman, Z. and Tester, K. (2001), *Conversations with Zygmunt Bauman*. Cambridge: Polity.
Bauman, Z. (2004), *Wasted Lives: Modernity and its Outcasts*. Cambridge: Polity.
Bauman, Z. (2005), 'The Demons of an Open Society', Ralph Miliband Lecture, LSE, 20 October.
Beck, U. and Grande, E. (2004), *Das kosmopolitische Europa*. Frankfurt: Suhrkamp.
Beilharz, P. (2006), 'The Worlds We Create'. *Polish Sociological Review*, 3 (155): 325–36.
Chardel, P-A (2005), 'Quelle morale pour le temps présent? Lecture de Zygmunt Bauman'. *L'Esprit*. février, 196–204.
Desaunay, C., Foessel, M. and Padis, M-O (2005), *'Les usages de la peur dans la mondialisation. Entretien avec Zygmunt Bauman'*. *L'Esprit*, juillet, 71–8.
Habermas, J. and Michnik, A. (1993), 'Mehr Demut, weniger Illusionen'. *Die Zeit*, 51, 17 Dec., 9–13.
Habermas, J. and Derrida, J. (2003), 'February 15, or what Binds Europeans Together'. *Constellations*, 10 (3): 364–70.
Heller, A. (1978), 'Marxist Ethics and the Future of Eastern Europe'. *Telos*, 38: 153–74.
Jacobsen, M. H. and Marshman, S. (2008), 'The Four Faces of Human Suffering in the Sociology of Zygmunt Bauman – Continuity and Change', *Polish Sociological Review*. 2008, 1(161): 3–24.

Joas, H. (1998), 'Bauman in Germany: Modern Violence and the Problems of German Self-Understanding', *Theory, Culture & Society*. 15: 47–55.

Junge, M. (2006), *Zygmunt Bauman: Soziologie zwischen Moderne und Flüchtiger Moderne*. Vs Verlag.

Junge, M. and Kron, T. (eds) (2002), *Zygmunt Bauman: Soziologie zwischen Postmoderne und Ethik*. Opladen: Leske + Budrich. 2nd edn 2007.

Le Guay, D. (2007), 'Le philosophe polonais Zygmunt Bauman', http://www.canalacademie.com

Kastner, J. (2000), *Politik und Postmoderne. Libertäre Aspekte in der Soziologie Zygmunt Baumans*. Münster: Unrast.

Kilminster, R. and Varcoe, I. (eds) (1996), *Culture, Modernity and Revolution. Essays in Honour of Zygmunt Bauman*. London: Routledge.

Kolakowski, L. (1971), 'A Pleading for Revolution: A Rejoinder to Z. Bauman', *Archives Europeenes de Sociologie*. XII: 52–60.

Kron, T. (2001), *Moralische Individualität: eine Kritik der postmodernen Ethik von Zygmunt Bauman und ihrer soziologischen Implikationen für eine soziale Ordnung durch Individualisierung*. Opladen: Leske + Budrich.

Outhwaite, W. (2000), 'Towards a European Civil Society?'. *Soundings*, 16, November, 131–43.

Outhwaite, W. (2010), 'Legality and Legitimacy in the European Union', in Samantha Ashenden and Chris Thornhill (eds), *Legality and Legitimacy*. Baden-Baden: Nomos.

Ossowski, S. (1962), *O Obsobliwościach Nauk Społecznyk*. Warsaw: Państwowe Wydawnictwo Naukowne. (German translation: *Die Besonderheit der Sozialwissenschaften*. Frankfurt: Suhrkamp, 1973).

Satterwhite, J. (1992), *Varieties of Marxist Humanism. Philosophical Revision in Postwar Eastern Europe*. Pittsburgh and London: University of Pittsburgh Press.

Schmidt, V. (2006), *Democracy in Europe. The EU and National Polities*. Oxford: OUP.

Smith, D. (1999), *Zygmunt Bauman: Prophet of Postmodernity*. Cambridge: Polity.

Sztompka, P. (2008), 'Coming in from the Cold', in Mathieu Deflem (ed.), *Sociologists in a Global Age*. Aldershot: Ashgate, 189–202.

Tester, K. (2006), 'Intellectual Immigration and the English Idiom (Or, a Tale of Bustards and Eagles)'. *Polish Sociological Review*, 3 (155), pp. 275–91.

Tester, K. and Jacobsen, M. H. (2006), 'Bauman Before Exile – A Conversation with Zygmunt Bauman'. *Polish Sociological Review*, 3 (155), 267–74.

2

The Use-Value of Human Waste and the Currency of Waste-Disposal Sites in Liquid Modernity

Abby Peterson

In this chapter I will interrogate Zygmunt Bauman's provocative notion of human waste or wasted lives in liquid modernity – his metaphor for society's outcasts for which society no longer has use. 'They are useless, in the sole sense of "use" one can think of in a society of consumers or society of tourists' (Bauman 1998: 96). To engage with Bauman's metaphors, I offer other metaphors, not as elegant, but with the hope of continuing the analysis, which Bauman awakens with his 'use' of the metaphor of human waste, that is, people with no 'use'. In the following pages I will look more closely at the gradations in the hell of the wastelands where wasted lives are lived, and question the conception that human waste is indeed 'useless' in liquid modern times, that human waste is devoid of use-value.

The varied nature of liquidity/fluidity impacts on humankind. Liquidity's movements or flows – from the force of the rushing torrential waters of a deluge, to the sluggish swampy waters of the delta – inexorably divides humanity and defines their social, alternative non-social, conditions; or rather, in liquid modernity humans have no condition, only the lived experiences of processes. Bauman claims that it is the speed of movement that has today become the dominant factor of social stratification and the hierarchy of domination.

> People whose hands are untied rule over people with tied hands. … People who move and act faster, who come nearest to the momentariness of movement [instantaneity, my comment], are now the people who rule. And it is the people who cannot move quickly, and more conspicuously yet the category of people who cannot at will leave their place at all, who are ruled. Domination consists in one's own capacity to escape, to disengage, to 'be elsewhere', and

> the right to decide the speed with which all that is done – while simultaneously stripping the people on the dominated side of their ability to arrest or constrain their moves or slow them down. ... In 'liquid' modernity, it is the most elusive, those free to move without notice, who rule.
>
> (Bauman 2000: 119–20)

The rulers travel light, trimmed and downsized; far from 'soft', but rather lean and mean, they surf the torrential waters, while the ruled travel (if they travel at all) heavily burdened with their memories of belonging and senses of loss (Peterson 2006), their hands tied in their attempts to navigate and plot a course through the rush of the waters around them. There are simply no courses left for them in liquid modernity; to be more precise they are set adrift, unmoored from the quays of courses and maps. There are no ultimate landing docks for the mass's migrations and no hopes after a perilous crossing. These are categories of people Bauman calls 'human waste/wasted humans' who are relegated to the swampy delta waters, as the sludge left in the wake of torrential global flows.

Tourists and vagabonds

Bauman posits a new 'grand narrative' of liquidity, mobility and fluidity as the pervasive condition in today's globalized modernity. His approach both subverts the spatial through processes of global 'flows' and, at the same time, reinstates spatiality in space-fixing localizing processes. These dual processes of deterritorialization and territorialization differentiate humanity, polarizing the human condition (Bauman 1998: 2–18). In Bauman's narrative of our present stage of modernity, everyone is on the move – some quicker and by their own choices, while others merely wander or are thrown aimlessly about by forces beyond their control. Mobility in this world has become the most powerful and coveted stratifying factor (p. 9), with speed of mobility lending it force.

According to Bauman (1998), liquid modern consumer society is divided between a first world of those 'high up' and a second world of those 'low down', plotted along a dimension of mobility, more specifically their degree of mobility – their freedom to choose where to be. The ideal types of travellers in liquid modernity that Bauman offers us are the tourists (high up on the freedom scale of mobility) and the vagabonds (low down on the scale). While all, tourists as well as vagabonds, are on the move, Bauman emphasizes the enormous differences in their experiences of their wanderings. Those 'high up' may leave (and they most often do) those 'low down' behind, but not vice versa. Societies construct territorial and cognitive abysses between these two categories. The tourist is more or less satisfied to travel through life picking and choosing their destinations according to the consumer delicacies and pleasures they are offered. They find a warm welcome wherever they travel. The vagabond finds himself time and again thrown out from the site they would rather stay in and with nowhere to go, or excluded from the site they would like to enter. The tourist travelling the fast track of global flows is living in a perpetual present and is perpetually 'short of time', but time is nevertheless under his/her control. Vagabonds live under the burden of abundant, redundant and useless time that they have nothing to fill with. 'They can only kill time, as they are slowly killed by it' (Bauman 1998: p. 88). For the tourists living in time, space does not matter, distances are easily bridged, even instantaneously in cyber-time, and borders are easily crossed. The vagabonds live in space: 'heavy, resilient, untouchable, which ties down time and keeps it beyond their control. Their time is void; in their time, "nothing ever happens"'. If they travel, they

> travel surreptitiously, often illegally, sometimes paying more for the crowded steerage of a stinking unseaworthy boat than others pay for business-class gilded luxuries and are frowned upon, and if unlucky, arrested and promptly deported, when they arrive.
>
> (p. 89)

In short, vagabonds are travellers refused the right to turn into tourists. The vagabonds are the waste of the world, which in liquid consumer societies is dedicated to providing tourist services unavailable to the vagabonds.

The ideal types of tourists and vagabonds are perhaps unwieldy categories if we are to analyse and better understand the highly differentiated human conditions among liquid modernity's travellers. Bauman emphasizes that there are degrees in the scale of freedom of mobility; there appears to be degrees in heaven among the tourists and degrees in hell among the vagabonds. Before we look closer at gradations in the hell of the global wastelands of human waste, we shall focus how speed becomes a force in the mobilities of liquid modernity.

Speed

Paul Virilio, French philosopher and social theorist, has in a series or works (for example, 1986 and 1983) expounded upon the West's obsession, since ancient times to the present, with movement and commitment to speed/penetration. Whether speaking of military warfare or economic warfare, but always warfare, Virilio follows the legacy of Sun Tzu: 'speed is the essence of war'. Speed is the motor of assault, penetration and domination and war is a 'speed factory' (Virilio and Lotringer 1983). The modern world of today is in a total and perpetual warring state of movement – aerial, spatial and now increasingly cyber spatial. 'All that counts is the speed of the moving body and the undetectability of its path' (Virilio 1986: 135). The speed of the movements of massed bodies, mechanized forces, capital and goods was long constrained by territoriality. Speed as the essence of war calculated to reduce spatial distances and thereby effectively penetrate and conquer territories/markets. Today the situation has changed. According to Virilio,

> [t]he reduction of distances has become a strategic reality bearing incalculable economic and political consequences, since it corresponds to the negation of space. The manoeuvre that once consisted in *giving up ground to gain Time* loses its meaning: at present, gaining Time is exclusively a matter of vectors. Territory has lost its significance in favour of the projectile. *In fact, the strategic value of the non-place of speed has definitively supplanted that of place*, and the question of possession of Time has revived that of territorial appropriation.
>
> (p. 133)

Virilio's diagnosis of the changes of social forms bears similarities with Bauman's, while differences remain. Virilio does not utilize the metaphor of liquidity, but his emphasis upon movement, vectors and speed dovetails with Bauman's notion of liquidity and the liquid modern society we are entering – a society that has ultimately negated space to privilege movement and above all speed of movement. To use Virilio's concept, the 'war of Time' has radically shifted gears – from hours and minutes to the simultaneity of the speed of light. The heavy or solid bodies/institutions/organizations of military and economic warfare have pared down their size and weights to move ever quicker in the race to be swiftest.

Warfare today, both military and economic, has, according to Virilio, taken logistical strategy to its absolute point, 'as the art of movement of unseen bodies' (for Bauman, 'those free to move unnoticed'); invisible bodies that can strike no matter where and no matter when, 'annihilating the enemy's will to power by creating a global zone of insecurity in which it will no longer be able to "decide" with certainty, to *want* – in other words, to win' (Virilio and Lotringer 1983: 38). Power is wielded for both theorists beyond the gaze of adversaries, but this is where the parallel ends. The state is still very present in the thinking of Virilio, not so in that of Bauman. In fact, this invisibility of the exercise of power through the speed of movements heralds the disintegration of politics as such, at least politics whereby the state can control the exercise of a power that flows beyond their reach and is wielded in the hands of undetectable actors. For Virilio (1986: 14ff) the State's political power is

> *[t]he polis, the police, in other words highway surveillance,* insofar as, since the dawn of the bourgeois revolution, the political discourse has been no more than a series of more or less conscious repetitions of the old communal poliorcetics, confusing social order with the control of traffic (of people, of goods), and revolution, revolt, with traffic jams, illegal parking, multiple crashes, collisions.

Not only Bauman, even countless police researchers (e.g. Garland, 1996; Bayley and Shearing 2001; Huysmans 2000) have pointed out the futility of the State's power to effectively control traffic of both people and goods, much less control traffic jams and illegal parking. The flows of people and goods in a globalized world are a global problem, which is more or less impervious to the local regulatory practices of states. *Per definition,* liquidity of a market is associated with free and laissez-faire markets, and hence with the absence of an intrusive institutional or regulatory apparatus (cf. Carruthers and Stinchcombe 1999: 353). So even if the discourse of regulatory exclusion is blooming as ever before, still attractive to the fortunate citizens of places who are demanding that unwanted and hence more unfortunate 'others' should be excluded entry (Bauman 2006), the discourse is increasingly difficult to realize in practice. Boundaries are progressively more penetrable to these global flows. Goods ooze in through ports of entry slipping through custom controls, and people are likewise oozing through these ports of entry.

This brings us to the lived experiences of the excluded in liquid modernity, the luckless 'vagabonds' on Virilio's 'highways', who in a liquid modern world are simply stuck in the mud left behind in the deluge of global flows. It is these unfortunate vagabonds, the human waste of liquid modernity, who have channelled the compassion of Bauman, not the fortunate 'tourists' in the fast lane through customs (Jacobsen and Marshman 2008: 23). The moral message of Bauman's work poses (again and again) the disturbing question as to the responsibility for the human waste – refugees, migrants, the unemployed and unemployable, drug addicts, single mothers – the nebulous category of the 'underclass' of poor clambering at our doors and appealing to our hearts.

The increasing numbers of outcasts – wasted lives – set adrift in the liquid forces of contemporary modernity is the gravest moral problem of our time. But who wants them? Who is willing to accept responsibility for them? If we do not need them, if their labour is not demanded, why should we shoulder the burden of caring for them? Bauman (2004) deliberates on these questions and finds little comfort in the hitherto evidence of concern for those left behind in the speed of societal changes. Of these unfortunate souls, he contends that 'we think only on the (fortunately not-yet-daily) occasions when the avalanche of leftovers descends from the refuse mountains and breaks through the fences meant to protect our own backyards' (p. 27). We, the privileged, lucky individuals on the inside of the human universe (riddled with fear that we, too, may lose our coveted places) refuse to acknowledge the cruel consequences of globalization's unremitting acceleration, 'negative globalization'. Or if we 'see' in media disclosures, we find comfort that the 'event' of being cast aside is 'far' from our protected 'homely' enclosures and the human outcasts are 'not like us'. If we (or some of us) suffer from guilty consciences, we put the sufferers in the hands of 'humanitarian workers' whose work is to dispose of the noxious human waste while gratifying our desire for moral righteousness. Those condemned to the outside of the human universe are to be kept at bay at all costs (and these costs are primarily moral). The boundaries must be relentlessly patrolled, for it is only these boundaries which divine the difference between the admitted and the rejected, the insiders from the outsiders – the fine (fuzzy and ambivalent) line between human lives and wasted lives which veils our common humanity. In the following pages we will turn our attention to human waste. And while their lives may indeed be wasted – condemned to the outside of the human universe, is human waste without use-value in liquid modern times? The moral costs of their subjugation are high for the fortunate tourists, but are there profits to be made from their exploitation?

Human waste stuck in the mud of the deltas

Bauman (2004) points out that the production of human waste is a predestined consequence of modernization and an indissoluble accompaniment of modernity. Modernity's twin pillars of order – building and economic progress inevitably led to the production of wasted humans – people found out of place, unfit, un-needed, or undesirable. In modern societies of producers the 'problem' of human waste could be at least partially remedied with emigration strategies (moving the 'excessive' people to less developed and populated parts of the globe) or simply retaining them as a reserve army of workers/soldiers, awaiting the time when they would be needed, or simply locking them away. But with the onslaught of the processes of 'negative globalization' and accelerated individualization, the 'human waste disposal industry' is experiencing a new, and acute, crisis. According to Bauman, '[g]lobalization has become the third, and currently most prolific and least controlled, "production line" of human waste or wasted humans' (p. 6). With the advent of liquid modernity, the vehicle of 'progress' is proceeding at such an unrelenting velocity that more and more of its passengers, unable to endure its speed, have fallen off, while more and more of those not yet inside cannot catch up and jump on – they too are left in its wake, on the 'outside', condemned to live as outcasts. Speed is the structuring factor making salient the borderline between 'the *comme il faut* and *comme il ne faut pas*, the inside and the outside of the human universe' (p. 28). Speed is a cruel and implacable force that is structuring our planet along a bipolar dimension, creating a hard and fast distinction between those who can keep up, the 'tourists' (and among those only the swiftest among them can feel more or less secure that they can retain their fortunate positions), and those who cannot, 'vagabonds', the tourist 'wanabees'.

Bauman (2002 and 2004) has placed refugees at the very bottom of the heap, 'outsiders incarnate' – those most stuck in the mud of the deltas and those most like mud: faceless, stripped of their identities. Refugees are human waste with no useful function to play in the country of their (temporary, indefinite) internment (they arguably might have a function for those more resourceful outcasts and/or bureaucrats through whose pockets humanitarian aid frequently passes). The refugee camp is a dumping site offering no return and no way forward for those hapless souls behind their fences; they are caught in a condition of the movement of non-movement, speed set in a state of limbo in the nowhere land of non-humanity.

> Refugees, the human waste of the global frontier-land, are 'the outsiders incarnate', the absolute outsiders, outsiders everywhere and out of place everywhere except in places that are themselves out of

> place – the 'nowhere places' that appear on no maps used by ordinary humans on their travels. Once outside, indefinitely outside, a secure fence with watching towers is the only contraption needed to make the 'indefiniteness' of the out-of-place hold forever.
>
> (Bauman 2004: 80)

If we continue to interrogate the strata of liquid modernity's human waste, the asylum seeker and the 'paperless' migrant must be next (only slightly up the rung) on the ladder down to hell. Asylum seekers and 'illegal' migrants arrive on the shores of 'fortress Europe' and at the airports of Europe's major cities, housed in improvised camps for their internment at the moment of their landing and until the moment of their probable deportation. Countless numbers (who can count the numbers of smuggled migrants within the borders of Europe; the European Commission only offers us their speculative figures to underline the 'threat') of people from the latecomers to modernity (excessive in their countries of origin, with little hope of acquiring the means to sustain themselves or their families or deemed there as undesirable for political or social/cultural reasons) are seeking new lives in the 'promised lands' of modernity (cf. De Genova 2002).

These are human waste on the move, seeking a haven within the European Union, and they do not enjoy a warm welcome, even if they make it alive to its shores or across its borders. Swedish legal scholar Gregor Noll (2003) has studied asylum policy discussions centred on 'protecting' the new expanded boundary of the European Union against the 'intrusion' of asylum seekers and migrants. He argues that a new politics of exclusion through creating a 'state of the exceptional' in the international refugee regime is taking shape and is being devised to more effectively close the external borders of the EU with the deployment of 'Regional Protection Zones' (in the protection seekers geographical areas of origin) as well as, 'Transit Processing Centres', which are closer to the external borders of the EU and will function as a first line of deterrence for unwanted migration. This state of the exceptional in policing migration portends a suspension of the Geneva asylum statutes and hints that human rights are routinely violated, but as Bauman (2004: 76) points out, refugees/migrants are more or less beyond the law as such; a condition which encourages states of exception.

If the European Union can do little to counter the threats of globalization which are eroding the durability of the social order on which the security of livelihood (income, employment) or survival in the case of invalidity or old age depend, it can transfer our fears of loss of security to the human waste clambering to enter our midst (Bauman 2006: 4). Relatively toothless to regulate the fast globalizing and increasingly extra-territorial markets, the European Union has shifted emphasis towards a defenceless, and in liquid modernity, immobilized category which is on the move. It is the human waste on the move towards 'us' who are posing threats to our livelihood, who are eager to scrounge off the benefits of 'our' labour or to take 'our' jobs. However, according to this discourse, the migration of human waste is not only threatening domestic and labour market stability. The migration of human waste poses even more sinister security threats. 'They', the human waste on the move towards 'us', pose an overriding danger to public order as well as 'European/Swedish/French/Greek/etc.' cultural identity (cf. Weber and Bowling 2004; Huysmans 2000; Garner 2007). On the one hand, migrants and asylum seekers have been 'criminalized' [*sic*], connected (collectively and *per se*) to terrorism, criminal activities, drugs and people trafficking, etc. 'They' threaten 'our' personal safeties. On the other, human waste bring with them deleterious and noxious cultural traditions, mores and ways of life that will pollute the purity of 'our' own. 'They' will undermine 'our', however shaky, place in the world. Human waste must be stopped and 'our' borders secured from their onslaught, even if exceptional measures should be taken (Bauman 2006: 153ff).

Refugees, asylum seekers and migrants are the ever-growing human waste commodities produced for export on the global production line of waste. If we continue to move upwards along the ladder of human waste strata, how is the situation for the redundant humans already 'inside' as there is no place else to deport them, and as the new 'fullness' of the planet bars their exclusion? Waste-disposal sites, according to Bauman (2004: 81), must be laid out inside the very localities which have made them supernumerary. These sites emerge either in or around most large cities across the globe. Whether we define them as slums, urban ghettos, 'hyperghettos' (Wacquant 2008), barrios, favellas, *quartiers*, shantytowns or simply depressed housing estates across the globe, these 'non-places' are all dumping grounds for those of whom, according to Bauman, the surrounding society has no economic or political use, that is waste-disposal sites for the surplus, redundant, unemployable and functionless population – domestic human waste. Agreed, the living conditions for domestic human waste relegated to these dumping grounds varies widely across the globe. There are even here degrees of misery (Webster et al. 2004). The economically and socially depressed housing estates surrounding Swedish urban centres, which are largely populated with ethnic minorities (the result of large-scale migration to Sweden during the last 30 years), are undeniably more attractive and comfortable than those offered to domestic human waste on the outskirts of Rio de Janeiro, but there are some similarities. The population housed in these stigmatized 'dumping grounds' are relatively immobile – escape to the 'other side' is limited to only the swiftest among them (the most notable of these 'escapees' is the Swedish striker Zlatan Ibrahimovic who has achieved celebrity tourist status). The lure of criminality for many of the young people (young men) is difficult to resist – it offers a short-cut to, and possibly the only 'cut' of, the consumer society harbouring their delectable wares. Welfare solutions to the problems arising from mass unemployment, poor education, crowded housing, drugs and petty crime are giving way to security measures lest these 'problems' should spread to the wider society; police crackdowns instead of increasing resources to the schools and youth centres in the 'problem' areas. In the thoroughly individualized world of liquid modernity, responsibility for 'personal' calamities is placed in the hands of the hapless 'losers' in the global reality game of exclusion (cf. Bauman 2004: 145). While some recycling among the redundant is successful, and some upon their own devices find the 'key' to entering the world of successful consumers, for the majority the prospects are dim for acquiring a secure position among the 'tourists' in Sweden (Peterson and Hjerm 2007).

Bauman (1998) explains that in the domestic dumping grounds, the vagabonds' experiences of territoriality, is far removed from the experiences of exterritoriality among the tourists.

> The territoriality of the rest [the vagabonds] feels less like home ground, and ever more like prison – all the more humiliating for the obtrusive sight of the others' freedom to move. It is not just the condition of 'staying put', being unable to move at one's heart's desire and being barred access to greener pastures, exudes the acrid odour of defeat, signals incomplete humanity … Deprivation reaches deeper. (p. 23)

Even in a more fundamental sense is immobility, being fixed in place, frustrating for those caught in what I call the deltas. Locality in the dumping grounds is not the locality of 'local community'. In today's world of high-speed mobility, locality is not what it used to be when information moved together with the bodies of the carriers. The public spaces of locality in general, and in the dumping grounds more specifically, have been stripped of their power. The public spaces where agendas are set, private concerns made public, opinions are formed, tested and confirmed, judgements are made and verdicts are passed – such spaces followed with the elites, the high-flying tourists, moving far beyond the reach of any territoriality and its residents, and most dramatically beyond the reach of the citizens of the deltas (p. 24). The residents of these dumping grounds, the immobilized domestic human waste, have lost the capacity to change the conditions of their plight. Power has moved at high speeds exterritorialy, beyond their grasp to influence and make their voices heard (cf. Bauman 1999 and 2002). They are left stuck in the mud with no way to gather their numbers and press their cause – this is the ultimate frustration of the powerless: stuck in the mud with nowhere to go and with no means to change the conditions where they are stuck.

The 'Big Brothers', old and new, are working at high speed together to police the borderline between the 'inside' and the 'outside' from intrusions. Human waste is to be kept 'in' place by the old Big Brothers – modernity's exemplary jailers – keeping people in and bringing them in line whenever they fall out. While the old Big Brothers are beefed up as never before with larger police forces, supplemented with a fast-growing private security industry and rising prison populations (Bayley and Shearing 2001), the old Big Brothers nevertheless, as Bauman (2004: 130ff) points out, play second fiddle today in liquid modernity to a new Big Brother – the Big Brother of exclusion (Bauman 2002: 65 and 2006: 25ff). The new Big Brother engages the same game rules as in the TV reality show and is preoccupied with *exclusion*:

> spotting the people who 'do not fit' into the place they are in, banishing them from that place and deporting them 'where they belong', or better still never allowing them to come anywhere near in the first place. The new Big Brother supplies the immigration officers with lists of people they should not let in, and bankers with the list of people they should not let into the company of the creditworthy. He instructs the guards about whom they should stop at the gate and not let inside the gated community. He inspires the neighbourhood-watchers to spy out and kick out suspected prowlers and loiterers – strangers out of place. He offers homeowners closed circuit television to keep the undesirables away from the door. He is the patron saint of all bouncers, whether in the service of a night club or of a State Ministry of Home Affairs.
>
> (Bauman 2002: 132)

Together the old and new Big Brothers, working in tandem, offer us a measure of security from the insidious threats posed by human waste.

They provide societies with its social order of exclusion, keeping at bay human waste and alleviating our fears (out of sight, out of mind) of falling victim to Big Brother too – of losing our place among the society of humans. What they appear to do rather poorly, the old and new Big Brothers, is to offer us a measure of security against the negative forces of globalization (see also Bauman 1999: 51). They cannot shield us from the consequences wrought upon us by high-flying tourists, for example, threats of being made redundant. They offer little protection from the global criminal 'samurai' ruling the global flows of human destruction.

Before we leave our interrogation of the rungs of misery among liquid modernity's global wastelands, we will contemplate the bottom of the heap, the lowest of the low, among society's domestic human waste – the heroin addict. Robert Saviano (2007) writes of the role played by the heroin addict for the international cocaine trade. Before cocaine is sent out from the warehouses in the districts surrounding Naples and distributed throughout Europe, it must be cut. One kilo cocaine costs the manufacturer one thousand euros; when moved to the distributor, the cost goes up to thirty thousand euros; after the first cut, thirty kilos becomes one hundred and fifty and its value on the drug market increases to approximately fifteen million euros So cutting the drug is important and the additive and its blend is fundamental. The concoction between the drug and the additive decides the quality of the product and a bad cut can mean death, hence the police and arrests, all of which clog the arteries of the distribution net. So the cut must be first tested and what better human guinea pigs than the heroin addict? Named after the characters from a popular 1980s TV programme where under false human skins lurked rats with slimy green scales, heroin addicts are referred to in the Camorra wastelands as the 'Visitors'. The heroin trade is dying out on the continent and the junkies are desperate. 'They stumble on buses, get on and off trains, they travel at night, they hitchhike and walk kilometre after kilometre in search of a fix' (Saviano 2007: 102). The Visitors are wandering human waste incessantly searching for their next fix. The Camorra drug clans send out a message that a free fix is available and the Visitors come – 'the green slimy untouchables, lower than monkeys', the truly expendables in the global human waste production line, which is this time intimately interconnected with the human destruction production line. One can't have customers with nosebleeds, foaming at the mouth and dying; better if the cut is tested first on a Visitor. If he/she dies, who cares? It would merely be an accidental case of overdose, with no subsequent criminal investigation. 'It is already a lot to lift him up from the ground, clean his face of vomit and piss and bury him' (ibid). Even the Visitors have a function, a 'use' on the global production lines of waste and destruction, which brings us to the question of the use-value of human waste.

The value of human waste

A key factor in Bauman's analysis of human waste is that they have played out their role in society, both economic and political. The wasted humans, vagabonds adrift in the masses' migrations – migrants, *sans papiers*, those people locked into the relatively immobile domestic dumping grounds – are, according to Bauman, of no use.

> They breach the norm and sap the order. They spoil the fun simply by being around, they do not lubricate the wheels of the consumer society, they add nothing to the prosperity of the economy turned into a tourist industry. They are useless, in the sole sense of 'use' one can think of in a society of consumers or society of tourists.
>
> (Bauman 1998: 96)

It is this point in Bauman's analysis of the labour value of human waste that I will in the remaining pages take issue. Human waste may very well be 'flawed consumers', but they very often provide the labour, which keeps societies of consumers or tourists running, adding to the prosperity from which they are cruelly excluded. Human waste regularly provides the concealed, out-of-sight labour upon which the cogs of the new wave of global neoliberalism are oiled and kept running. Saskia Sasson (1991 and 1998) has pointed out that in the 'global cities' – New York, London and Tokyo – the new global elite, tourists high up on the rungs of the ladder of mobility and speed, 'feed upon' an array of labour-intensive services that are most often provided by underpaid migrants – 'legals' as well as 'illegals'. The schools of high-flying tourists that swarm these global internodes of finance request the services of launderers, child carers, cleaners, caterers, tailors, exclusive restaurants and coffee houses; these are services often provided by migrant women. These women caring for the global elite's children very often leave their own children, on the other side of the globe, in the care of their mothers/grandmothers thereby maintaining a global domestic service exchange. The urban sociologist Mike Davis (2007) writes in the introduction to the anthology *Evil Paradises – Dreamworlds of Neoliberalism*:

> Many of the 'dreamlands' described in the pages that follow are, in fact, iterations of Los Angeles, or at least 'California lifestyle', as a global phantasmagoric ideal, which the nouveaux riches pursue with the same desperate zeal in the desert of Iran and the hills of Kabul as they do in the gated suburbs of Cairo, Johannesburg, and Beijing. But, as in autochthonic Los Angeles, Hell and the Mall are never more than a freeway drive apart. Thus the real housewives of Orange County, like their counterparts in Hong Kong's tony-phony 'Palm Springs' or Budapest's neo-Hapsburg gated communities, exploit the same labour of maids who themselves live in slums or even chicken coops on the roofs of mansions. The Metropolis-like phantasmagoria of Dubai's super-skyscrapers or the Olympic megastructures in Beijing arise from the toil of migrant workers whose own homes are fetid barracks and desolate encampments. *In the larger perspective, the bright archipelagos of utopian luxury and 'supreme lifestyle' are mere parasites on a planet of slums.*
>
> (Mike Davis 2007: 4, emphasis added)

What is perhaps even more surprising is that within domestic dumping grounds the global capital of liquid modernity may even have (at least some of) its roots among the immobility of wasted humans with no other alternative, or vision of alternative, to find their livelihoods and a piece of the consumer cake on offer (Webster et al. 2004). Roberto Saviano (2007) in his global blockbuster *Gomorra* offers us a keen and penetrating picture of the social relations and social practices of the Camorra's organized crime networks in the economic frontier lands between the law and the unlawful or beyond the law. For the uninitiated eye, the depressed housing district of Secondigliano, on the outskirts of Naples, is Europe's ultimate ghetto, a place of misery incarnate. What one does not 'see' is that Secondigliano, a non-place for southern Italy's underclass, is, in fact, 'the pillars of economy, the hidden mine, the darkness where the market's pulsating heart finds its energy' (p. 123). Saviano begins his count of the death toll, the Camorra's victims, from the date of his birth in 1979 to 2005 when he completed his book: three thousand and six hundred dead. The Camorra has murdered more than any other crime syndicate in Europe and far more than any terror network working on the continent. But as Saviano points out, who hears about the Camorra? The Camorra operates within the heart of Europe. It is through Naples that the drug trade is organized and distributed across the continent. On the basis of its financial profits from the drug and arms trade, the Camorra extends its financial empire in confection, construction, 'tourist' services and real estate. Within the heart of Naples' surrounding housing estates, the dumping grounds of Italy's domestic waste, surges, paradoxically, the lifeblood of the Italian economy. But this appears to be a well-guarded secret. As Saviano points out, where the money comes from is unimportant. 'What matters is that the cannon fodder remained mired in the outskirts, trapped in tangles of cement and trash, in the black-market factories and cocaine warehouses. And that no one notices them, that it all seems like a war among gangs, a beggars' war' (Saviano 2007: 120). The 'beggars', the human waste of Secondigliano, are the foot soldiers in the economic warfare waged by the Camorra on the global economic battlefield – expendable and readily replaceable. Secondigliano, and similar dumping grounds, breed the potential foot soldiers in places where hope of a 'tourist ticket' to the consumer wonderlands is cruelly limited. A position in 'the System' can bring at least a motorbike and pocket money, and offers, in any case, a dream of a life as a 'tourist'. Saviano quotes a letter that a young man who was confined to a juvenile correction centre left to his priest.

> Everyone that I know is either dead or in jail. I want to become a boss. I want to own supermarkets, stores, factories, I want to have women. I want three cars and when I go into a store I want to be treated with respect, I want warehouses all over the world. Then I want to die. But like a real man, like someone who truly commands. I want to be killed.
>
> (Saviano 2007: 114)

This is the ambition of a young man, a 'clan kamikaze', who can choose a life as a Camorra soldier on the 'wrong' side of the law or a life on the 'right' side of the law as a 'nobody' scraping by on a pittance in an illegal factory; the dumping ground does not offer anything else for the immobile youth living in its swampy delta waters. Stuck in the mud they dream of a life on the fast track as a tourist.

Bauman (2004) compares classical frontier-land conditions with the frontier-land conditions of liquid modernity. In the classical frontier land, cattle barons and outlaws were in tacit agreement that the absence of a government of law was good for both their 'businesses'. They had a convergence of interests in a condition, which valorized the absence of routine, on fluidity of alliances and front lines and on the overall frailty of commitments, rights and obligations. 'It made the frontier-land a site of perpetual uncertainty and at the same time made insecurity immune to all effective intervention. Insecurity could not be confronted at its source: like the coalitions and the battlefields, the resulting anxiety was free-floating, unsure of its targets and selecting them at random' (pp. 87–8). This is a more or less accurate description of the conditions in Secondigliano. Whereas Bauman argues that the place of cattle barons has been taken by global manufacturing, trade and capital, and terrorists have taken the outlaws' place (ibid.), he is ignores the place taken by Camorra and its counterparts in the global economy of liquid modernity. They are the ultimate liquid cattle barons, operating fast and furiously within, outside and, above all, *beyond* the law in a grey zone of 'legitimate' enterprises, lawlessness and mayhem. Saviano's (2007) vivid account of the Camorra's battlefield and its code of battle resonates with Bauman's description of the classical frontier land.

> Kill them all. Every one of them. Even if you have doubts. Even if you don't know which side they're on, or if they're even involved. Shoot! They're slime, nothing but slime. In the face of war, danger, and defeat, allies and enemies are interchangeable. They're no longer individuals, but elements for testing and expressing your strength. Groups, alliances, and enemies will take shape afterward. But first the shooting has to start.
>
> (p. 80)

It is only their speed of mobility, and their invisibility, which can keep the liquid cattle barons and their foot soldiers alive and their economic empires afloat. Contrary to Bauman's (2004) contention that the refugees, in their state of 'liminal drift' *outside* the law as such, are outlaws of a novel kind and are 'the fullest epitome and incarnation of its frontier-land spirit' (p. 76), I would argue that it is the liquid cattle barons, the Camorra samurai and their kind, that are in fact the quintessence of liquid modernity's frontier-land spirit. The power of their assault and penetration of global markets rests upon the speed with which they operate beyond the law as such.

The tourists surfing the rushing waters of exterritoriality

Bauman invokes the image of Henry Ford as an exemplary symbol for classical or solid modernity's ruler. Virilio (1986) in turn invokes the image of Howard Hughes, the 'invisible citizen':

> This completely de-socialized man, who vanished from the earth, who avoided human contact for fear of germs, who was terrified by

> the very breath of his rare visitors, nonetheless thought only of the media, from the aerospace industry to the cinema, from gasoline to airfields, from casinos to the star system, from the design of Jane Russell's bra to that of a bomber. His existence could be considered exemplary. Hughes cared only about that which passes in transit. His life rebounded from one vector to another, as has, for two hundred years, the power of the American nation he adored. Nothing else interested him. He died in the open sky, in an airplane.
>
> (pp. 108–9)

Hughes can be regarded as a harbinger of what would later materialize in the persona of Bill Gates, a model ruler in liquid modern times – the consummate tourist. Bauman (2000) comments upon Gate's

> unashamed, outspoken, even boastful willingness to destroy what he has made, given the demands of the immediate moment. Gates appeared to be a player who flourishes in the midst of dislocation. He was cautious not to develop attachment (and particularly a sentimental attachment) or lasting commitment to anything, including his own creations. He was not afraid of taking a wrong turn since no turn would keep him going in one direction for long, and since turning back or aside remained constantly and immediately available options.
>
> (p. 124)

Bill Gates, and Howard Hughes before him, are indeed high-flyers in the exterritorial flows of liquid modernity, unfettered by spatiality with no (apparent) fixed ties to localities, bravely surfing uncharted flows in their search for opportunities for power. What Bauman has neglected in his accounts of the tourists, those 'high up' on the scale of freedom of movement, is the necessity of spatial, infrastructural and institutional moorings that configure and enable mobilities – enabling what Harvey (1989) called the 'spatial fix'. Hannam, Sheller and Urry (2006) emphasize that there are no forms of detachment or 'deterritorialization', no liquid modern tourists, without extensive systems of immobility, interdependent systems of 'immobile' material fixtures, for example, transmitters, roads, aerials, airports, docks, factories, satellites, etc. The 'mobile machines' which generate and make possible the liquid flows of people, goods and especially capital – mobile phones, cars, aircraft, trains and computer connections – presume 'these over-lapping and varied time–space immobilities' (p. 3). These are the territorially fixed systems or infrastructures of mobility, which enable or afford different degrees of 'motility' or potential for mobility and speed of mobility.

If we turn our attention from the exemplars of Bill Gates and his precursor Howard Hughes as ultimate tourists to the Camorra samurai Salvatore Giuliano, Francesco Schiavone 'Sandoken', Vincenzo Zagaria, Dante Passarelli and countless other clan bosses that Saviano (2007) has so vividly written about, another aspect of liquid modern territoriality, of fixed locality, emerges as a prerequisite for these warriors on the global economic battlefield. They rely, in addition to the moorings of a communication infrastructure, on the moorings of a 'culture of misery'. Saviano argues that the Camorra and its leadership of 'industrialists' draw their lifeblood, their power, from the soil, the amalgamation of social relations of family, friends and enemies, and most importantly, from the history of their territorial roots in Campania in southern Italy. In the domestic dumping grounds of Casal di Principe, Villa Literno, Castelvoltorno, Gricignono, San Tammaro, Mondragone, Carinola and in the provinces surrounding Naples, the global networks of the arms trade, drug trade, construction businesses, industrial waste disposal, tourist industry, etc. flourish. With the power of the Camorra clans grounded in these specific territorialities and within their close-knit systems of family and friends/allies, the global flows from their production lines of waste and destruction branch out to the rest of Italy, Spain, Bolivia, Serbia, Scotland, China, Romania, Somalia, Peru, Venezuela, Germany, Poland, the Ukraine and Nigeria – in short, across the globe. Their exterritorial transactions operating beyond the law generates inconceivable wealth and power. Nevertheless their power stems from, and is rooted in, territory – a wasteland of wasted lives where they reign supreme. 'No boss can leave his roots for too long, because all his power is based on them' (Saviano 2007: 206). This is the paradox of organized crime's freedom of mobility. Their simultaneous fixation in locality, in place and its undergrowth of culture enables their exterritorial mobility and speed of mobility. It is not the industries, shopping malls, homes, warehouses or farms, that is, the physical materializations of their wealth wherein their power lies. The various anti-mafia commissions have repeatedly, throughout the last 30 years, confiscated the physical manifestations of their wealth and power to the tune of billions of euros, such economic catastrophes would have sunk most 'ordinary' global economic empires. The courts have imprisoned hundreds of bosses and thousands among their ranks of foot soldiers, a decimation of personnel and expertise which would have crippled most enterprises. Despite these measures, the Camorra lives on 'healthier' than ever. Despite these 'temporary' setbacks, they rise again and again from the ashes of their brutal wars like the Phoenix. It is the cultural and social undergrowth of these territorialities, which continues to provide the lifeblood for their existence and their means to move at great speed across the globe. They draw upon the cold currency of places of hopelessness and cultures of misery.

Bauman (2000: 14) claims that 'any dense and tight network of social bonds, and particularly a territorially rooted tight network, is an obstacle to be cleared out of the way' for power to flow smoothly. Bauman (2003) further alleges that

> power rules *because* it flows, because it is *able* (beware ever forgetting it!) to flow – to *flow away*. Power superiority, domination, consist these days in the capacity of *disengaging* – the capacity that territorially defined places and people, whose lives are circumscribed by those places, are conspicuously lacking.
>
> (p. 15)

For mafia-like networks across the globe this would appear not to be the case, nor is it the case for terrorist networks. They are literally grounded in the soil (and Saviano (2007: 214) would argue, 'concrete', Southern Italy's 'crude oil') of their family's or clan's territorial roots in a culture of misery that provides them with both the foot soldiers and social support – a community of accomplices (Bauman 1999: 16) – with which they can conquer global exterritorial spaces, which they assault and penetrate at great speeds. Their power *flows from* the territorially defined places and people in wastelands of human destruction – the global samurai both *engage with* these roots of their power and *disengage from* the consequences of their actions.

Conclusion

Bauman (2004: 64–5) argues that contrary to the popular notion of the 'globalization of crime', what distinguishes negative globalization is the annulment of the distinction between 'legal' and 'illegal' which only an abiding and enforceable law may draw. There is no global law in operation that could permit the setting apart of mafia-style criminal pursuits from 'normal business activity' (ibid.).

There is no effective Big Brother patrolling the global space in which the mafias and the Camorra operate; it is according to Bauman a 'politics-free' zone, beyond the sovereignty of nation states. Not only is there no Big Brother out there in the global flows, there are no political institutions to set the agendas, to legislate and regulate the global frontier land. We are experiencing an ongoing separation of power from politics. What remains of all extant political (electable, representative) institutions is stoutly local, virtually *glaebae adskripti* (Bauman 1999: 75), incapable of taking on the exterritoriality of global flows as their speed of action comes to an abrupt halt at their borders.

According to Bauman (2002: 4), the right to draw the line between legitimate (permissible) and illegitimate (impermissible) coercion is the prime stake of all power struggles. However, what is permissible violence in specific contexts is not necessarily state-approved violence. In the wastelands alternative regimes of violence can come to coexist alongside the state. Saviano (2007) points out that today's Camorra bosses rarely take a stand against the state aiming to directly challenge and undermine the legitimacy of state-approved coercion; rather they pride themselves by working with, or perhaps more accurately, working alongside the state. They mobilize their surrogate regimes of violence during their internal wars over markets; the power struggles between the family clans, joined in temporary warring coalitions, are, as a matter of course, necessary for their grip on power. These internal wars and the murders of their adversaries are regarded (by the Camorra and their community of accomplices) as more or less permissible. Saviano (2007: 190ff) has written about the so-called Spartacus trials, the most extensive and far-reaching legal process initiated by the Italian State during the last 20 years. The 'maxi-process', which dragged on for over ten years, resulted in 21 lifetime sentences and 70 more convictions with varying lengths of sentences. After the sentences were read at the trial, the principal boss in the area of Caserta, Sandoken, began to scream his frustration with the trial's outcome, claiming that the judgement was unjust. He and his companions were merely successful businessmen, not criminals. The trial was, in fact, a colossal conspiracy of Marxist judges jealous of their economic power in the region. In Sandoken's worldview it was their entrepreneurship and economic talents that laid the ground for their financial empires; all of the murders in the area were simply expressions of the region's peasant culture. In Caserta, murdering of rivals was simply the way things were done – it was the justice of the soil of Caserta, which nourishes its own 'legal codex'. In their codex, murder and intimidation do not breach laws; murder and intimidation are acts of necessity and not criminal acts.

Of course, the Spartacus process, spectacular as it was, did not destroy the power of the Camorra in Caserta. It instituted a shift of power, and according to Saviano, actually rejuvenated the network. 'Every arrest and maxi-trial seems more like a way of replacing capos and breaking business cycles than something capable of destroying a system' (p. 202).

Bauman (2002) offers us little choice but to resume the battles against the globalizing forces of destruction; we either chose to place our solidarity with the forces of mutual destruction *or* place our solidarity in our common humanity, assuming responsibility for the wasted lives of the world. In the words of Bauman:

> [I]n the new frontier-land of the full planet, evil – any instance of evil, wherever it is gestated and whoever may be its intended or 'collateral' victim – affects us all. A global world is a place where, for once, *the desideratum of moral responsibility and the interests of survival coincide and blend.* Globalization is, among other things (perhaps above all), *an ethical challenge.*
>
> (p. 17)

Or in the words of Roberto Saviano:

> [t]o set oneself against the clans becomes a war of survival. ... Knowing is thus no longer a sign of moral engagement. Knowing – understanding – becomes a necessity. The only necessity if you want to consider yourself worthy of breathing.
>
> (p. 300)

If the global space lies beyond the reach of all extant institutional guardians of standards of decency and ethical responsibility, we must take up the challenge and invent them. The underlying creed in Bauman's sociology is that whatever human kind has made can be remade.

Bauman's path-breaking work on society's outcasts, those excluded from partaking in the pleasures of consumer society or tourist society, poses a critically important challenge for social scientists. Research is gravely needed that can better map the 'use-value' of human waste for liquid modern times. More attention should be directed towards the exploited labours of migrants, both 'legals' and 'illegals', in order to access the degree to which today's consumer society in fact depends upon them. How are migrants providing the services in the global tourist industry? The production lines of human waste and destruction, the drugs trade and arms trade, generates unheard of wealth and power for rulers of global flows upon which liquid modernity's global flows of finance may very well rest. These are cynical times when humanitarian aid to suffering refugees is filtered through the greedy pockets of those mobile enough and fast enough to ensconce them; where the contracts to 'build up' war-savaged territories fall in the hands of the privileged elite, the high-flying tourists, who are eager to exploit the situation. The waste-disposal industry, both material and human, produces massive profits for the swift and ruthless tourists. In liquid modernity the labours of many vagabonds are providing for increasingly fewer tourists. In short, we need to better understand the contributions of wasted lives to the global economy of liquid modernity.

References

Bauman, Z. (1998), *Globalization: The Human Consequences.* Cambridge: Polity Press.

Bauman, Z. (1999), *In Search of Politics.* Cambridge: Polity Press.

Bauman, Z. (2000), *Liquid Modernity.* Cambridge: Polity Press.

Bauman, Z. (2002), *Society Under Siege.* Cambridge: Polity Press.

Bauman, Z. (2003), *City of Fears, City of Hopes.* London: Goldsmiths College, University of London.

Bauman, Z. (2004), *Wasted Lives. Modernity and its Outcasts.* Cambridge: Polity Press.

Bauman, Z. (2006), *Liquid Fear.* Cambridge: Polity Press.

Bayley, D. and Shearing, C. (2001), *The New Structure of Policing: Description, Conceptualization, and Research Agenda.* Washington D.C.: National Institute of Justice.

Carruthers, B. G. and Stinchcombe, A. L. (1999), 'The Social Structure of Liquidity: Flexibility, Markets, and States'. *Theory and Society*, 28: 353–382.

Davis, M. (2007), 'Introduction', in Mike Davis and D. B. Monk (eds) *Evil Paradises. Dreamworlds of Neoliberalism.* New York: New Press.

De Genova, N. P. (2002), 'Migrant "Illegality" and Deportability in Everyday Life'. *Annual Review of Anthropology*, 31(1): 419–47.

Garland, D. (1996), 'The Limits of the Sovereign State: Strategies of Crime Control in Contemporary Societies'. *British Journal of Criminology*, 40(3): 347–75.

Garner, S. (2007), 'The European Union and the Racialization of Immigration 1985–2006'. *Race/Ethnicity*, 1(1): 61–87.

Hannam, K., Sheller, M. and Urry, J. (2006), 'Editorial: Mobilities, Immobilities and Moorings'. *Mobilities*, 1 (1): 1–22.

Harvey, D. (1989), *The Condition of Postmodernity.* Oxford: Blackwell.

Huysmans, J. (2000), 'The European Union and the Securitization of Migration'. *Journal of Common Market Studies*, 38(5): 751–77.

Jacobsen, M. H. and Marshman, S. (2008), 'Bauman on Metaphors – A Harbinger of Humanistic Sociology', In Jacobsen, M. H. and Poder, P. (eds) *The Sociology of Zygmunt Bauman: Challenges and Critique.* Aldershot, UK: Ashgate, pp. 19–40.

Noll, G. (2003), 'Visions of the Exceptional: Legal and Theoretical Issues Raised by Transit Processing Centres and Protection Zones'. *European Journal of Migration and Law*, 5: 303–41.

Peterson, A. (2006), 'Minnesresor – Mellan försök att minnas och glömma', in D. Mulinari och N. Räthzel (eds), *Bortom etnicitet.* Umeå: Boréa.
Peterson, A. and Hjerm, M. (2007), *Etnicitet: Perspektiv på Samhället.* Malmö: Gleerups.
Sasson, S. (1991), *The Global City: New York, London, Tokyo.* Princeton, N.J.: Princeton University Press.
Sasson, S. (1998), *Globalization and its Discontents.* New York: New Press.
Saviano, R. (2007), *Gomorrah. Italy's Other Mafia.* London: Pan Books. Originally published as *Gomorra viaggio nell' imero economico e nel sogno di dominio.* Milan: Arnoldo Mondadori ditore S.p.A. (2006).
Virilio, P. and Lotringer, S. (1983), *Pure War.* New York: Semiotext(e).
Virilio, P. (1986 [1977]), *Speed & Politics.* New York: Semiotext(e).
Wacquant, L. (2008), *Urban Outcasts. A Comparative Sociology of Advanced Marginality.* Cambridge, UK: Polity Press.
Weber, L. and Bowling, B. (2004), 'Policing Migration: A Framework for Investigating the Regulation of Global Mobility'. *Policing & Society,* 14 (3): 195–212.
Webster, C., D. Simpson, R. MacDonald, A. Abbas, M. Cieslik and T. Shildrick (2004), *Poor Transitions: Young Adults and Social Exclusion.* Bristol: Policy Press.

3

Bauman and the Drama of Abu Ghraib

Stjepan G. Mestrovic

Among the many contributions that he has made to sociology, Zygmunt Bauman is known for his dualisms, which include modernity versus postmodernity, legislators versus interpreters and solid versus liquid modernity. He has published extensively on Communism, the Holocaust, modernity, postmodernism, bureaucracy and ethics among other topics. But there exists a fruitful ambivalence in how he can be interpreted in these and other regards. Is he claiming that the Holocaust and Communism were the result of order-seeking modernity, the final effect of so-called Enlightenment narratives? For example, regarding the Holocaust, he writes, 'The Nazi vision of a harmonious, orderly, deviation-free society drew its legitimacy and attractiveness from ... the century and a half of post-Enlightenment history' (Bauman 1993, p. 29). Similarly, according to Bauman, 'communism was modernity's most devout, vigorous and gallant champion – pious to the point of simplicity' (Bauman 1991, p. 179). In these and other passages, it is difficult to determine whether Bauman is claiming that Nazis, Communists and other modernists were sincere disciples of an emotion-free, hyper-rational vision of the Enlightenment, or, if they were pretending to be sincere. This is difficult to determine because he does not raise the issue of sincerity in relation to the topics that interest him. By contrast, Erik Erikson (1958) focuses on the issue of 'meaning it' versus 'faking it' when it comes to understanding the motives of the leaders as well as the followers of the Reformation, Enlightenment and other social movements that Western culture has enshrined.[1] One cannot fail to notice the ambiguity in Bauman's emotion-laden vocabulary ('attractiveness', 'devout', 'gallant' etc.) in describing the apostles of an emotion-free ideology allegedly derived from the Enlightenment. Does Bauman 'mean it', in Erikson's sense, with regard to his descriptions of modernity? The best answer seems to be that analysts rarely, if ever, pose this question publicly. To be sure, some have questioned Bauman's Communist past, but not his sincerity regarding his alleged commitment to Communism, as in this reply he gave to a journalist:

> If you looked at the political spectrum in Poland at that time, the Communist party promised the best solution. Its political programme was the most fitting for the issues which Poland faced. And I was completely dedicated. Communist ideas were just a continuation of the Enlightenment.[2]

How 'completely' dedicated was he, or anyone else, to Communism? Where are the nuances one expects in any description of a person's commitment to anything? Contrast Bauman's self-assessment with those of the ex-Communist Milovan Djilas, who was imprisoned for changing his mind about Communism. Much of Bauman's intellectual career centres on the truth aspects of Communism and modernity. But Djilas claims that 'the will to gain and hold power is the strongest motivation and basic essence of contemporary communism' (Djilas 1984, p. 53). Bauman has made a tremendous contribution to knowledge by depicting Communism, not as the Evil Empire (in Ronald Reagan's words), but as Western modernity's close kin. But should we believe Bauman that Communism was 'just' a continuation – with no added elements – of the Enlightenment? Again, nuances seem to be missing in Bauman's assessments of the social world.

Late in his intellectual career, Bauman seems to have moved his attention from the 'solid modernity' associated with Nazism and Communism to the new, 'liquid modernity' that he associates with a plethora of phenomena, ranging from postmodernism to the abuse at Abu Ghraib and Guantanamo. For example, Bauman writes in *Liquid Modernity*:

> The stories about the sinister exploits inside the Guantanamo camp or Abu Ghraib prison, cut off not only from national or international law, and about the gradual but relentless descent into inhumanity of men and women appointed to perpetrate or supervise that lawlessness, have been publicized in the press widely enough to save us from repeating them here. What we think of less often, however, and what we seldom hear, is that the demons that surfaced in those remote places may be only some particularly extreme, radical and imprudent, wild and reckless specimens of a larger fury of lemurs that haunt the attics and cellars of our homes right here – in the

> world where few if any people continue to believe that changing the life of others is of any relevance to their own life. In a world, in other words, in which each individual is left on his or her own while most individuals are tools of each other's promotion.
>
> (Bauman 2007, p. 23)

In this provocative passage, Bauman seems to connect Abu Ghraib to his other, larger concerns about 'liquid society' in which 'solid' ethics seem to have disappeared. He may be correct that the abuse and social dysfunction at Abu Ghraib is only a reflection of a much more widespread spread of general abuse and dysfunction, including dysfunctional families whose members feel increasingly alone and emotionally abandoned. But how does one connect Bauman's earlier concerns with Nazism and Communism as vehicles for discussing solid modernity based on the Enlightenment to his later concerns with Abu Ghraib as a vehicle for discussing liquid modernity based on postmodern rebellion against the Enlightenment? Is one to believe that Nazi and Communist societies were as solid as he purports, and that these legislative, 'solidly' modern societies had minimal dysfunction, disorder and emotion? Bauman writes that this past version of modernity was one in which most people apparently believed that 'the moral world can only be, therefore, a regular, orderly world' that was 'bent on the eradication of emotions or at least keeping them off limits' (Bauman 1996, p. 10). On the other extreme, is one to believe that the 'liquid' evil at Abu Ghraib was truly 'cut off' from 'any' law? Is one to believe with Bauman that the media has relayed to us all the details that we need to know about how the abuse at Abu Ghraib kept itself in a self-perpetuating cycle of dysfunction? (This, in opposition to the famous idea by Talcott Parsons (1937) that modern societies are 'self-correcting' systems.)

I hope to avoid becoming trapped in the labyrinth of trying to pursue the orderly and 'solid' versus the ambiguous and 'liquid' aspects of Bauman's provocative paradigm. As I have stated at the outset, I intend to treat Bauman's own ambivalence in writing about ambivalence as fruitful and productive. Here again, one may take a cue from Erik Erikson's (1958) monumental study of Martin Luther: Erikson is respectful of Luther's ambivalence, and concludes that Luther resolved his personal issues with authority by changing the social world with regard to papal and spiritual authority. Perhaps, in this sense, Bauman's magnificent and numerous writings are an effort to resolve his personal issues with Communism and modernity, and like Luther long before him, Bauman has changed the social world, at least within a huge portion of sociology. In any event, one should take careful note of Bauman's ambivalence about ambivalence – and by 'note', I mean that one should observe in a neutral fashion, without prejudice and not in a pejorative sense – illustrated in this passage, which purports to 'define' postmodernity:

> Postmodernity ... is modernity which goes beyond its false consciousness and *comes to understand* what it actually was doing all along, i.e., *producing ambivalence and pluralism*, and also *reconciles* itself to the fact that the purposes which were originally set, e.g. rational order and absolute truth, will never be reached.
>
> (Bauman 2001, p. 19, my emphasis)

It is one thing to claim that liquid modernity is the ambivalent end point of modernity. But in his typically complex style, Bauman seems to imply that human agents, in the age of liquid modernity, both comprehend *and* are reconciled to their state of ambivalence, and to a future whose exits have been pitilessly blocked. It is possible to imagine the comprehension of such an existential situation, but if the agent is also 'reconciled' to this dismal fate, he or she is no longer ambivalent. The fatalistic[3] acceptance of a state of permanent ambivalence without the possibility of parole is no longer ambivalence. It is the acceptance of defeat. For these reasons, I shall strive to avoid trying to force Bauman into either the solid modernist or the liquid postmodernist camps in intellectual discourse. In this essay, I will limit myself to the abuse at Abu Ghraib vis-à-vis Bauman's social thought. But this connection is itself fundamentally ambivalent because, as Bauman suggests, the abuse at Abu Ghraib spills over into abuse at Guantanamo and other U.S. military detention facilities, as well as widespread abuse in dysfunctional families. I agree with Bauman that the abuse at Abu Ghraib is a vehicle for discussing much more widespread, contemporary issues and contemporary society as a whole. But I disagree with Bauman in at least three basic assumptions. First, I disagree with Bauman that the Enlightenment was ever as orderly or emotion-free as he purports. Moreover, I regard this false depiction of the Enlightenment as an example of 'postemotional' chicanery (Mestrovic 1997).[4] Second, I deny that the social setting at Abu Ghraib was purely lawless, chaotic and 'liquid'. I shall argue that Abu Ghraib was simultaneously chaotic and orderly, 'solid' and 'liquid' at the same time, and that this seemingly illogical, ambivalent state of affairs was made possible by postemotional, 'fake sincerity' regarding American and Enlightenment ideals. Finally, I disagree with his often-repeated conclusion that the human agent must resign, rejoice, or otherwise reconcile his or her self with a dismal state of existence that is either purely 'solid' or 'liquid'. If the fundamental ambivalence that Bauman sincerely uncovers is the result of 'fake sincerity' within the social fabric, as I will argue that it is, then there exists the possibility of breaking through to authentic, albeit dormant, emotions and narratives. Of course, it is beyond the scope of this essay to venture into the details of how this depiction of Abu Ghraib as a vehicle for a much broader discussion of contemporary societies applies to other social issues, but this assumption is implicit in the rest of this discussion. To be clear on this point, like Bauman, in writing about Abu Ghraib, I am writing about far more than Abu Ghraib.

To rephrase my take on Bauman in a different form, I would urge the reader to compare and contrast Bauman's overall work with David Riesman's *The Lonely Crowd* (1950).[5] In many ways, Bauman's (1989) distinction between 'legislators' and 'interpreters' correspond with Riesman's 'inner-directed' (solid) and 'other-directed' (liquid) social types. Both Bauman and Riesman foreshadowed a social world which is often labelled as postmodern. But there exist some key differences between Bauman and Riesman. One is that like Erikson, Riesman questions what lies beneath the veneer of modernity, and is mindful of insincere manipulation by self, others and society as to what is true concerning the modern world order, whereas Bauman does not venture into questions of what is sincere versus insincere about solid or liquid modernity, or the human agents who inhabit these social worlds. Another difference is that Bauman does not see and does not seem to seek a way out of liquid modernity whereas Riesman – while he believes that a backward-looking retreat to inner-directedness is both impossible and unwanted – leaves open the possibility that new forms of autonomy and authenticity may emerge in the future. To be sure, Riesman does not spell out how the ambivalent, anomic, apathetic, and otherwise distressed other-directed type can find a way out, but he does admit the possibility of hope.[6]

Order and chaos at Abu Ghraib

In summary, so far I have indicated my admiration for Bauman's bold yet ambivalent critique (of sorts) as well as defence (of sorts) of both solid and liquid modernity. I criticize him in one major regard: he neglects the issue of 'sincerity' versus chicanery regarding both individual human agents as well as social institutions.

Let us turn now to Bauman's take on Abu Ghraib as an exemplar of liquid modernity. The most striking thing about the social conditions at Abu Ghraib, as shown through testimony in open trials, sworn affidavits, government reports and other evidence is precisely this: Abu Ghraib was simultaneously bureaucratic and chaotic, orderly and disorderly, modern and postmodern, an example of the Enlightenment-based 'orderly garden' as well as a 'weed' infested space that supposedly produced 'a handful of rotten apples'.[7] On the one hand, a recent report issued by the US Senate Armed Services Committee, co-authored by Senators Carl Levin and John McCain, is blunt in its assessment that the infamous abuse at Abu Ghraib was *not* the result of deeds dreamt up by a few bad apples, but was the direct result of unlawful policies that were established at the White House, then travelled through the bureaucratic, modern chain of command, down to the low-ranking soldiers who carried out the unlawful orders and were eventually sent to prison.[8] This conclusion seems to support Bauman's version of Nazi and Communist methods of committing evil: rational, hierarchical, orderly and in other ways, 'solidly' modern. Moreover, this report makes it clear that these unlawful policies 'migrated' (this is the precise word that is used, migration) from the US-run prison facility at Guantanamo Bay to prisons in Afghanistan, and then to prisons across Iraq, including Abu Ghraib. This report is substantiated by other government reports, numerous film documentaries such as 'Taxi to the Dark Side', and my own direct experiences with testimony in my role as an expert witness for the defence in three Abu Ghraib courts-martial (see Danner 2004, Mestrovic 2007, Strasser 2004).

On the other hand, it is equally true that the soldiers at Abu Ghraib were unable to name their commanding officer or their particular chain of command. The supply officer, Major David DiNenna, testified in open court that he felt 'abandoned' by the army, which failed to supply the soldiers as well as the prisoners with adequate food, water, toilets, light bulbs, generators, bullets and other necessities. I shall probably never forget the moment of this testimony in court, because it was heart-wrenching to hear a commissioned officer accuse the army of 'abandoning' him and the soldiers under his command, and because the idea of a hyper-modern, organized, 'solid' army being unable to provide its soldiers and prisoners with the necessities of life seemed so terribly incongruous. Furthermore, I learnt from testimonies at the trials that soldiers at Abu Ghraib slept in jail cells. This fact was not broadcast far and wide by the media that Bauman assumes is performing its social role adequately. Testimony revealed that Iraqi men were routinely stripped naked and forced to wear panties on their heads. Seemingly countless other details of everyday chaos seem to explain why soldiers and officers described Abu Ghraib, in their own words, as 'a crazy place', 'Bizarro world' and 'a Mad Max movie'.

Thus, if one is to believe the Levin-McCain and other government reports, the abuse at Abu Ghraib was the result of what Bauman calls 'solid' modernity: it was caused by clearly defined yet unlawful policies that emanated from the White House and migrated down the chain of command. Using Riesman's vocabulary, it seems that unlawful policies became the inner-directed, gyroscopic standards for US policy towards prisoners in the war on terror. Through Bauman's own writings on the Holocaust, such reports make one shudder at the thought that Nazi-like policies had infiltrated the US government. On the other hand, if one is to believe the officers and soldiers who testified at the Abu Ghraib trials, Abu Ghraib was a 'Bizarro World' of filth, chaos, depravity and emotional as well as physical abandonment – in a word, it was the poster child for Bauman's 'liquid modernity'. Similarly, and harking back to Riesman, the abuse at Abu Ghraib was motivated in large measure by conformity: other-directed soldiers used their metaphorical 'radars' to detect new, unlawful policies, which they followed as they would any fashion or other trend in contemporary society.

But which version of Abu Ghraib is correct, and which version of Bauman (the early theorist of solid versus the late theorist of liquid modernity) applies to which version of events? How is it possible that the US Army would be solidly modernist with regard to its abusive policies yet hopelessly 'liquid' with regard to food, water, generators, and other necessities for accomplishing its mission (albeit, a perverse mission)? Again, I urge the reader to resist the temptation to opt for easy, well-trodden answers, namely, to choose between order versus chaos in explaining or understanding the abuse at Abu Ghraib vis-à-vis Bauman or in general. This is the very trap that continually leads academics to impose a false sense of order onto reality for the sake of elegance and parsimony based on a fake understanding of Enlightenment-based traditions of thought. In other words, Bauman, like Anthony Giddens (1990), Jean Baudrillard (1986) and other contemporary social theorists, is typically interpreted as intending to claim that societies are moving towards 'liquid modernity' or that modernity is an unstoppable 'juggernaut' or that societies are inevitably heading towards or have already arrived at an age of 'rootless, circulating fictions'. One important theoretical voice in the sociological wilderness that all of these thinkers and mainstream sociology in general omit from their theoretical scaffolding is that of Thorstein Veblen. Veblen ([1899] 1965) pointed out the obvious: the so-called Enlightenment was limited historically and geographically to the Northwest corner of Europe, and was simultaneously an age of science *and* witch hunts, of predatory, barbaric tendencies *and* the 'machine age'. David Riesman ([1960] 1995) captured Veblen's intent with the pithy observation that for Veblen, modernity was only a latter-day barbarism. The key point here is that the phenomenon of barbarism is omnipresent and universal in human history, but the *style* of barbarism changes. Verification for Veblen's unorthodox views can be found in historical accounts such as James Loewen's (1995) *Lies My History Teacher Told Me*. However, and despite Loewen and other authors who seek to deconstruct the false version of the Enlightenment as an idealized state of order, the false version is repeated endlessly in textbooks and so-called mainstream social theory. In other words, it is impossible to arrive at a 'solid' take on what the Enlightenment was 'really' like because such a goal is already based on the fake premises of the Enlightenment, and ignores the emotional investment of those who uphold this fake version.

Despite these theoretical obstacles, let us persevere, and hold the ambivalent thought that Abu Ghraib was simultaneously orderly and chaotic, based on empirical evidence. Thus, Abu Ghraib simultaneously exhibited all of the fruitful oppositions and tensions that interest Bauman, from legislators versus interpreters to solid versus liquid modernity. For example, Abu Ghraib had three commanders ('legislators') simultaneously, yet no one was certain who was in charge (multiple 'interpreters'). Once this accurate and empirically verifiable view is accepted – even though it is contradictory by Enlightenment narrative standards – it leads to other considerations which expose further ambivalence. First, one must examine the courts-martial for the Abu Ghraib trials. Ostensibly, these trials were a celebration of Enlightenment-based principles such as the 'rule of law', yet they resulted in the scapegoating of a few low-ranking soldiers who were sent to prison while their many commanders (legislators) were merely reprimanded and none went to prison. The analogy I want to pursue is that this state of affairs is not fundamentally different from the infamous Salem witch trials that were orchestrated by the Puritans. The Puritans, too, had their lofty, Enlightenment-based culture based on science, freedoms and rationality at the same time that they irrationally persecuted selected human beings as witches (Demos 2004). And it cannot be coincidence that the 'witches' were 'low-ranking' members of Puritan society – their 'rotten apples.' The more important point is that before they executed the alleged witches, the Puritans ensured that these humans were given 'fair trials', had lawyers for their defence, and that evidence was presented by physicians and other experts. In the words of another neglected voice in the sociological wilderness, Alexis de Tocqueville, the Puritan 'founders of New England were both sectarian fanatics and noble innovators' (Tocqueville [1845] 2003, p. 55). One should linger on Tocqueville's arresting choice of words: he describes the Puritans much like contemporary writers describe today's Taliban (sectarian fanatics) while at the same time praising their noble commitment to the Enlightenment. Could it be that the Enlightenment was something like American Civil Religion, as described by Robert N. Bellah (1967)? I argue that Tocqueville's depiction still applies to the fundamentally ambivalent manner in which the Abu Ghraib trials were conducted: the military judge, prosecutor, defence attorneys and all who were involved knew of government reports which existed at the time of the trials which admitted that the soldiers were following policies established by the White House, yet they went through all the bureaucratic, 'rational', procedural and 'legislative' motions described by Bauman in order to treat a handful of low-ranking soldiers as if they were 'witches' from the Puritan days. This was an exercise in what David Riesman calls fake sincerity: 'Just because such a premium is put on sincerity, a premium is put on faking it' (Riesman [1950] 2002, p. 196). Without wishing to deviate too much from the present discussion, the important point is that 'fake sincerity' is itself an oxymoron and an ambivalent concept, not to be reduced to simple deceit. 'Fake sincerity' involves the intricate manipulation of one's self and others (what Riesman [1950] 2002, p. 266 calls 'false personalization') so that the painful cognitive dissonance of exposing either the order or chaos of the ambivalent situation is avoided. For example, the Puritans did not need to examine their hypocrisy (that they were children of the Enlightenment) and barbarism in killing people whom they labelled as 'witches' because they gave them ostensibly 'fair trials'. Similarly, the Abu Ghraib saga was closed in the eyes of most people once the so-called rotten apples went to prison: there was no perceived need and no incentive to hold civilian and military leaders high in the chain of command as responsible for the unlawful policies they had unleashed, despite the doctrine of command responsibility which calls for precisely such an accounting of leaders. Weren't the 'rotten apples' given 'fair trials' in one of the most lawful nations on the planet?

Second, the role of the media and other professions with regard to the war on terror, the abuse at Abu Ghraib, the trials of Abu Ghraib and other events in this overall drama was and continues to be ambivalent. Journalists are trained to be objective, present at least two sides of every story and eschew emotion in their reports for all the other legislative aspects of solid modernity described by Bauman. These are also throwbacks to the inner-directed practices of journalism described by Riesman, such that journalists print 'all the news that is fit to print'. In practice, it is well-known that the media acted largely as cheerleaders for the war on terror, supported corporate interests, and often failed to follow the norms, obligations, and procedures of their profession. Specifically with regard to the Abu Ghraib trials, I witnessed journalists who came in late for trials and left following lunch break, not returning for the afternoon sessions. The trials ran from 9 am to 5 pm, but the media was present for and reported primarily testimonies that occurred between 10 am and 12 noon. Most journalists simply missed some extremely important testimonies, including the fact that the army confiscated 18,000 photos from Abu Ghraib, while only about two hundred photos, at most, were revealed to the public. Some of the unknown photos display facts that are further unknown: that there were women and children imprisoned at Abu Ghraib, that soldiers slept in jail cells, that there was sexual abuse of women and that murder and other heinous crimes at Abu Ghraib were never prosecuted. Bauman seems naïve to believe that the press did its solid duty in reporting on the abuse or the testimony at the trials.

But instead of endlessly returning to the Enlightenment-tainted concepts of order versus chaos in explaining the behaviour of the media, I believe that Riesman's idea of 'fake sincerity' or what I call postemotionalism[9] offer better explanations. In summary, the media presents a faked-sincere façade that it is motivated to find all the news that is fit to print, as journalists succumb to pressure to compete with other journalists in sending their story by the 1 pm deadline. The ambivalent coupling of order and chaos at Abu Ghraib was repeated in the courtroom by journalists reporting on both the abuse and the trials. And in all these layers of analysis (the site of abuse, the courtroom, the media), one would be mistaken to conclude that either the 'legislators' or the 'interpreters' were entirely sincere. Like so many other contemporary social theorists, Bauman seems to assume sincerity, whereas I question it.

Postemotional responsibility

At stake in this discussion is Bauman's overall assessment, made in a long series of books, that liquid modernity has led to the abandonment of the lonely individual such that he or she alone in making ethical decisions and being responsible for them. In Bauman's words,

> [t]he authority of churches, political parties, academic institutions and so on is clearly declining. The responsibility which was taken away from the individuals is coming back – you and I are very much felt alone with our decisions. We do not have a moral code which has all the visibility of being absolute and universal. We confront moral problems again as if modernity had not happened: we are thrown back on individual responsibility.
>
> (Bauman 2001, p. 22)

I do not agree with Bauman's assumptions regarding modernity and the Enlightenment on the one hand, or postmodernity, liquid social forces and the resultant solitary individual on the other. It cannot be true that the survivors of the real Enlightenment or its fanatical champions who later pursued so-called Enlightenment narratives were as exclusively devoted to order, harmony, science, and other virtues as he contends. Chaos, both private and social, always accompanies apparent order. On the other extreme, it is not possible for the solitary individual to be the sole arbiter of morality and ethics. Durkheim (1912) and Veblen (1899) are convincing in their arguments that even the seemingly most private habits, actions, wishes and behaviours of the individual owe an unknown debt to posterity and previous generations. For example, we do not invent language as children, but inherit language which is a social product. Similarly, human agents are never solely responsible for something, but are always connected to notions of collective responsibility. It is an empirical fact that contemporary lawyers routinely sue corporations and institutions in addition to holding individuals accountable for their decisions. Religion is not, as William James (1902) argued, a purely private matter of devotion, but necessarily involves social rituals. Even the most extreme example of Bauman's solitary judge of morality, the narcissist, is at bottom a *social type*: narcissists believe that they are special and unique in being outside the law and of society, but in the end – and quite ironically – they are easily reduced to other narcissists who believe and behave in remarkably similar patterns. And such allegedly solitary and solipsistic individuals are the products of a culture of narcissism which pushes them into the direction of competing with each other on the basis of the narcissism of small differences (Lasch 1974).

Nevertheless, there seems to be a grain of truth in Bauman's depiction of contemporary society: it certainly feels as if the Geneva Conventions, professional ethics, the regulations that are supposed to guide Wall Street investors and other 'solid' moral codes are deteriorating rapidly.

But again, such arguments and counter-arguments are immobilized in the straitjacket of false depictions of the Enlightenment and its alleged opposite, the 'state of nature' depicted by Hobbes, and dutifully cited by Bauman, other theorists and sociology professors around the world. Are the only alternatives an idealized and false vision of Enlightenment order versus a Hobbesian 'war of all against all?' I propose a new theoretical solution to this age-old conceptual dilemma. Suppose that one side of the solid-liquid, society-individual and other dualisms is practicing fake sincerity. To return to Abu Ghraib as a vehicle for discussion, it is not the case that the Geneva Conventions ceased to exist at the prison, as Bauman claims, but that they were not posted and not followed, even though officers and soldiers were fully aware of their existence. When the Taguba Report (in Strasser 2004) exposed this empirical fact, the Bush Administration resolved the cognitive dissonance that ensued with the fake-sincere claim that 'America does not torture people'. If that is true (and it is clearly not true), then the postemotional 'solution' to the problem of explaining the coexistence of the Geneva Conventions and the verifiable abuse is simple: it was the result of 'a few bad apples'. American society cannot tolerate the truth that the U.S. government wrote abuse into its official policies, so it scapegoated a handful of vulnerable, low-ranking soldiers. The irony here is that by placing all responsibility on the lonely individual, Bauman inadvertently [illegible] individual for policies that were not th[illegible]l. (It should go without saying that I [illegible] intention.) Of course, the counter-a[illegible]ual has an ethical duty to disobey an u[illegible]e question: who or what social institu[illegible]e unlawful order in the first place? [illegible] social responsibility with individual, [illegible]

[illegible] in of such abstract arguments, issues [illegible]ate the issue that is at the heart of [illegible]ance to contemporary society. I shall [illegible]n expert witness in and observer of three Abu Ghraib trials, and cite two pieces of testimony as illustrations of these dilemmas. My intention is to show, as I have indicated all along, that solid and liquid modernity coexist in every situation, and that this intolerably ambivalent, dramatic situation is maintained by 'fake sincerity'. Once a portion of the chicanery is exposed, a portion of the ambivalence that haunts Bauman and other contemporary social theorists is also eliminated.

For example, the Company Commander at Abu Ghraib, Captain Donald Reese, was asked to explain on the witness stand why prisoners at Abu Ghraib were stripped naked and forced to wear panties on their heads. He testified that he enquired about this as well, because he thought it was very strange the first time that he walked through the prison. He testified that he was told by his superiors that the 'technique' of forcing naked men to wear panties on their heads was 'an MI [military intelligence] thing' or a 'supply issue'. The 'MI thing' explanation is a vague attempt to claim that wearing panties on one's head was an interrogation technique, even though such a technique is not listed in any official army manual, no rational-legal authority exists to support it, and above all, the prisoners were wearing panties on their heads even when they were not being interrogated. The 'supply issue' explanation is the backup rationalization: one is expected to believe that the U.S. Army was unable to procure blankets and clothing for prisoners, so it had them wear women's panties (which were purchased in Baghdad) to protect them from the cold. The obvious, common sense explanation for women's panties in this context, admitted to me privately by soldiers and officers, is that the Army was seeking to humiliate the Iraqi prisoners. But this simple, obvious, and non-ambivalent explanation was never made in court, and is not really obvious in postemotional society that is based upon chicanery and the manipulation of fake emotions as well as rationalizations. Instead, witnesses resorted to tortured logic and preposterous claims, which were not challenged by the judge, the attorneys, jury, or even the media. The captain's explanation was accepted without emotional reaction, as if he had said something to the effect that he drank from a glass of water. Postemotional society has the feel of living in the Twilight Zone. Preposterous, 'crazy' explanations and behaviours are tolerated so long as they can be explained with reference, however tangential, to some technique which implies 'solid modernity', and without expressing emotional fire, which would be an indicator that the witness has overcome the 'state of nature' and is firmly under the control of Enlightenment narratives. In a word, Captain Reese was *pretending* that obviously irrational, 'liquid modernity' behaviour was in fact 'solid' by resorting to rationalizations of Military Intelligence techniques and 'supply issues'. The postemotional element here is the manipulation of self and others in the courtroom – including the media – to the effect that *real* Enlightenment narratives of order, rationality, and control were the explanation for what otherwise came across as crazy behaviour. Why didn't Captain Reese simply say in open court that the behaviour in question was crazy? Part of the answer is that his performance in open court was part of a rehearsed, orchestrated, and what I call postemotional morality play based upon false depictions of Enlightenment narratives.

Let us dissect this example more closely. One of many insincere and largely unknown elements in the testimony described above is that the Company Commander had been promised immunity from prosecution in exchange for his testimony. But this meant that he promised to give the army the testimony or 'truth' it wanted in order to avoid prosecution against him. In the falsely 'solid' social world of the U.S. Army, there exists the doctrine of command responsibility. This doctrine holds that commanders are responsible for acts of commission (giving an unlawful order) as well as omission (failing to take steps to prevent unlawful acts which they did not order). This is one of those 'open secrets' so reminiscent of Communist regimes: everyone knows the real truth, but no one dares speak it. In his book, *Nineteen Eighty-Four*, George Orwell illustrates this phenomenon with regard to the central character, Winston, who feels spiritually free so long as he knows that 2 + 2 = 4, even though he must proclaim publicly for Big Brother that it equals 5. I brought up the doctrine of command responsibility during my expert witness testimony, and it was simply ignored by the judge, prosecutor, and everyone else. It was as if I had said nothing at all. The doctrine of command responsibility could have been invoked against Captain Reese. Moreover, had this doctrine been invoked in prosecuting the Company Commander for the abuse at Abu Ghraib due to lack of leadership, it automatically would have opened a Pandora's Box of questions concerning similar command responsibility for his commanders, all the way up the chain of command to the Commander-in-Chief (see Hersh 2004). In Bauman's vocabulary, the possible invocation of the falsely 'solid' doctrine of command responsibility would have made the situation seem 'liquid' by raising questions of how the unlawful policies that erupted at Abu Ghraib originated and 'migrated' down the chain of command while the United States was claiming officially and formally that it was following the Geneva Conventions as a matter of policy. Here again apparent 'order' and 'chaos' came down to how 'legislators' chose to 'interpret' a situation they controlled. There can be little doubt that the simplest solution to this dilemma was to preserve the false image that the 'solid' Geneva Conventions were followed by officers and disobeyed by low-ranking soldiers who engaged in 'liquid' abuse. While the prosecutor allowed officers to state their case in 'solid' terms – following MI policy and 'supply shortage' – he went out of his way to portray the 'rotten apples' as acting in a 'liquid' or what he called frat-party, jovial, irrational manner of sadistically engaging in abuse for no rational reason at all. Logically, low-ranking soldiers could have been given immunity from prosecution in order to testify against commanders in their chain of command for ordering, condoning, and failing to prevent the abuse – but this option was closed due to the fake-sincere script that the army chose to present to the world. And the more important point is that this chicanery involves far more than a particular prosecutor, judge and set of trials regarding Abu Ghraib. The judge self-consciously stated, 'The army is not on trial here!' He did not need to state, but we may infer, that he also did not want the Enlightenment to be on trial either. Using Riesman's wonderful concept of 'jury of one's peers' to refer to all of other-directed society, which acts like a real jury through the media, one may conclude: the entire world was the 'jury' watching these trials, and the outcome had to be predictable, namely, that the abuse was the result of a few 'rotten apples', but not of 'legislators' who misused the Enlightenment narratives.

There are many more layers of fake sincerity in this one example of testimony, but in the interest of space, I shall analyse only one more aspect before moving to another example. Sworn statements as well as testimonies by others revealed that MI was aware of the unlawful orders that followed General Geoffrey Miller's infamous visit in August of 2003 for the expressed purpose to 'Gitmoize' Abu Ghraib (see Karpinski 2005). 'Gitmoization' refers to the explicit decision to transplant policies from Guantanamo Bay, where the Geneva Conventions were ruled not to apply, to Abu Ghraib, where the Geneva Conventions were supposed to apply. In Bauman's terminology, a 'liquid', unlawful policy (itself an oxymoron) was deliberately transferred to a site that was supposed to be 'solidly' under the sway of the Geneva Conventions. But MPs (Military Police) at Abu Ghraib was not aware of these secret orders to which MIs were privy. The over dozen government reports on Abu Ghraib routinely cite friction and misunderstanding between MIs and MPs at Abu Ghraib, without admitting that the MI were acting under 'liquid' policies while MPs were trying to behave under 'solid' rules. The Company Commander was in charge of an MP group of soldiers, and was apparently genuinely shocked by the sight of naked, shackled Iraqi prisoners with panties on their heads. He testified that he knew such actions were against the Geneva Conventions, but when he confronted his MI superiors, he was told to go along with the 'MI thing'. In a 'solid' military unit, he could have protested all the way up the chain of command, but as I have mentioned previously, the chain of command at Abu Ghraib was so 'liquid' that no one was certain as to who was in charge of this prison facility or prison facilities in Iraq generally. Brigadier General Janis Karpinski (2005), who was in charge of all MPs in Iraq, similarly wrote a book in which she claimed that MI officers above her in the chain of command circumnavigated her 'solid' authority.

In sum, the parameters of individual versus collective (command) responsibility by MI versus MPs vis-à-vis the façade that the United States was following the Geneva Conventions in Iraq but not in Guantanamo Bay created an intricate, complex situation that was simultaneously 'liquid' and 'solid', chaotic and orderly. Perhaps the more important point is that the situation could not have been 'liquid' and chaotic without the chicanery and fake image of being 'solid'. All this was known to the prosecutors and defence attorneys at the trials, but for the most part, was forbidden from being disclosed in testimony. I will elaborate on this point later. The trials of Abu Ghraib as well as the abuse at Abu Ghraib were both elaborate exercises in fake sincerity, such that 'liquid' and 'solid' elements coexisted in the presentation of reality.

The drama of torturing 'Gilligan'

Let us turn next to one of the most infamous photographs of the abuse at Abu Ghraib, that of the prisoner nicknamed 'Gilligan', who is seen standing on a box, wearing a hood and hooked up to electrodes. Testimony revealed that the electrodes were not hooked up to electricity, but it is not clear whether Gilligan knew this fact. Why would soldiers engage in such chicanery? Testimony revealed that three low-ranking soldiers were given an order by a commissioned officer to keep Gilligan awake as part of a 'sleep deprivation plan' with the specific words, 'I don't care what you do to him, just don't kill him'. Ironically, the commissioned officer who gave this unlawful order was also a CID special agent, which means that he later interrogated soldiers and gathered evidence against them for following his unlawful orders, while he was never charged with wrongdoing. Among other soldiers, Sabrina Harman was charged with 'maltreatment' for participating in this episode at Abu Ghraib. Her civilian defence attorney, frank Spinner, made claims in the courtroom that seem preposterous at first glance: namely, that Harman struck up a friendship with 'Gilligan' and that they were joking while he was standing on the box, so that this incident did not constitute maltreatment. He argued that precisely because she did not want to hurt him or anyone else at Abu Ghraib, but was ignored when she tried to protest the abuse on other occasions, she convinced him to 'play along' with staged abuse so that neither one of them would get in trouble.[10]

On the one hand, there is something disturbing about using the word *friendship* to refer to a relationship between a soldier and prisoner in which the soldier seems to be forcing a frightened, hooded prisoner to stand on a box for hours at a time. If Gilligan really was joking and laughing, he must have been desperate. At first blush, it seemed simply crazy to refer to the relationship between 'Gilligan' and Harman as a friendship. On the other hand, it seems that Spinner was touching upon a creative attempt by a powerless, low-ranking soldier to exert some autonomy and responsibility in a situation she felt she could not control: she could be and apparently really was 'friends' with a prisoner that she was pretending to 'abuse'. As an MP, she was ordered by MI to 'soften up' a prisoner (with no clear end-point or solid 'interrogation plan') and she decided to make the 'torture' as pleasant as possible under the brutal circumstances.

The prosecutor retorted that even if this explanation was true, the very act of photographing 'Gilligan' in this situation constituted the crime of maltreatment. 'Maltreatment?', Spinner asked. 'That's where the fight is', he said. The prosecution would have one believe that taking the photographs was maltreatment. Spinner said he would concede that she took the photos. But he would fight the idea that taking the photos constitutes maltreatment. A plethora of other reasons for taking the photos emerged during testimony, ranging from whistle-blowing to passive conformity. Herein lies another ambivalent circumstance that involves chaos and order simultaneously: The prosecutor argued that the photographs were part of the 'liquid' and irrational abuse, but he used them as part of 'solid' evidence to prosecute his case. On the other hand, the low-ranking soldiers testified that they took the photographs to document the abuse because their objections to the abuse were ignored and no one would believe their stories without the 'solid' proof of the photos. There is no adequate explanation for why they took the photos, how the photos were edited, framed and used against them, and how journalists arrived at seemingly 'solid' interpretations of the meaning of the photos without reporting on the intricate testimony that surrounded the photography.

In summary, the Abu Ghraib trials were carefully scripted and controlled at the same time that they offered a dramatic spectacle of chaotic, competing interpretations. No officers were put on trial, to prevent uncomfortable questions as to who gave orders for or set the stage for the abuse. The lowest-ranking soldiers were court-martialled, with a script prepared for them that obeying unlawful orders is not an excuse. All the officers and fellow soldiers who testified against the 'rotten apples' did so out of fear and intimidation that they could be prosecuted for the same offences: dereliction of duty, conspiracy, and maltreatment. Neither the trials nor the abuse at Abu Ghraib were examples of what Durkheim ([1912] 1965) called *spontaneous*, genuinely emotional, collective effervescence. Rather, Harman was found guilty of these crimes even though she did not yell or shout at anyone, did not punch anyone and did not participate in the sexual and violent abuse other than pose in photographs. By these standards, most soldiers at Abu Ghraib were guilty for simply being there during abuse and not stopping it, though most testified that they felt helpless to stop it. For the most part, the courts-martial of all seven rotten apples were a non-Durkheimian scripted performance in carefully orchestrated, postemotional imitation of 'collective effervescence'. More importantly, the documented facts concerning similar abuse at Guantanamo, in Afghanistan and in Iraq other than at Abu Ghraib were strictly kept out of the courts-martial. Such evidence points to widespread and systematic abuse, which ruins the storyline of the seven rotten apples acting on their own. The seven rotten apples were sent to prison, and the larger story of how the abuse was ordered, as well as its widespread nature, was largely forgotten. Bauman's ambivalent stand on ambivalence and liquid versus solid modernity fits various facts in the Abu Ghraib drama, but does not capture the overall thrust of the drama. One has to question the relative degree of sincerity versus insincerity of all the actors involved in order to grasp, emotionally as well as rationally, the dynamics of the abuse and the subsequent cover-up. It is worth repeating that the cover-up was performed in an 'open' courtroom, reminiscent of Communist regime show trials.

Conclusions: The end of truth?

If it is a truism that postmodernists write about the 'end of truth', it is also true that the meaning of this claim is debatable. Bauman's particular take on this subject is typically ambivalent, as when he writes,

> Postmodernity does not seek to substitute one truth for another, one standard of beauty for another, one life ideal for another. Instead it splits the truth, the standards and the ideal into already deconstructed and about to be deconstructed. It denies in advance the right of all and any revelation to slip into the place vacated by the deconstructed/discredited rules. It braces itself for a life without truths, standards, and ideals.
>
> (Bauman 1991, p. ix)

Let us skip the seemingly nihilistic consequences of Bauman's claim, which might suggest that we will never know the truth about Abu Ghraib. The more relevant point, as it pertains to the present discussion, is that the military judge and prosecutor tried their best to keep out of the courtroom various truth-claims that would damage the government's position. At the same time, they participated in an imitation of a Durkheimian ritual (namely, a trial) whose aim was supposed to be a re-enactment of the Enlightenment drama in bringing out the 'truth, the whole truth, and nothing but the truth'. During the three courts-martial in which I participated as an expert witness in sociology for the defence, the military judge and the prosecutor would not allow the words 'Guantanamo' and 'Afghanistan' to be mentioned in any testimony, including my own. The judge ruled from the bench that the abuses at Abu Ghraib had no connection to abuses in Guantanamo and Afghanistan. As a matter of fact, he was wrong in making this consistent ruling. The Levin–McCain Report, issued in 2008, has connected the abuses at all three sites to a widespread US policy that promoted torture and abuse. But this information – that the abuse among these three sites was connected – was already available at the time of the courts-martial in the year 2005 in the Schlesinger Report. The defence for all the 'rotten apples' hinged on the fact that they did not individually dream up the abuse on their own but were following unlawful policies that had 'migrated' from installations at Gitmo and in Afghanistan. This is the truth-claim that shatters the government's 'fake sincerity' in prosecuting the low-ranking soldiers, and was treated as dangerous.

When I mentioned on the witness stand that these abusive techniques did, indeed, originate in and migrated from Gitmo and Afghanistan, the military judge stopped the trial and ordered the jury to leave the courtroom. He argued with the one and only defence attorney who challenged him in any of the seven trials on this ruling, Frank Spinner, at length as to whether I should be permitted to state this documented fact in open court. The judge demanded to know my evidence. Spinner responded that it came from a U.S. government report authored by James Schlesinger. The prosecutor argued that the Schlesinger Report is not a bona fide learned treatise, and is inadmissible as evidence. They argued back and forth until the judge finally admitted that a U.S. government report is on par with learned treatises. He called the jury back into the courtroom and ruled that I would be permitted to restate the obvious fact that the abuse at Abu Ghraib, Gitmo, and Afghanistan was connected. When I began to speak, the prosecutor again objected, and this time the judge sent me out of the courtroom while the attorneys argued some more. Eventually, I was called back into the courtroom and allowed to state this obvious fact. By this time, the military jury was clearly attentive. Although the prosecutor asked for a sentence of five years, the jury returned a sentence of three months.

How can one explain all this drama over stating an obvious truth that has been verified many times by multiple sources? To be sure, some modernist, 'solid', 'legislator-type' academics will be tempted to fall back on seemingly 'solid' rules of evidence and procedure that judges and lawyers use, and which are often incomprehensible to the lay person. But such recourse to alleged Enlightenment narratives (rules and procedures) begs multiple questions: How enlightening can the Enlightenment narratives be if they can be understood only by legal specialists, who, in turn, argue with each other as to their meaning? The most obvious, common sense explanation appears to be far more convincing: the military judge and prosecutor attempted to engage in a postemotional, 'open-secret' type cover-up of information that would 'illuminate' the government's pernicious role in the abuse at Abu Ghraib. They orchestrated this cover-up by manipulating Enlightenment narratives. There was no need for the government to engage in Orwellian, draconian suppression of the media, because the media itself is part of postemotional society's manipulations. My testimony occurred after lunch, so that the media was not present in the courtroom for the one time in the courts-martial that the government's efforts failed. The opposing, postmodern point of view (that there are no truths, only apparent truths ready to be deconstructed) is negated by the simple fact that the military judge and prosecutor invested so much *emotional* energy into keeping certain truth-claims out of the courtroom. If the postmodernists were correct that there is no truth, there would be no threat to the power elite (see Mills 1959) from admitting any and all truth-claims into discourse, since none would be privileged and all would be subject to deconstruction. But, in fact, not all truth-claims are equal, and some are dangerous to the status quo.

The notions of 'sincerity' and 'meaning it' are essential for the sorts of discussions that involve Enlightenment narratives versus 'liquid modernity' and which animate Bauman's interests. Without the added, emotional element of sincerity, such discussions come across as grand, but overly abstract. If Bauman is correct (and I believe he is) that Enlightenment narratives eschew human emotion, then one should pay attention to how passion enters into discourses that involve such narratives, and holds the potential to sabotage[11] such fake discourses. My point is that if Bauman is correct about Enlightenment narratives, then any genuinely spontaneous, imaginative, emotional, and sincere departure from the Enlightenment script is sufficient to expose the postemotional, false premises of Enlightenment narratives. For my final illustration, I will cite the closing exchange between the prosecutor and myself in Sabrina Harman's court-martial.

The prosecutor pointed to the door in the courtroom, and asked me forcefully, 'Doctor, just tell me why Harman didn't walk out that door?' He was grandstanding, as lawyers often do in the courtroom, and clearly he was referring to the door in the courtroom as a metaphor for why this soldier did not leave the scene of abuse at Abu Ghraib. Of course, intuition and emotional intelligence are required to grasp that he was not talking about the specific, actual door in the courtroom with his reference to 'that' door. (One should keep in mind Jean Piaget's writings on 'concrete reasoning', which are purely rational, in opposition to 'formal operational' thinking, which involves imagination.) The prosecutor departed from his script, and created an emotional moment in the courtroom. Typically, lawyers ask witnesses concrete questions which are supposed to be answered with a 'yes' or 'no' answer. But at this moment in the drama, the prosecutor decided to pose an open-ended question, which calls for imagination and emotion as well as logic. I answered: 'Captain, I can't walk out that door either, because the judge has to dismiss me first. I could walk out physically, but there are social norms in this room, just like there were social norms at Abu Ghraib that prevented Harman from walking out the door.' The judge nodded in agreement. I did not have to explain further to the judge or the jury all the human, passionate elements that go into 'walking out' of a metaphorical door into freedom and genuine Enlightenment ideals. The prosecutor sat down, and the judge dismissed me. I turned to the judge and asked, 'Your Honour, does this mean I may now walk out that door?' He answered, 'Yes, Doctor, you may walk out that door.' He could have chastised me for my impish, even mildly sarcastic behaviour, but he allowed it. I left the witness stand, and walked through the door, which was held open for me by a military guard who smiled at me. Of course, on a concrete level of abstraction, I merely walked out of a physical door. But it was clear to everyone in the courtroom, and especially to the jurors, that I was making the intuitive point that the accused, and I, and everyone else depend on authority and society and other people in exercising our limited options for freedom and responsibility.

And this is the point at which Bauman's hyper-impressive 'grand theory' of solid versus liquid modernity, order versus chaos, modernity versus postmodernity, and other dualisms reaches its breaking point.

I would extend the metaphor of the door to the situations created by Bauman's social theory, and ask: Where is 'the door' by which human agents may exit the intolerable situations of a purely solid or liquid society? Bauman's theory neglects to point to a door for us to use as an exit. Human agents do not inhabit exclusively one pole *or* the other pole in his many dualisms. In fact, they experience order *and* chaos, solid *and* liquid modernity, collective *and* individual responsibility and so on, at all times. And they navigate these cognitive dualisms at all times with various mixtures of emotions, sincerity, 'meaning it' and 'not really meaning it', among other components of Nature that champions of Enlightenment narratives, in fact, have not squelched.

For these reasons, the reality of Abu Ghraib comes across as a human drama, not an abstract test or falsification of any theory about Enlightenment narratives or postmodernism or any other abstraction. One suspects that if one were to look for emotional and postemotional elements in Communism, the Holocaust and other sites of human abuse, one would find similar human drama. Finally, one should enquire into the drama of Zygmunt Bauman, the person who created so much rich social theory, albeit, most of it in an ambivalent vein. Is he like a prosecutor who is putting the Enlightenment narratives on trial, metaphorically speaking, and if so, why? Is he like a judge who tries to act like a neutral referee in deciding between 'solid' versus 'liquid' modernity? Is he like a defence attorney who is defending a client, and if so, against whom, and who is the client? As I have stated at the outset, Bauman is ambivalent – even so far as to be ambivalent about ambivalence – so that it seems impossible to answer these questions at the present time. Nevertheless, I think these are important questions to raise. Ultimately, these questions come down to the fundamental question: Does Bauman 'mean it?' Is he being sincere in his claims about the Enlightenment? In the end, Enlightenment – socialized scholars, who gives us 'blear-eyed wisdom out of midnight oil', – would do well to ponder the imaginative dimensions of the immortal, concluding line from the poem, 'Among School Children', by William Butler Yeats: 'How can we know the dancer from the dance?' This question pertains to Bauman as well as the abuse at Abu Ghraib.

Notes

1. It is beyond the scope of this essay to explore the concept of 'sincerity' sociologically in a satisfactory way. It is worth noting that sincerity is the crux of Erikson's influential study of Martin Luther and the origins

of Protestantism, and Max Weber's famous study, *The Protestant Ethic and the Spirit of Capitalism*, is important for understanding the importance of 'faith' in modernist religion as well as capitalism. David Riesman (1950) also focuses on the interplay of these concepts in his study of the modernist, 'inner–directed' social type in his *Lonely Crowd*.

2. Aida Edemariam, 'Professor with a Past', *The Guardian*, 28 April 2007.
3. There are many versions of fatalism in the literature. I am referring to Emile Durkheim's neglected definition of fatalism as an attitude 'of persons with futures pitilessly blocked and passions violently choked' ([1897] 1951, p. 276). Durkheim even referred to 'fatalistic suicide' as a neglected, fourth type to complement his descriptions of anomic, egoistic, and altruistic suicides. But it is safe to conclude that Durkheim's concept of fatalism has been largely ignored by sociologists.
4. I am using the antiquated word, 'chicanery', based upon the entire thrust of Thorstein Veblen's ([1898] 1965) use of this word in *Theory of the Leisure Class* to capture multiple aspects of a false existence within modern society, ranging from emulation to the dominance of prestige and status-seeking to cover up barbarian, predatory tendencies.
5. Here again, we must bracket a potentially interesting discussion of Bauman's and Riesman's starting points and assumptions, because it is beyond the scope of this essay. But I will mention briefly that Bauman and Riesman share, to some extent, the intellectual scaffolding of critical theory and the Frankfurt School of sociology. Riesman was especially influenced by Erich Fromm's particular brand of Marxism. Bauman is open about Marx's influence upon him. But unlike Bauman, Riesman was also influenced by Thorstein Veblen, Alexis de Tocqueville, and Sigmund Freud (an unlikely and diverse set of influences). Thus, Riesman and Bauman overlap as well as differ in their fundamental assumptions concerning 'rationality' and 'emotions'.
6. Contrast Riesman with Bauman (2001) in passages where he describes liquid modernity in terms of 'mental depression, the feeling of one's impotence' such that 'to be adequate to the tasks of life becomes the emblematic malaise of postmodern times' (p. 43). He uses the slogan, 'Individually we stand, individually I fall' to capture the mood of liquid modernity.
7. It is beyond the scope of this essay to support this claim fully. These claims are documented extensively in Mestrovic (2007), Mestrovic and Lorenzo (2008), and Caldwell and Mestrovic (2008).
8. See http://levin.senate.gov/newsroom/supporting/2008/Detainees.121108.pdf
9. 'A working definition of postemotionalism might be that it is a neo-Orwellian mechanism found in Western societies in which the culture industry markets and manipulates dead emotions from history that are selectively and synthetically attached to current events' (Mestrovic 1997, p. 11). It is beyond the scope of this essay to delve into the theoretical scaffolding for postemotional social theory, which includes Durkheim, Freud, Riesman, Veblen, and Orwell. It will suffice to say that, for the present discussion, the concept applies to the confusion, hypocrisies, nostalgia, ironies, paradoxes, and neo-Orwellian manipulation regarding the so-called Enlightenment.
10. I cannot avoid citing Carol Gilligan's famous polemic against Lawrence Kohlberg's excessively rationalistic, Kantian, explanation of morality as being patriarchal. Gilligan argued that in approaching moral issues, women

resort to dialogue and 'relational' tactics. Harman seems to exhibit the traits that Gilligan describes. In addition, Harman seems to be exhibiting 'expressive' or emotional aspects, as described by Talcott Parsons, in opposition to typically masculine, 'instrumental' dimensions of social life. For further discussion, see Caldwell and Mestrovic (2008).

11. I use the term 'sabotage' along the lines of Thorstein Veblen's fascinating use of this term 'to describe any manoeuvre of slowing-down, inefficiency, bungling, obstruction' (in Mestrovic 2003, p. 85). For Veblen, sabotage can be benign or sinister, in service of the 'common man' or the 'leisure class', depending upon its usage.

References

Baudrillard, J. (1986), *America*. London: Verso.

Bauman, Z. (1987), *Legislators and Interpreters*. Ithaca: Cornell University Press.

——— (1989), *Modernity and the Holocaust*. Ithaca: Cornell University Press.

——— (1991), *Intimations of Postmodernity*. London: Polity Press.

——— (1993), *Modernity and Ambivalence*. Ithaca: Cornell University Press.

——— (1996), *Alone Again: Ethics After Certainty*. London: Demos.

——— (2001), *Individualized Society*. London: Polity.

——— (2007), *Liquid Modernity*. London: Polity.

Bellah, R. N. (1967), 'Civil Religion in America'. *Daedalus, Journal of the American Academy of Arts and Sciences*, 96 (1): 1–21.

Caldwell, R. A. and Stjepan Mestrovic (2008), 'The Role of Gender in Expressive Abuse At Abu Ghraib'. *Cultural Sociology*, 2 (3): 275–99.

Daedalus, Journal of the American Academy of Art and Sciences, Vol. 96, No. 1, pp. 1–21.

Danner, M. (2004), *Torture and Truth: America, Abu Ghraib and the War on Terror*. New York: New York Review of Books.

Demos, J. (2004), *Entertaining Satan: Witchcraft and the Culture of Early New England*. New York: Oxford University Press.

Djilas, M. (1984), *Of Prisons and Ideas*. New York: Harcourt Brace.

Durkheim, E. [1897] (1951), *Suicide: A Study in Sociology*. New York: Free Press.

——— [1912] (1965), *The Elementary Forms of the Religious Life* New York: Free Press.

Erikson, E. H. (1958), *Young Man Luther: A Study in Psychoanalysis and History*. New York: W.W. Norton.

Giddens, A. (1990), *The Consequences of Modernity*. Stanford: Stanford University Press.

Hersh, S. (2004), *Chain of Command: The Road From 9/11 to Abu Ghraib*. New York: Harper Collins.

James, W. [1902] (1965), *The Varieties of Religious Experience*. New York: Longman.

Karpinski, J. (2005), *One Woman's Army: The Commanding General of Abu Ghraib Tells Her Story*. New York: Hyperion.

Lasch, C. (1974), *The Culture of Narcissism*. New York: W.W. Norton.

Loewen, J. (1995), *Lies My Teacher Told Me: Everything Your American History Textbook Got Wrong*. New York: Touchstone.

Mestrovic, S. (1997), *Postemotional Society*. London: Routledge.

——— (2003), *Thorstein Veblen on Culture and Society*. London: Sage.
——— (2007), *The Trials of Abu Ghraib*. Boulder: Paradigm.
Mestrovic, S. and Ronald, L. (2008), 'Durkheim's Concept of Anomie and the Abuse at Abu Ghraib'. *Journal of Classical Sociology*, 8 (2): 179–207.
Mills, C. W. (1959), *The Power Elite*. New York: Oxford University Press.
Orwell, G. (1949), *Nineteen Eighty-Four*. London: Penguin.
Parsons, T. (1937), *The Structure of Social Action*. New York: Free Press.
Riesman, D. [1950] (2002), *The Lonely Crowd*. New Haven: Yale University Press.
Riesman, D. [1960] (1995), *Thorstein Veblen*, New Brunswick: Transaction Publishers.
Strasser, S. (2004), *The Abu Ghraib Investigations: The Official Reports of the Independent Panel and the Pentagon on the Shocking Prisoner Abuse in Iraq*. New York: Public Affairs.
Tocqueville, A. [1845] (2003), *Democracy in America*. New York: Penguin.
Veblen, T. [1899] (1965), *Theory of the Leisure Class*. London: Penguin.

4
Another Bauman: The Anthropological Imagination

Peter Beilharz

Zygmunt Bauman who is widely known as the postmodern sociologist is now also known as the theorist of liquid modernity. My sense is that he really is neither. Bauman's project is mobile, as befits its object. Modernity moves. The earlier enthusiasm for the postmodern, from *Legislators and Interpreters* (1987), was in part a reaction to the sense of sea change. After communism, modernity was bound to mean something different. But the postmodern was also a cultural phenomenon with a use by date, except in the most general sense, that of following modernism. The idea of the liquid modern, in turn, refers both to the sense of heightened mobility associated with revived uncertainty – all that is solid melts into air – and to the closer, post-war sense that the robust institutions associated with Fordism and Keynesianism now dissolve before our eyes. Whatever happened to full employment and the social regime which constructed it? There is your answer.

What is the liquid modern? It is an emblem, or a symbol rather than a theory or a social phase of development. It represents a way of seeing where what was taken for granted after World War II now seems mercurial, perhaps especially to those of us who have lived through this. For those born into this present, this acute anxiety and sense of insecurity must surely seem normal, normalized, simply the way the world works. For those born into the 80s, this world must seem speedy, busy, bubbly and demanding, but essentially modern, representing the now, the *Jetztzeit* rather than the new revolution; it must feel rather like the revolution of the modern itself.

The image of liquidity in social theory has, however, become a new scholarly commonsense. Liquidity has become a futurist version of the zombie metaphor when often all that is indicated is the sense of process and movement which sociologists have always sought to grasp, though it is again mercurial. This is not, then, an indication that all that is solid melts into air; Bauman's intention is not to turn the idea of liquid modernity into a hard, or soft phase of development that separates it from what came before, it is rather to seek to capture its present tangibility. 'All that is solid melts into air' is not the new mantra; it is the significant period mistranslation of Marx's image, which refereed rather to the standing and estate-like character of the earlier, pre-locomotive period (Beilharz, 2005).

Perhaps, then, Bauman is (as he is given to insist) after all a sociologist, an analyst and critic of modernity. Of course; yet there is so much more in his work, a surfeit of meanings, arguments, ideas and thinkers. Evidently Bauman's work is more than a sociology, though it could also be seen as a sociology in the general, everything-that-is-social, rather than specific post-war disciplinary sense. Bauman is, among other things, a 19th-century figure, a sage and professor of things in general.

He is also a continental sociologist, which means that he draws no hard lines between sociology and philosophy. The affinity here is with other East-Central European writers including sociologists like Agnes Heller and Ivan Szelenyi. And because his background is continental, he also presumes that insight appears often in literature. His earlier explicit enthusiasm for hermeneutics in *Hermeneutics and Social Science* (1978) tells of his commitment to both those fields of understanding. To introduce hermeneutics into social sciences is to add into it respect and curiosity for the book of life. One book then leads to another; biblical hermeneutics opens up into the art of reading texts in general, including literary as well as sociological texts.

The broader issue is that truth, insight or wisdom can be found variously, in all kinds of places. As Keith Tester then observes, Bauman can find as much power in a line from Kundera, Borges or Musil as in the imagery of Gramsci, Simmel or Marx (Tester, 2004). This should come as no surprise to us, for it is consonant with the continental approach itself. Shakespeare and Goethe might be its early modern pioneers. S. S. Prawer makes plain the extent of this wisdom in his classic *Karl Marx and World Literature*, which is still one of the very best books ever written about Marx (Prawer, 1978). For both in detail of line and grandeur of vision, Marx draws fundamentally on literature in the creation of his science. And as Wolf Lepenies shows on the broad canvas of the book called *Between Science and Literature*, there is distinct sense in which sociology emerges in hands like John Stuart Mill's in his *Autobiography* through to Beatrice Webb in her *Apprenticeship* as the bridge or third plane which seeks to connect and mediate science and literature more conventionally defined (Lepenies, 1988).

Beyond the question of disciplinary history, Bauman's attraction to hermeneutics represents an attitude, rather than an orthodoxy or a method. Bauman is deeply committed to the conversational model in social sciences. Hermeneutics is central because interpretation is fundamental, and it is processual, circular, characterized by movement rather than by axioms or truth claims. Human beings tell stories, and seek out stories. This is why ethnology matters, as mythology, as storytelling.

The stories that show in Bauman's work are many and various. This sense of diversity of insights sometimes generates the charge of eclecticism. When it comes to stories about others, however, many of Bauman's interlocutors are anthropologists. At a random glance, there is Marx, whose own enquiry resembles philosophical anthropology, and is interested in beginnings especially early; and then the others: Lévi-Strauss, Mary Douglas, Paul Radin, Rene Girard, Gellner, Kluckhohn, Morgan. Along with the anthropologists, there are other precedents, storytellers of the other: Rabelais, Herodotus, Montesquieu in *The Persian Letters* and of course Montaigne, the greatest exemplar of the essay as the attempt at understanding. In a completely different register, and connecting across the kinds of fields conventionally thought of, literary and anthropological, there are the echoes of Bauman in the work of Georges Bataille, on sacrifice and excess.

On occasion Bauman employs anthropologists to develop particular insights. In *Legislators and Interpreters* Radin is used to work the problem of primitivism, or the modernity of the primitive. Radin writes, for example, that primitive man is afraid of only one thing, the uncertainties of everyday life (1987: 15). Perhaps uncertainty is an anthropological universal, across primitive, modern and liquid modern times. In Bauman's case, the connection is to Freud, across to the volume of essays called *Postmodernity and its Discontents* (1997), where the desire for freedom leads to the desire for security after World War II, and then, again, to the increased popular desire for freedom, even at the expense of increased insecurity, more for some than for some others. More, intellectuals work as mythologists, in this broad scenario, for it is they who develop and propagate myths of foundation, as the inventors of modern tradition. Ernest Gellner is also set to work in Bauman's garden in *Legislators and Interpreters*. This image has travelled further, in the idea that wild culture, or the culture of the gamekeepers, is brought to curb by gardeners and gardening culture, the culture of control. Elsewhere, later, Girard comes to work alongside or nearby Agamben. Modern cultures still have their sacrifices, their scapegoats. Sacrifice is always sacrifice of the others (Beilharz, 2006).

Two anthropologists are relied upon more substantially in Bauman's work. These are Mary Douglas and Claude Lévi-Strauss. Mary Douglas' classic *Purity and Danger* (1966) becomes central to *Modernity and the Holocaust* and its sequel, *Modernity and Ambivalence*. In Bauman's working, this logic points to a larger project, to the sociology of violence.

The central clue for Bauman in *Purity and Danger* is obvious. Dirt is essentially disorder. Dirt is therefore relative to time and place. Uncleanliness is matter out of place. It is but a short step for people, out of place, also to become dirt, the object of the project of social hygiene. Slime is liquid dirt; and this is the theme Bauman uses to connect to anti-Semitism and its exterminatory version, via the work of Sartre. The conceptual Jew was *visqueux*, in Sartrean terms, slimy, in those of Mary Douglas (Bauman, 1989: 39). Viewed as dirt or as weed, the conceptual Jew was a threat to the Nazi conception of order. So did masses of Jews become its victims. Matter out of place, people out of place: all this would have to be sorted, put into order, first by plans of expulsion, then by death camps and roving battalions.

Bauman pursues this idea from *Modernity and the Holocaust* through to its annexe, in *Modernity and Ambivalence*. Here it is the larger concept of the stranger which, or who works as the *visqueux* or slime, both indicating the ineradicable ambivalence of the category and the position. Plainly Bauman's use of Douglas is selective; this is the way he thinks, associates and operates. Similarly with Lévi-Strauss.

The pertinence of Lévi-Strauss for Bauman's project shows especially in two ways. The first is in Bauman's sociology of culture, where structuring works not as result but as activity. This interest arcs back to Bauman's earlier work, in *Culture as Praxis*, and is echoed in the significant essay that attends its second edition, published in 1999. Contrary to the logic of Lévi-Strauss, however, Bauman reads structures as process, as endless beginning rather than as categorical logic. The second use of Lévi-Strauss for Bauman is in the sociology of the other. The text which fascinates here is not *The Elementary Structures of Kinship* but the wonderfully wistful memoirs of *Tristes Tropiques*. The particular image which detains Bauman is in Lévi-Strauss' distinction between anthropoemic and anthropophagic strategies. Bauman anticipates the theme in a footnote to *Modernity and the Holocaust* (1989: 237, n. 27). Here it is Lévi-Strauss' interviews with Charbonnier which act as the prompt. Bauman discusses liquidity in the context of the Nazi gas vans. Fluids of the human kind would flow more or less easily from the vans, depending on their thickness. People about to be murdered lose control of their bodies; for the technologists, these were technical problems of thin and thick liquids, not desperate human problems of excreta and vomit. In Lévi-Strauss' discussion with Charbonnier, Bauman recollects, the indication is that our modern civilization is anthropoemic, as opposed to anthropophagic 'primitive' cultures; they 'devour' their adversaries, while we vomit them up (separate, segregate, evict, exclude from our universe of obligation).

Bauman returns to Lévi-Strauss in 'The Making and Unmaking of Strangers', reprinted in *Post Modern and its Discontents* (1997). Now the frame of reference is firmly modern. Modern strangers, for Bauman, are the waste of the state's ordering zeal. Order-building is a war of attrition waged against the strangers and the strange. In this war (to borrow Lévi-Strauss's concepts) the alternative, but now also complementary strategies are intermittently deployed. In detail:

> One was *anthropophagic*: annihilating the strangers by *devouring* them and then metabolically transforming into a tissue indistinguishable from one's own. This was the strategy of *assimilation*: making the different similar; smothering of cultural or linguistic distinctions; forbidding all traditions and loyalties except those meant to feed the conformity to the new and all-embracing order; promoting and enforcing one and only one measure of conformity. The other strategy was *anthropoemic: vomiting* the strangers, banishing them from the limits of the orderly world and barring them from all communication with those inside. This was the strategy of *exclusion* – confining the strangers within the visible walls of the ghettos or behind the invisible, yet no less tangible, prohibitions of *commensality, connubium* and *commercium*; 'cleansing' – expelling the strangers beyond the frontiers of the managed and manageable territory; or, when neither of the two measures was feasible – destroying the strangers physically.
>
> (1997: 18)

Bauman's claim is that in our times political regimes combine these two strategies, rather than choosing between them. Modernity is always also traditional, always mixed. Modern states then combine the politics and administration of assimilation and expulsion. In Bauman's work this points to a larger project, towards a sociology of surplus populations. The field of a possible sociology of surplus populations is animated by the idea of waste, including human waste and wasted humans. Bauman develops this theme in *Wasted Lives* (2004), though its earlier impulses go back to the images of the Enclosure Acts and 'masterless men' in *Between Class and Elite* (1972), which is given a Foucauldian overdrive in the images of factory discipline in *Memories of Class* (1983).

Behind this image of waste, of excessive and rapacious consumption, of the waste of humans as well as piles of trash and discards that ascend towards heaven is what I would call a critique of modernity as a potlatch culture. This is, of course, a pre-eminently anthropological idea. Its *locus classicus* is with Marcel Mauss, in *The Gift* (Mauss, 1966). There potlatch is distant, rather than present. It combines images of gifting and destruction, which is sacrificial. Potlatch refers both to the senses, to nourish and to consume. It involves killing wealth; and it arouses violence, rivalry and antagonism. Potlatch demonstrates the future of the strong by expending it, to the humiliation of others. Humans celebrate waste transhistorically, when they are blessed by excess abundance, and to show their temporal status and power. The result divides the planet into those who contribute to the garbage heaps and those who work them. Even those who work them, in a perverse way, are surrounded by abundance, by the detritus of plastic, obsolete technologies stacked in waste piles from B-52's to car hulks and computer frames, dead computer screens and hard drives. Bauman wants us to confront the fact that we are awash in shit, where our own refuse, human and material, tells us much of our civilization as the wonders of electronic communication and BMW's, high fashion on high streets. If our lives are indeed mercurial, liquid modern, then we are also surrounded by shit. Dirt is famously, per Mary Douglas, matter out of place, but you do not drown in it. This new culture of liquid modernity is something else.

There are, finally, two other senses in which Bauman's project works anthropologically. The first has to do with Bauman's fascination with the other understood as the realm of radical possibility or imagination. Bauman's fascination with other also manifests as utopia. This means that the other is not only understood negatively, as stigma, within a sociological critique of power, but also positively, as elsewhere, in time and space. The other is routinely reduced in contemporary sociology to the victim, as enemy, outsider, stranger and alter ego. The idea of alterity as utopia in contrast is open to value as well as stigma. The connection of utopia to literature, fiction and satire returns us again to Tester's enthusiasm for the idea of Bauman's project as literary, and not only sociological.

The second sense has to do with Bauman's insistence on the exoticization of the ordinary. The best example of this approach is in his remarkable textbook, *Thinking Sociologically* (1990), whose principal purpose is to present and advocate the purpose of sociology as the 'defamiliarisation of the familiar'. *Thinking Sociologically* is also, almost, thinking modernity anthropologically. This is clear already from its table of contents: freedom, and dependence; us and them; strangers ... gift and exchange, self preservation and moral duty, nature and culture, order and chaos, and so on ... going about the business of life, knowing how to go on, to deal with anthropological universals of life and death as well as modern contingencies, mobile phones and reality television. We could always do other; the message persists.

Elsewhere Bauman describes what he calls the 'sweet scent of decomposition' (1993). Here he connects back to a radically underdeveloped sensibility in social criticism, to the significance of the senses and the sense of smell in particular. Orwell used smell as an indicator; the smell of decomposition we might, in contrast, connect with warmer climes than Wigan Pier or Leeds. The logic of the curiosity remains powerful, and its interests remain suggestive of what could be an urban ethnography. Whatever the case, as I hope to have shown in this essay, Bauman's work is also suggestive of an anthropological imagination. Whatever the status of sociology or literature here, Bauman also behaves like an anthropologist of modernity. In this, the nature of his curiosity coincides with what Joel Kahn calls for, as an anthropology of modernity (Kahn, 2001). The conversation with the other is also a conversation with ourselves.

References

Bauman, Zygmunt (1972) *Between Class and Elite*. Manchester: Manchester University Press.

Bauman, Zygmunt (1973), *Culture as Praxis*. Second edition, London: Routledge and Kegan Paul.

Bauman, Zygmunt (1978), *Hermeneutics and Social Science*. London: Hutchinson.

Bauman, Zygmunt (1982), *Memories of Class*. London: Routledge.

Bauman, Zygmunt (1987), *Legislators and Interpreters*. Oxford: Polity.

Bauman, Zygmunt (1989), *Modernity and the Holocaust*. Oxford: Polity.

Bauman, Zygmunt (1990), *Thinking Sociologically*. Oxford: Polity.

Bauman, Zygmunt (1991), *Modernity and Ambivalence*. Oxford: Polity.

Bauman, Zygmunt (1993), 'The Sweet Scent of Decomposition', in C. Rojek and B. S. Turner (eds), *Forget Baudrillard?*. London & New York: Routledge, 22–46.

Bauman, Zygmunt (1997), *Postmodernity and its Discontents*. Oxford: Polity.

Bauman, Zygmunt (2004), *Wasted Lives*. Oxford: Polity.

Beilharz, Peter (2005), 'Postmodern Socialism Revisited', in P. Hayden and C. El-Ojeili, *Confronting Globalization*, New York: Palgrave Macmillan.

Beilharz, Peter (2006), 'The Worlds We Make – Fabric, Camp and Polis in Zygmunt Bauman's Critical Theory', in M. H. Jacobsen & P. Poder (eds), *Om Bauman-Kritiske Essays*. Copenhagen: Hans Reitzels.

Douglas, Mary (1966), *Purity and Danger*. London: Routledge.
Kahn, Joel (2001), 'Anthropology and Modernity'. *Current Anthropology*, 42, 651–680.
Lepenies, Wolf (1988), *Between Science and Literature*. Cambridge: Cambridge University Press.
Mauss, Marcel (1966), *The Gift*. London: Routledge.
Prawer, S. S. (1978), *Karl Marx and World Literature*. Oxford: Oxford University Press.
Radin, Paul (1987) *The Method and Theory of Ethnology*, New York: Bergin and Garvey.
Tester, Keith (2004), *The Social Thought of Zygmunt Bauman*. Basingstoke: Palgrave Macmillan.

5
Bauman's Challenge to Sociology

Tony Blackshaw

One of the most striking characteristics of sociology in recent years is the speed with which sociologists in the English-speaking world – including while we're on the subject Bauman – have jettisoned postmodernism. It is hard to believe that in a period of less than 20 years postmodernism went from being a revolutionary practice to an art form, from an art form to a sociological sensibility, from a sociological sensibility to a domesticated sociological perspective and finally became a form of contempt. Indeed, if postmodernism began as a programme of disruption in sociology, it is today a way of thinking that is largely derided. No less interesting is the concurrent revival of the ideas of the 'founding fathers' in sociology. One need only mention the emergence over the last ten years or so of publications such as *Classical Social Theory* (Craib, 1997), *Classical Sociology* (Turner, 1999), *Theorizing Classical Sociology* (Ray, 1999), *Classical Sociological Theory* (Calhoun et al., 2002) and *Understanding Classical Sociology: Marx, Weber, Durkheim* (Hughes, Sharrock and Martin, 2003) (reprinted six times since 1995 and now its second edition) and the *Journal of Classical Sociology* (2001) to make the point. A further parallel is suggested by the fact that a revival in empirical studies has taken place in sociology, which has also had a substantial impact on recent developments in sociological thought.

The appearance of these two parallels, however, is misleading. For, while it is undeniable that the revival of the ideas of the 'founding fathers' and the revival of applied empirical research can both be seen as intellectual and ethical responses to the implications of postmodernism for sociology, there is an unarticulated contradiction connecting the two. This is that the kind of sociology practiced by the 'founding fathers', which as that most astute chronicler of the unit ideas of the sociological tradition Robert Nisbet once observed, provides the well-spring of the sociological imagination (that intuitive and ethical frame of thought through which sociological ideas are arrived at) that is markedly at odds with the ethos that underpins empirical sociology, which is dedicated first and foremost to the 'scientificity' of its methods (Bauman, 1989). Indeed, there is little to connect these two trends in sociology except the nostalgia for an imaginary past when the 'founding fathers' were out in the 'field' generating grounded theory (Glaser and Strauss, 1968) out of data which had been obtained through systematic empirical research. This is something that we all know did not happen. As Nisbet (1967: 19) points out, each of the 'founding fathers' was instead, 'with deep intuition, with profound imaginative grasp, reacting to the world around him, even as does the artist, and, also, like the artist, objectifying internal and only partly conscious, states of mind'. In the words of Bauman, it is this contradiction that represents the 'irreparable and irredeemable ambivalence' of sociology today, whose siren call might well be: 'We cannot give up the unit ideas of the "founding fathers", but we must at all costs resist the kind of sociology that they practiced, because it does not have any link to the empirical world – which means that it is bereft of any value'.

For while the sociological imagination only has its few practitioners around today, there seems widespread resistance to the idea that it has any substantial role to play in the development of contemporary sociological thought. Given that the sociological imagination is the source of Zygmunt Bauman's opus, there is widespread scepticism in sociology circles that his work is of genuine sociological relevance, whatever his popular reputation as a social theorist. Indeed, if there is an 'official' view among English-speaking sociologists of Bauman's work, it is perhaps best stated by Larry Ray (2007: 77) in his chapter in *The Contemporary Bauman*, in which he says of it, reducing the *modus operandi* of *Thinking Sociologically* (1990) to 'Bauman's metaphors': 'However useful they may be in stimulating imaginative enquiry they are not a substitute for rigorous conceptualization and research into the social'.

In some respects, this reaction to Bauman's sociology is not surprising. In the 1980s, when Anthony Giddens was generally understood as the most important sociologist in the English-speaking world, his work was treated in much the same manner (see Held and Thompson's (1989) collection *Social Theory of Modern Societies: Anthony Giddens and his Critics*). What this suggests is that perhaps the problem here is not the fallout from postmodernism at all, but something far deeper. The issues associated with the poetical sensibility of sociological imagination, it might be argued, are universal, or at least not distinctive to sociology, and can be traced back to Plato's admonition in the *Republic* that the poets' imaginative capacities are essentially amoral. Whatever is the case, there is no doubting the fact that sociology's view of the sociological imagination has a superficially parochial character, which is reflective of a discipline that is not only sure that any social theory that is at all genuine must have emerged out of empirical research, but is also intent on preserving the unit ideas of the 'founding fathers'.

However, what sociology today chooses to forget is that the creative blend of ideas behind the 'rigorous conceptualizations' developed by the 'founding fathers' were all reached through the kind of 'stimulating imaginative enquiry' that draws on the playfulness of language of that of the poets, or in other words, metaphors and metaphoricity. This is not only because metaphor is unavoidable, but also because it renders insights and revelations far below the surface of words. Consider one example: the view of society that underpins Marx's theory – 'class', 'capitalism', 'base and superstructure', 'struggle' and so on – is metaphorical through and through. The thing is these concepts developed by Marx are used so habitually in sociology that we forget that they are just metaphors. Sociological language is full of metaphors.

The key message emerging out of Bauman's sociology is that the metaphors of the 'founding fathers' don't work as well as they once did. Metaphors are important to telling stories, not only because they use language in magical and enlivening ways, but also because they are edifying and enlightening. But when metaphors fail to cast a spell, people don't listen to them. To return to the sociology of Marx once again, class is a metaphor whose magic still burns brightly for many in sociology, but it is by now too faded to resonate with the lives of the majority of people today, who do not experience the world in the way that people of a class society did. As Agnes Heller (1998) points out, one of the upshots of this is that class no longer has any emancipatory force, which means that Marx's distinction between the idea of a 'class in itself' and a 'class for itself' does not carry any great weight – if it ever did. For Bauman, it is simply the case that sociology underpinned by the grammar of metaphors of the 'founding fathers' does not have within its grasp an overarching narrative of sufficient power, simplicity and wide appeal to compete with the recent changes with modernity and it is getting further and further removed from any kind of social reality. What Bauman does in his work is challenge sociology to give up some of its old metaphors and adopt some new ones: metaphors that are not only better adapted to the world today, but are also receptive to a world that is constantly changing.

The trouble is that sociology has become a device for sustaining old habits of thought and it relies on its old metaphors to the extent that they have become part of its *doxa* (the knowledge it thinks with but not about), which is the understanding of the world its protagonists have before they even start to contemplate the world as it is today. To misquote Wittgenstein, sociology seems to have given up the struggle against the bewitchment of its intelligence by means of its language. This state of affairs not only signals that the past is needed by sociology's present that wants to go on in the way of the 'founding fathers', but is also most informative about sociology's problem with the work of Bauman, whose fate it has been to make sociology more poetically expressive at the same time when the sociological imagination of the discipline as a whole is running on empty.

What the following discussion demonstrates is that contrary to the received wisdom in sociology, Bauman's sociology is not only 'up there' with the 'founding fathers' – the likes of Durkheim, Marx, Simmel and Weber – in terms of the originality of its form and content, but that it also offers new ways of challenging, stretching and redefining how sociologists carry out empirical work in sociology. What it also demonstrates is that the 'official' view among English-speaking sociologists of Bauman's work is inadequate, since its conception of his sociology is too simple. What I argue below is that what we need to do instead is look at the total design of Bauman's work. By this I mean not so much the title he gives it – after all, we don't know what kind of palimpsest is going to emerge next – but his main themes and his point in writing it. If we can pinpoint these, then we will see that what his sociology does is make a breakthrough into a new sociological world, which is intent on filling in sociology's by-now-opaque shapes with sharper light and deeper shadows.

The way I go about developing this critique is to first of all offer a critical analysis of the ways and means of Bauman's sociology in order to give the reader a clear view of his ferocious intellect, his profound humanism, his skill in depicting the world in thought and his ingenuity in structuring these into sociological narratives. The central aim of this first part of the chapter is to give the reader the sense of his hermeneutical insight, narrative skill and keen moral awareness. In other words, it explores what it means to Bauman to go about the task of sociological hermeneutics. The second part of the chapter argues that because he breaks sociological conventions by making meaning in order to find it, following the currents of his sociological imagination as they reveal themselves to him, and, through his sociology, to us, demonstrating that it is connection, not 'data', where sociological meaning lies, Bauman's contribution to more empirically focused sociological work has not been widely acknowledged. As a critical response to this state of affairs, the analysis focuses on the way in which Bauman volunteers himself for service as a cultural intermediary, between sociological hermeneutics and hermeneutic sociology, most certainly, but also, and more importantly for the purposes of the present discussion, for the relationship between social theory and empirical research. The way I go about this to critically examine the connection between Bauman's sociological hermeneutics and my own hermeneutic sociology in my ethnographic study of the 'the leisure life-world of "the lads", which is the basis of my book *Leisure Life* (2003). In so doing, I demonstrate that what Bauman offers empirically minded sociologists is an original way of thinking sociologically wherein new layers of meaning are always on the verge of making an appearance: frames of reference full of allusions and contradictions, contingencies and ambivalences, as they coil and uncoil through 'real' lives, which in their liquid modern guises, are restless and urgent, complex and contradictory, both knowable and unknowable.

Sociological hermeneutics: Or sociology freed from the problematic of the subject-object and fiction-reality dichotomies

To borrow one of late Richard Rorty's favourite aphorisms, the difference between Bauman and most other sociologists writing today is the difference between a man who can remember and use a range of different vocabularies at the same time and those who can only remember and use only one. He is, as Hegel would have said, one of those thinkers who are always looking for new ways to capture his own time in thought. To this extent what Bauman offers sociology is an *orientation* rather than a perspective; he is the sociologist as poet who is keen to use words in ways they have never been used. His mission is to shape the old language of sociology into new ways that he imagines will extend the possibilities of civic engagement. To this extent, in the manner of the sociology of the 'founding fathers', Bauman's work is metaphorical rather than literal, its objective being to sweep you into a world you think you already know and make you see it all with a startled second sight. Its ethos is hermeneutical: metaphor trips a switch and a connection is made.

Doing things Bauman's way means working with the assumption that the fundamental job of sociology is to produce, out of the society we live in, a vision of the society we want to live in. As Keith Tester (2007: 81) points out, Bauman's work 'is *committed* and never deviates from its *dedication to human freedom*'. Obviously that vision can't be separated from society itself, so we have to understand how to relate the two. This is where hermeneutics comes in. Bauman's body of work is a conversation of concepts and ideas drawn from the *social sciences* (sociology, philosophy, politics etc.), *literature* (Blake, Borges, Calvino, Dostoyevsky, Kafka, Klima, Kundera, Ranke, Scheler, Shakespeare, Shaw, Stevenson, to name some of the literary greats who appear in his last two books, *The Art of Life* (2008a) and *Does Ethics Have a Chance in a World of Consumers?* (2008b)) and *society*, a vision that not only resists pigeonholing, but which smudges the usual dividing lines between sociology and the other social sciences, between academic book and novel, between fiction and reality.

The line between fiction and reality is like a door than Bauman chooses to walk in and out of all the time. Most sociologists begin with the world as it is, while the starting point of Bauman's sociology is the world he wants us to have. He begins with the world he constructs, not with the world he sees. In other words, he starts with his imagination, and then works towards ordinary experience. This is a sociology that thrives, not on revealing empirical truths, but by demonstrating the endless, boundless possibilities of the sociological imagination. The assumption that we can achieve some direct correspondence with 'reality' is replaced by a richer sense of knowing that assumes that there is more to language than just happening upon some aspect of human life and naming it. This is because Bauman is the sociologist as a poet – someone for whom the life of the mind is emotionally important – who writes for an audience as intellectual and well versed in the sociological imagination as him. For Bauman, sociology is truthful when it is hermeneutical, not in the self-regarding 'data discourse' style of the sociology journals (which is just plain ordinary), but in the way that it sparks connections, like poetry. In other words, just like the founding fathers – Durkheim, Marx, Simmel, Weber – he supplants the false coherence of empirical-evidence-tacked-on-to-social-theory-thought with the contrariness of cross-grained human narrative. Out of the crooked timber of humanity, as Immanuel Kant once wrote, nothing straight was ever made: this is sociology that so bristles with knotty knack and know-how that it breaks free of these two dimensions into the three where the art of the sociological imagination is unbridled and original ideas flourish. What is worth fighting for is humanity, not the identity of sociology – whatever that might be.

To paraphrase what the great Canadian literary critic Northrop Frye (1963: 24) in his Massey Lecture *Giants in Time*, drawing on Aristotle's idea of the 'universal event', said of poets generally, and what can be said of Bauman's sociology specifically: what we meet in it is neither real nor unreal: it is the product of his sociological imagination. Bauman's sociology is not fixed and definitive. It is, on the contrary, a place of perpetual deliberation, speculation calmed by an awareness of the 'facts of life', the 'facts' that lie behind what is often naively called 'reality' *and* the human imagination, and which makes them one and indivisible. Quite simply, Bauman recognizes that sociologists make a good deal of assumptions about everyday life and that there is a good deal of truth behind these, and he works with the assumption that his own assumptions are as good a place to start as any.

To continue with Frye's synopsis, Bauman never makes any real statements at all, certainly no particular or specific ones. He believes that his job is not to tell you what *happened*, but what *happens*: not what *did* take place, but the thing that *always does* take place. It says 'the biggest charlatans in sociology are the empiricists and the realists: the ones who claim that they are telling their readers how it 'really happened'. Bauman is that most honest sociologist, the hermeneutician, who says, 'This is my interpretation of the world and I'm going to try like hell to make you believe that it's true; all I ask is that you suspend your own epistemological and ontological assumptions for a little while until I have told you my story.' In other words, he challenges his readers to engage in what Rorty (2007) calls 'cultural politics': the beginning of a conversation about what words to use to create a better vision of the society we want to live in. What this tells us is that we should not trust what Bauman says; we should instead trust his story. This is because sociology conducted under the auspices of cultural politics can only be good or bad in its own categorization. Bauman knows that what he is presenting us with is both a superior and an inferior world than the one we usually live with, and he demands that we keep looking steadily at them both. For Bauman, no idea of reality is final and no interpretation, however good, is going to pronounce some final absolute truth. Every new interpretation, every new formulation emerging from that interpretation has the potential to change our understanding. Sociological hermeneutics is simply the sparkling statement of a valuable point of view; it is, to borrow a turn of phrase from Lionel Trilling, about sincerity and authenticity.

The 'dialectic process of reciprocal determination' (Bauman, 1992a: 11) that underpins this sociological hermeneutics is facilitated through an *ideal typical* analysis in the Weberian meaning (*ideal types* are not a descriptions of reality, but analytical tools sociologists use to try to understand it), which attempts to locate the impressions of the bits and pieces of real life Bauman has picked up one and by one, and which remain for most of us agonizingly confused, contradictory and incoherent. In other words, he creates from extant understandings and his own observations certain theoretical models of social life and its institutions to make comparisons in order to create his own hypotheses about social patterns of continuity and change.

These relations form a double hermeneutic. *Ideal types* such as solid modernity and liquid modernity are the inventions of Bauman's sociological imagination, but they carry their own sense of 'reality'. Together they ask, 'Is modernity in its liquid stage different from solid modernity?' Sociology gives us no straightforward answer. However, the idea that it likely is increases nonetheless liquid modernity's potential as a concept, because it is precisely the same kind of possibility which attends to our experience of everyday life. In this dialectical process Bauman's *ideal types* and 'real' life are continually changing places, each under the scrutiny that produces sociological hermeneutics. In theory, we can know everything about *ideal types* – after all they are only analytical tools – and still know very little about 'real' life. But in Bauman's hands, 'reality' is availed of its inability to speak for itself, and under his sure guidance, is enriched.

What the foregoing discussion suggests is that turning 'reality' into sociology is hermeneutics, and as to what triggers this shift, into the language of sociology, depends on the sociological imagination of the sociologist. Notwithstanding this observation, we need to understand that the world of the sociological imagination is neither an objective nor a subjective world. On the contrary, it is one that sociologists construct through their imaginations, which means that it makes no distinction between categories such as object and subject. This is not to say that Bauman does not aspire to objectivity, but that the important categories of the sociological imagination are *what you have to do* and *what you want to do* – in other words, necessity and freedom (Frye, 1963: 4). Whereas orthodox sociological thought is concerned with questions of epistemology and ontology, truth or reality, sociology made to measure of the sociological imagination never wastes time in contemplating concerns of that kind. Instead, like other forms of art, it fixes its own rules for itself as a source of freedom.

To this extent what Frye said of the educated imagination is true of the sociological imagination: it is something that affects the whole person, not bits and pieces of him or her. It doesn't just train the mind, it is also a social and moral development, which leads to the discovery that the imaginative world and the world around us are different worlds, and that the imaginative world *is more important*. The world in which we reside might look like the 'real' world, but it is always an ideal world of our imaginations; it has no reality except what we put into it – as Milan Kundera (2007) puts it his celebration of the novel *The Curtain*, it is always 'made-up', 'masked' or 'pre-interpreted'. This is not to say that there isn't a real world, but to acknowledge that there is always an unedited version of it hidden behind the one we see.

As Bauman sees it, sociology is hampered by the curtain of pre-interpretation given to us by the 'founding fathers', which by now occludes our view of the real world. This curtain is made of 'heavy' and 'solid' stuff, 'woven of legends', as Kundera would say. Bauman tears through it, freeing sociology from the edicts of this formidable past. 'Only by ripping down the curtain of sociology's respectability', Bauman's sociology says, 'can sociologists ask the questions about identity, family, community and destiny, mortality, love and so on that define the worlds of men and women today'. He knows that those questions can never be answered in the unambiguous ways that defined the sociology of the 'founding fathers', because we live in 'light' and 'liquid' times that require us to be content with the uncertainty of our understandings, to accept the apparent absence of certain meaning. But what Bauman shows us is this: By drawing sociology back once more to an intimate connection with the sociological imagination, we should not only be defying those who insist on maintaining the ideas of the 'founding fathers' (and conforming to their uniformity), we should be arriving at a new sociological world without which sociology cannot pass for a discipline whatsoever.

Juxtaposition, metaphor and the sociological imagination

One of the key things the discussion hitherto makes clear is that sociology after the 'founding fathers' must inevitably follow a dichotomous thread. Indeed, in developing new habits that are respectful of sociology's past, but better adapted to life's present, the need to gain a clear view of societal changes and the patterns of human life emerging out of these exhort it to constant juxtaposition. It should come to us as no surprise then that Bauman's most compelling insights always come from his attempts to isolate and compare historical and sociological processes: society's different historical trajectories, namely community, modernity and postmodernity; the effects of industrial production versus post-industrial consumption; mixophobia versus mixophilia; the shift from social control based on repression to that based on seduction; sociological hermeneutics versus hermeneutic sociology and so on; and as his 'millennial' work attests, solid modernity versus liquid modernity. From all this shuttling between concepts he weaves a larger fabric, a sustained deliberation on some key themes, to be precise, a picture of the always unrestful and disjointed modernity. By way of these juxtapositions he uses 'liquid' uncertainty, and its unformed and unstable nature, and makes something formed and stable out of it, raising sociology to a new level of intellectual achievement.

What the discussion so far also makes clear is that when the reader enters Bauman's sociological world, he or she is also entering into a world in which the whole world of literature is also a part. For Bauman, the particular literary conventions he adopts are, for him, part of the facts of life. For example, in the books of the novelists-cum-philosophers, Milan Kundera and Italo Calvino, he finds a foil for his sociological imagination, as well as the perfect conduit for his current sociological trajectory: liquid modern lives chime with Kundera's (1985) exploration of emptiness and meaning – 'lightness' and 'weight' – in the novel *The Unbearable Lightness of Being* and stated virtues that appear in all Calvino's work: *lightness, quickness, visibility* and *multiplicity*.

As good a place as any to begin understanding how Bauman uses these metaphors is the Foreword 'Being Light and Liquid' in *Liquid Modernity* (2000). In this short prelude to his deeper exploration of the major issues at stake in the latest changes associated with the relentless process of modernization, Bauman argues that we have recently seen a shift from a 'heavy' and 'solid', 'hardware-focused' modernity to a 'light' and 'liquid', 'software-focused' modernity. What sets liquid modernity apart from solid modernity is that it is a social formation that does not, cannot even if it so wanted, resist changes to its shape. And what distinguishes our lives from those of our solid modern counterparts is their utter contingency: no matter what our current circumstances or how certain we individually feel about our lives at the moment, things could always be different. We might have an experience in a couple of hours, next week or 20 years from now that will place us squarely in a new and previously unimagined place. One experience at the right moment might change everything. A liquid life, Bauman suggests, might not always feel like a freely chosen one, and when considered over a period of time it would probably look like a fairly stable existence; however, depending on our individual state of affairs, and who we might happen to meet, all of this can suddenly and unexpectedly change.

Living a liquid modern life means that the *habitus* into which we are born has less of a constraining influence on our lives than would have been the case even 20 or 30 years ago. In other words, liquid modernity has converted necessity into contingency, which means that our *habitus* is experienced as accidental rather than inevitable. Bauman knows, of course, that liquid modern lives are not completely free of their social class, gender and ethnic statuses, but he knows that by now these markers of identity and difference flow into each other more than they did once upon a time in the not too distance past. He also knows that today our lives have a more in-between, DIY ready-made feel about them, and to this extent that they are better understood as individualized existences. A liquid modern life, in other words, has no solid ontological status (just like the sociology that names it), something that is given, is inevitable, we are predisposed to or firmly believe in. Without any firm centre of gravity, a liquid modern life is one whose basis of authority is visibility, which challenges individuals to perform their identities in order to make themselves palpable. Some lives are no doubt more liquid than others and some individuals are more adept at performing their identities than others, but anyone's *habitus* is just something that is until further notice. In other words, it seems to fit us as a person who chooses to live this kind of life rather than another.

What Bauman is really interested in is the slippage between the gaps of daily interaction – the things we don't see, as well as the half-hidden truths that sustain everyday life. As we have seen, Bauman is more at home with razor-sharp interpretation than the ostensible clarities of social science. We have also seen that his sociology dresses the details of 'reality' with atmosphere from literature. However, it is always 'real' world affairs that are its beating heart. This is sociology in the hermeneutic mode; it employs a dominantly metaphorical rendering of 'reality', to give poetic intensity to its representation. In other words, it is a sociology more fully felt than that normally found in the sociology journals. Bauman may start with the plain sense of basic definitions, but no sooner has he noted down his initial observation than he begins to question it, to investigate its meaning until what at first seemed a simple assessment is no longer so. Bauman knows that, like art, sociology has to invent metaphors for those ineffable individual and collective experiences – the things we can see, hear, taste, touch, smell, but cannot say exactly what it is, its precise meaning always evading our attempts to put it into words – for which we do not have words. Think about the way that he interrogates the idea of community in the following quotation, for example:

> To start with, community is a 'warm' place, a cosy and comfortable place. It is like a roof under which we shelter in heavy rain, like a fireplace at which we warm our hands on a frosty day. Out there, in the street, all sorts of dangers lie in ambush; we have to be alert when we go out, watch whom we are talking to and who talks to us, be on the look-out every minute. In here, in the community, we can relax – we are safe, there are no dangers looming in the dark corners (to be sure, hardly any 'corner' here is 'dark').
>
> (Bauman, 2001: 1–2)

As Agnes Heller (1999) would say, this definition presupposes that there is *something* in the concept of community (its *unknown known*) that cannot be disciplined – it's *secret*. The secret of community is beyond straightforward interpretation, and we do not know, cannot know about its secret; rather we *feel* its warm glow, we *sense* it. Here Bauman knows that a sociology made to the measure of understanding community must have a ways and means for dealing with the ineffable, precisely because there is a great deal to know about it that says no to conceptualization.

Of course, Bauman also wants his sociology to leap out and grab his readers, in the hope that it will teach them the power of storytelling. However, he also hopes that it will provide them with intimations of how it feels to live in a moral world. The aim of the sociological imagination should be to defamiliarize the familiar by colouring it with the strange (Bauman, 1990), but in this sociology, excitement and empathy mix and are guided by an unfailing moral compass. Indeed, Bauman uses metaphor, not just to tell sociological stories, but to make things happen with words and make his readers feel in a special way. What he shows his readers is that what *thinking sociologically* entails is trying to put ourselves in the shoes of others, which also means using our sociological imaginations to shed our own identities. This is a way of *thinking sociologically* that is not only insistent on our feelings, our empathy, our solidarity, our *kindness* for others – as Bauman puts it 'loving others as you love yourself'– but also our acceptance that for all our cultural differences as human beings we have a responsibility for each other, because we are, after all, one of a *kind*. In insisting on our *human kindness* Bauman is suggesting that human faces come before everything else: in looking into the face of the other we are reminded that we are engaged in a human encounter, person to person, that comes with the face (Blackshaw, 2007). It is the moral message of his sociology that it should help us to feel for the Other, that it should touch our human capacity for kindness in an important way. This is a complex understanding of feeling and the revelation of depth to which few other sociological accounts could aspire.

An interim summing up

What we can conclude from the discussion so far is that what Bauman seeks in his sociology is to express a poetic response to modernity in its liquid modern stage. Unlike most other sociologists, however, he is not content trying to reproduce the world's outer appearances; he also seeks to capture the ascent of the inner existential nature of modern life in the presence of culture and the quotidian. Indeed, with the sociological imagination as its backbone, its relationship to the dichotomy between social theory and empirical evidence is uncompromising: the two might be conjoined twins, but the sociological imagination prospers at the expense of both. It is the skill with which Bauman opens up the gap between perception and the 'real' world that is the point. This is because, for him, there is always much more to 'what you see and hear than meets the eye, that the most important part is hidden from view, and that there is a huge and dense tissue of inter-human connections below the visible tip of the iceberg. An insight that triggers imagination that, if worked on properly, sediments sociology' (Bauman in Blackshaw, 2002: 2).

These observations notwithstanding, what is very clear is that empirical research does not really interest Bauman: it has too little to do with his sociological imagination. However, this doesn't mean that his sociological hermeneutics doesn't have any relevance for empirically minded researchers. On the contrary, it is simply that we have to look at what his sociological hermeneutics has to offer hermeneutic sociology. It is in this relationship that we find the epistemological transformation of empirical sociology. Whereas orthodox empirical sociology portrays the everyday worlds of men and women simply *there* in time and space, hermeneutic sociology subverts the idea by suggesting that the everyday is not to be found in the world, but on the contrary always open to different interpretations. In other words, just like sociological hermeneutics, hermeneutic sociology shakes and wakes the sociological imagination and in the process, doesn't so much attempt to define and describe the world it comes across in the field as an objective reality, but instead attempts to give it its own living, breathing presence, by summoning it alive through the medium of language. Here, as with sociological hermeneutics, 'reality' is availed of its inability to speak for itself.

What is hermeneutic sociology?

Hermeneutic sociology might be defined as an attempt to show its readers what it is like to tumble through a hole in the world into another world that is just as brightly coloured and fully felt as their own. According to Bauman (1992b: 42), what its adherents are after is a 'mimetic representation' of the social world. To put it another way, hermeneutic sociology works with the assumption that it has the ability to tell its readers things about human life that they wouldn't, couldn't get in another way. Along with this intuitive insight, hermeneutic sociology operates with a keen moral awareness. This is because it recognizes that the world as an object of investigation is in fact the globality made up of a countless number of worlds, cultures and communities, which as a result of the historical process to date appear to each other as at once familiar, but also fascinatingly Other. In this sense it recognizes that the world is in fact a multitude of alternate universes sometimes intersecting with each other to create an infinite number of slightly different versions of reality.

The conspicuous implication of hermeneutic sociology is that since we cannot know everything, we cannot know anything for sure; but its actual effect – and its success – is to suggest something different: that hermeneutics confirms the idea of truth instead of dissipating it, that the difficulty of explaining 'how things really happened' doesn't disprove those things but authenticates them. The watchword of hermeneutic sociology is the mindfulness of its own contingency, or in other words the need to be aware that there is an unbridgeable gap between what it says about the world and what might be going on in the world. Indeed, it is the acceptance of this kind of responsibility 'over meaning-production and truth-validation' that casts the hermeneutic sociologist into the role of the interpreter, of the cultural intermediary, whose specific role it is to facilitate communication between different communities (ibid.).

Hermeneutic sociologists not only recognize that their research findings will always remain partial, but they are also cognizant of the limitations of orthodox sociological forms of writing up research, which suggest that the meticulous and gradual observation of social phenomena provides a grounding for theory *vis-à-vis* Glaser and Strauss (1968) – an approach which assumes that theory emerges from research 'data', which is typically illustrated with characteristic examples of 'data' from field notes, such as interview quotations. Instead hermeneutic sociologists look to develop writing techniques that attempt to reflect the worlds of those under sociological scrutiny. This hermeneutic way of writing sociology revels in accretions of detail and theory, speaking to the important things that govern men and women's lives: their loves, their memories, their families and the many other beauties and truths and quidities and epiphanies that give meaning to their individual and shared existence. It also works on the basis that the best sociology works its magic through the ability of its author to *convince* its readers about the reality under scrutiny, rather than through any direct correspondence with that reality. This approach works with the assumption that like all good novels empirical sociology must be well written, but its real strength and power lies in researcher's sociological imagination. That is, its thick descriptions, as Geertz (1973) called them, should be free of sociological jargon and editorializing, and capable of engaging the reader with what makes life for men and women intimate and real, by evoking the actual feeling of day-to-day, week-to-week, year-to-year of everyday life.

In this way the compositional practices of hermeneutic sociology offer creative ways of telling factual stories. This suggests a shift in the writing of empirical sociological research, which means that if hermeneutic sociology is as compelled as orthodox sociology ever was in its ambition to capture everyday life, it also has an ambition to create atmosphere, whether it is a single consciousness or the atmosphere of a shared consciousness – even the consciousnesses of liquid modern lives that are contingent, shape-shifting rather than enduring. In my book *Leisure Life* (2003) I argue that it is that only by such staging that researchers can reach a more profound level of truth that cannot otherwise be found. This is because hermeneutic sociology relishes the task of transporting its readers by telling them how people who share a particular fate think, speculate, desire, understand, live their lives but in a way which makes every gesture, every attitude and every word spoken by its respondents part of its imaginative and deliberate study.

Hermeneutic sociology in action: the leisure life—world of 'the lads'

Leisure Life, which is an ethnographic study of an imagined community based on working-class men's leisure, is a good example of hermeneutic sociology. The thesis underpinning the book is developed through a hermeneutic sociological approach to make knowable the leisure life-world of a group of working-class 'lads' with whom I had grown up. This meant that the study was about their leisure life-world, my leisure life-world, but also our leisure life-world. I was an 'inmate' who had become a 'spectator' – Tony Blackshaw as an insider and Tony Blackshaw the sociologist as an outsider on the inside. I was and was not part of the leisure life-world I was exploring. The ethnography nonetheless involved me attempting to literally go out of the singularity of my own conscious mind, shedding for the time being my own sense of self and entering the world that I was researching *verstehen* in Max Weber's meaning. To paraphrase Bauman (1992b: 42), it involved me as someone securely embedded in his own 'native' tradition penetrating deeply into successive layers of meanings upheld by that tradition. What this practically entailed was me trying to accumulate in my mind the ins and outs of what I had seen, heard, tasted, touched and smelt and linking it with what I knew already and had imagined as a consequence. This also involved a process of penetration which was simultaneously that of translation because in the person of the hermeneutic sociologist, I had as a consequence of the research brought together two traditions in a communicative contact – and thus opened to each other their respective contents which otherwise would have remained opaque. In this way I was also 'giving voice' to a culture which without my help would have remained numb or stayed inaudible. In effect I was operating at the interface between 'language games' or 'forms of life', with the explicit aim of enriching both sides of the interface.

I knew that the key to the success of this ambition would lie in my ability to grasp a sense of the trajectory of the lived experience of the leisure life-world, because this would in turn allow me as researcher to grasp some understanding of the influences that move it. One of the first things that became clear to me was that the community underpinning this leisure life-world was imagined as a double movement: back in time, and back to a particular place. Drawing on Bauman's distinction between solid modernity and liquid modernity, the crux of the thesis I developed was that 'the lads' collective leisure experiences are animated by their belief in an imagined community which is perceived as the cornerstone of their shared masculine working-class existence. 'The lads' only feel 'real' in relation to this leisure life-world. There is a warmth, a particular feeling of home about this life-world, which offers 'the lads' a protective cocoon where they are 'naturally' safeguarded from the uncertainties of liquid modern change. They close its shutters to guard against their mutual home-made models of themselves losing credibility and the intricate cogs of their masculine realism from being damaged or lost. The leisure life-world enables them to keep these ready-made narratives alive in their collective memory, their own private gallery, which is the legacy of their youth.

My central argument was that it is this shared passion for a *solid modern* missing world, sometimes proudly resurrected and celebrated, sometimes merely borne out of the private burden of individuality, which gives this shared leisure life-world its weight and its depth. The book charts 'the lads'' intermittent forays into Leeds city centre on Friday, and Saturday nights which constitute a memorable vindication of this missing world. Nights out with 'the lads' tend to spin themselves out into a familiar web which feels like one of those reunions which famous rock bands have when the group gets back together after playing with other people. When 'the lads' are on stage together once again, it feels great and everything just clicks into place. They drink their beer faster than is good for them and conversation moves from subject to subject. They finish each others' sentences, and communicate, more remarkably, without speaking at all. With a real affinity, and in the spirit of the communion that exists between them, they use gestures known only to them.

'The lads', in a collective act of nostalgic remembrance, conjure the leisure life-world, in the process restoring a past reality, if not in its entirety, as a form of resurrection, which is another expression for a life beyond death, but carrying with it a kind of immortality. Here community closes the gap between the then and the now in the minds of 'the lads'. Near and far become elided, then is juxtaposed with now and a version of community arises in the form of the leisure life-world, which gives 'the lads' a secular version of Tillich's (1952) 'power of being', which, as the philosopher Martin Heidegger would have said, enables them to overcome the threat of their non-being.

This leisure life-world operates in the cusp between imaginary reality and the really existing reality, which pass through each other, their shapes muddled, not a perfect fit, but awfully close. To arrive in the leisure life-world is to pass through a chink in the gates of reality and enter a liminal, around the corner universe. What excitement. But also what a relief. To leave the uncertainties of liquid modernity and to arrive in predictable, certain, histrionic 'lad world'. Here, the virtual and the actual are hard to prise apart: as a result we are insistently forced to acknowledge that there is no solid ground of unassailable truth on which this leisure life-world rests; it blurs the boundaries between the virtual and the real. It is a remarkable creation, not quite of the world. The gap, the slippage, the contingency of the discourse of the leisure life-world and the already existing reality itself is the point.

However, on these nights out 'the lads' do not so much relive their youth as recreate it through their leisure its unheroic aftermath. In truth the leisure life-world has, to use the rock band analogy once again, been turned into a sort of heritage museum for ageing lads, which, I argue, in recent years has become more a duty than a pleasure and whose nagging subliminal power reverberates only on the edges of individual lives lived in the main elsewhere. Indeed, although it is the ultimate experience of a solidly modern leisure life 'the lads' desire, but cannot really capture, it does not deter them from endeavouring to regain the power and certainties of its past, and seeking a realm of mutual happiness that was once upon a time theirs.

Outside the leisure life-world, resignation and disillusionment are the nearest things 'the lads' have to freedom – or so it seems. In the fluidity of liquid modernity they have to watch powerless as the Other invades uninvited into their existential and material realms: women controlling their bedrooms and telling them what to do, women and black people taking their jobs, buying their houses, taking over their shops and their schools. But in the leisure life-world 'the lads' are in control. Here 'the lads' are determined to ensure that their leisure lives are unaffected by difference. In the leisure life-world the features of the Other begin to elongate and liquefy, swell and then re-solidify, like Sartre's *le visqueux,* they are transformed into 'the lads' own DIY custom-made creations. Take for example, women, who can never exist as cheerful subjects of their own lives in the leisure life-world, but exist merely as scaffolding for 'the lads'' shared dreams – happy and loving shags without another single care except perhaps 'to go down on' working-class white blokes. That these characterizations are not 'real' is neither here nor there, 'the lads' simply have to be convinced that they are. What is important for 'the lads' is the *meaning for them* of these characterizations to their version of truth, which is something that enables them to form what they recognize *is* the world when they are at leisure together. Women have to be wiped out from a solid modern story in which they have no place, excluded from the leisure world that has created them.

These characterizations of the Other become symbols of subjugation, power and knowledge, the luscious fruit of a solid leisure life lived in a solid version of truth. The 'universal' truth of the rationality which divides 'the lads' and Others into two categories: us and them, same and Other.

By alternating perspectives in the book, seeing events unfold through 'the lads'' eyes and then from the view of the research, I try to do more than simply analyse this leisure life-world; I also attempt to coax the reader into walking in the shoes of 'the lads' to experience the 'lad-like' worldview. The leisure life-world is more real than the flesh and blood characters that are 'the lads'; its discourse more alive, more interesting and more nuanced than the characters speaking it. This is nothing less than about reinventing the empirical sociologist's writing craft by making fact read like fiction, using language charged and poetic, which takes its readers on a cultural ride in order to find truth – physically transporting them. In this way hermeneutic sociology permits and requires greater descriptive detail than is the case in more conventional empirical sociological accounts.

There are critics who will no doubt argue that the borrowed prestige of fiction can limit as well as liberate hermeneutic sociology. That is, to liken sociology to literature may suggest that it verges on fiction. But such a reaction fails to recognize that even the most positivistic of accounts are prey to cosmetic enhancement. The real world is contingent, chaotic and crowded with inessentials while sociology requires order, themes and structure, so researchers can transform the accumulation of their experiences into an object of analysis. 'One of the upshots of this', the critic might ask, 'is that there must be a temptation to sharpen an observation here or make better a quote there'. What such criticism ignores is that such a thing can be tempting to *any* researcher. Readers do not have to be reminded that they are reading 'fact': but this way of writing shows them how close facts relate to fiction.

The critic might retort: 'At what point does fact pass into the fiction?' In *Leisure Life* I sidestep this question by stressing that this hermeneutical way of writing empirical sociology should not be understood as in any way deceitful on the part of researchers, but more precisely sociology looking at itself in the mirror and recognizing that it can still do everything it used to be able to do *and* much more. The trick of hermeneutic sociology is that it is able to tell the 'truth' about the social world while not being exactly deceitful, but embellishing that 'truth'. In this sense, rather trying to make the reader believe in the 'facts' of the reality it deals with in its pages, it simply conjures the 'real' instead. This changed economy of narration simply leads hermeneutic sociologists to write in self-consciously literary ways, which, in common with Bauman, tend to draw on rhetorical devices, such as metaphor, which they use *not* to replace the real, but to clarify, reinforce and enhance our understanding of it. In order to get to grips with the leisure life-world of 'the lads' all you have to do is accept a world which is figurative. In other words, in the place of methodological reliability and validity there is only the literariness of hermeneutic sociology, which holds its own uncomplicated magic – the kind that can't be deconstructed.

Conclusion

To complete the above analysis would surely require a critical assessment of a third moment, namely, in the parlance of Hans Gadamer, the 'fusion of horizons' spiralling from hermeneutic sociology to sociological hermeneutics. For the present purposes, however, this is unnecessary. Our basic task has been two-fold: on the one hand to flesh out and assess the merits of Bauman's sociology – *pace* Ray (2007), not merely its metaphors, but its hermeneutics, its main themes and his point in writing it – and on the other hand to demonstrate what it has to offer empirically minded researchers. What we have discovered is that although Bauman has every faith in the power of his own senses to tell his own truths, he also knows that there are many other roads that the sociological imagination can follow, and that contrary to what his critics suggest, his sociology does not signal any 'significant loss of interest in the role of empirical research as a standard against which to establish the adequacy of theories' (ibid.: 64). All you need to do is put your own epistemological and ontological assumptions on hold and listen to what Bauman has to say. As was demonstrated above, when I applied Bauman to the dynamics of the leisure life-world of 'the lads', everything was all of a sudden clear. Until that moment I did not know how that world worked; Bauman confirmed to me that I did know.

What we have seen is that it is actually the discursive formation known as sociology that needs to overcome its estrangement from the everyday worlds of men and women and recognize that individualization is today *the* shaping force in the narrative of human existence and that *all* men and women are contingent people living contingent lives, and that from now on it will always be like this. It seems to me that the major task facing sociology today is how to re-acquaint itself with the habit of acquiring new metaphors made to the measure of lives that are DIY, decentred, episodic, fragmented, consumerist and sometimes magical, but always subject to uncertainty, anxiety, indecision and change. In other words, what sociology needs are new ways of conveying the world that men and women today can follow, and which will lead them to realizations which are very much a part of their everyday existences.

What this also means is that sociology needs to start paying proper respect to Bauman, who knows that metaphor is becoming of increasing importance in a world in which life's central challenge has been turned from a given into a task, or as Bauman (2008a) himself would say, into a work of art, which entails that men and women are confronted daily with the task of setting themselves challenges, targets and standards of excellence that are all too often well beyond the wherewithal of individuals alone. Engaging with Bauman might make sociology uncomfortable, but hopefully it might also provoke it – and jog its memory about how to make some of its own art with words that might just trip a switch and connect with the lives of ordinary men and women. I cannot overemphasize the importance of this necessity, for what the foregoing discussion of Bauman's work makes very clear, to paraphrase what Malcolm Bradbury once said of Salman Rushdie's historical novels, is that it is the tricks of literature that show us with what fantasy the 'real' world must now be written – if, that is, we are to penetrate it, and in the process save sociology.

References

Bauman, Z. (1989), 'Hermeneutics and Modern Social Theory', in D. Held, D. and J. B. Thompson, *Social Theory of Modern Societies: Anthony Giddens and His Critics*. Cambridge: Cambridge University Press.

Bauman, Z. (1990), *Thinking Sociologically*. Oxford: Blackwell.

Bauman, Z. (1992a) *Mortality, Immortality and Other Life Strategies*. Cambridge: Polity Press.

Bauman, Z. (1992b) *Intimations of Postmodernity*. London: Routledge.

Bauman, Z. (2000) *Liquid Modernity*. Cambridge: Polity Press.

Bauman, Z. (2001) *Community: Seeking Safety in an Insecure World*. Cambridge: Polity Press.

Bauman, Z. in Blackshaw, T. (2002), 'Interview With Zygmunt Bauman', *Network: Newsletter of the British Sociological Association*, number 83, October.

Bauman, Z. (2008a) *The Art of Life*. Cambridge: Polity Press.

Bauman, Z. (2008b) *Does Ethics Have a Chance in a World of Consumers?* London: Harvard University Press.

Blackshaw, T. (2003), *Leisure Life: Myth, Masculinity and Modernity*. London: Routledge.

Blackshaw, T. (2007), 'Zygmunt Bauman', in R. Stones (ed.) *Key Sociological Thinkers*. Second Edition. Basingstoke: Palgrave Macmillan.

Calhoun, C., Gerteis, J. M., Pfaff, S., Schmidt, K. and Virk, I. (2002), *Classical Sociological Theory.* London: Pluto Press.

Craib, I. (1997), *Classical Social Theory.* Oxford: Oxford University Press.

Frye, N. (1963), *The Educated Imagination.* Toronto: Canadian broadcasting Corporation.

Geertz, C. (1973), 'Thick Description: Towards an Interpretive Theory of Culture', in *The Interpretation of Cultures.* London: Hutchinson.

Glaser, B. and Strauss, A. (1968), *The Discovery of Grounded Theory.* London: Weidenfield and Nicholson.

Held, D. and Thompson, J. B. (eds) (1989), *Social Theory of Modern Societies: Anthony Giddens and His Critics.* Cambridge: Cambridge University Press.

Heller, A. (1998), Simon Tormey: Interviews with Agnes Heller. See http://homepage.ntlworld.com/simon.tormey/articles/hellerinterview.html

Heller, A. (1999), *A Theory of Modernity.* Oxford: Blackwell.

Hughes, J., Sharrock, W. and Martin, P. (2003), *Understanding Classical Sociology: Marx, Weber, Durkheim.* Second Edition. London: Sage.

Kundera, M. (1985), *The Unbearable Lightness of Being.* Translated by Michael Henry Heim. London: Faber and Faber.

Kundera, M. (2007), *The Curtain: An Essay in Seven Parts.* Translated by Linda Asher. London: Faber and Faber.

Nisbet, R. A. (1967), *The Sociological Tradition.* London: Heinemann.

Ray, L. J. (1999), *Theorizing Classical Sociology.* Buckingham: Open University Press.

Ray, L. (2007), 'From Postmodernity to Liquid Modernity: What's in a Metaphor?', in A. Elliott (ed.) *The Contemporary Bauman.* Abingdon: Routledge.

Rorty, R. (2007), *Philosophy as Cultural Politics.* Cambridge: Cambridge University Press.

Tester, K. (2007), 'Bauman's Irony', in A. Elliott (ed.) *The Contemporary Bauman.* Abingdon: Routledge.

Tillich, P. (1952), *The Courage to Be.* New Haven: Yale University Press.

Turner, B. S. (1999), *Classical Sociology.* London: Sage.

6
Bauman's Implicit Theology

Kieran Flanagan

Mixing sociology with religion and theology generates a cocktail very few English sociologists care to sip, even after 9/11. The bartending activities producing such toxic cultural and political mixtures violate the foundational aspirations of English sociology which sought to overthrow an establishment patrician culture, in which the theology of Anglicanism played a significant legitimizing part (Halsey 1987). Theology is treated as incredible, archaic and regressive. Most English sociologists are pleased to act as bouncers on the field of culture, regarding those who would plant the seeds of faith there as representing all the discipline was formed to denounce and replace. A strange land now, English society conceives of itself as living in a state of post-secularity, beyond religion and rendering civil inattention to any of its activities. Thus, in times when identity politics is shaped by inclusiveness for all, religion is bracketed with suspicion and designated as 'unrecognised' and somehow unfit for inclusion in civil, refined life.

Few protest at this state of affairs, a notable example being the Scottish Catholic composer James Macmillan. In a widely publicized lecture, he hit out against the 'ignorance fuelled' hostility to faith, notably of Christianity, among 'metropolitan arts, cultural and media elites' (Macmillan 2008). Religious events of inescapable cultural and political significance are ignored, such as the 260,000 who turned out at the *Esplandes des Invalides* in Paris to hear Pope Benedict XVI speak in mid-September 2008, twice the numbers who heard Obama in Berlin earlier in the year (Ziegler 2008: 17–20). But, again to invoke Macmillan, despisers of believers have not quite succeeded in 'beating religion into a pulp'.

Despite atheistic exhibitionists and the cultural clones who seem to dominate the mass media, religion displays an embarrassing resilience not only in providing indispensable means of securing social solidarity, but also of marking the sacred even in a civil society where all gods are supposedly vanquished. Were religion to be confined to civil designations of the sacred and to supplying ceremonial repairs when solidarity is fractured, then few might object. But something brooding, deeper and unsettling is sensed in the subterranean depths of modernity and bizarrely, it has fallen to sociology to pick up these resonances of a Divinity stirring. Zygmunt Bauman is hardly associated with religion, let alone theology, so it might seem perverse to suggest that he, perhaps the last great living sociologist, gives an unexpected witness to these theological resonances in modernity in the variety of forms he has sought to encapsulate over a long career.

Polish, Jewish, living in exile in Leeds for forty years, long retired, but still highly productive, Bauman has accomplished a long march through the epochs and paradigms of sociology over half a century and has left numerous tracts and tomes to mark his steps. He has supplied the biography of sociology over epochs. His journey marks a long sociological retreat from acknowledgement of the absolute claims of reason to a stance of disenchantment which denotes it as dangerous, tyrannical and totalitarian in outcome. This leads him to a defence of ambiguity as an antidote to reason and its deterministic powers that exclude and classify so dangerously. More than any other sociologist, Bauman has explored what Tester terms the social suffering that emerges as an outcome of postmodernity that signifies the power of self-constitution in the marketplace (2004: 153). Rather than securing happiness, freedom and self-emancipation, the traits of modernity, consumption and consumerism have produced cultural mirages that distort realizations of loneliness and hopelessness in a world increasingly denoted as having one human property in short supply: love.

Having ascended to the peaks of reason, Bauman finds himself sliding down the smooth paths of modernity into the quagmire generated by its liquefaction. In the swamps, he faces, though with reluctance, matters the light of reason supposedly had expelled: death and evil. The antinomies of the human condition remain unresolved, inconvenient and mysterious in their intractability. As a result the self feels vulnerable. In the vertigo of its self-propelled ascent into a divine status, the self finds it is no god. Frustratingly, the quest for independence has yielded a heightened sense of dependence, a realization that stresses on embodiment, of necessity and gives rise to concerns with suffering and death. This realization of frailty so embedded in what it is to be human leads on to questions generated by theodicy. For some, this rude, crude insertion might be profoundly archaic and deeply unsociological, yet theodicy was a domain concern of Weber. Perhaps reflecting the needs of the age, Durkheim's work has been reinterpreted in relation to evil and suffering (Pickering and Rosati 2008). It might seem that the forces of modernity that displace God peculiarly generate a longing for His return.

Concerns with the self were one of the unexpected outcomes of postmodernity, but Bauman gives their 'discovery' a novel twist. Initially his purpose was to steel the self to stand stoically and steadfast in life to be lived with God denoted as missing in action, believed to be slain in modernity. This insight led to a realization that as modernity matured into postmodernity, the crucial question emerging was not one of power but of ethics. How were mutuality and solidarity to be secured when the individual had no necessary interest or duty to the other, or the Other? This question reverts back to the unfinished business of Durkheim, whose vision of and for sociology was to provide what theology was denoted as incapable of supplying: a reason to live in sociability. But what is remarkable in Bauman is the way he is forced to look more starkly at the consequences of an absent God in a modernity which, itself, seems fated to dissolve.

Unlike Durkheim, whose concerns were confined to religion, Bauman's realizations are theological. In his scrutiny of modernity in post and liquefied versions, Bauman comes upon the characterizing theology of their moments. This form is apophatic theology. It illustrates the way the absence of God provides a proof of his existence. It was the Renaissance German theologian Nicholas of Cusa who marked apophatic theology as the trait of modernity. Later, in sociology, Simmel was to grasp this point. But Bauman never set out explicitly to employ apophatic theology in his characterizations of modernity in its unfolding forms. The realization of this theology emerged in another and perhaps unexpected context.

Modernity and the Holocaust generates two unsettling and inconvenient questions (1989). The first question relates to theology. A problem is presented, the absence of God felt by many amidst the suffering and death of the camps. It might be resolved by reference to negative theology. What cannot be resolved is the theodicy of the Holocaust. Whether God is deemed dead or alive, the issues that require reference to theodicy persist, all the more so as generated by the Holocaust. For what reason, did the innocent suffer and die so horribly in these camps? For some reason, reason had no answer to this reasonable question, simply because it was the unfettered application of reason that generated it.

But the second question Bauman generates unsettles sociology itself. God might be condemned over indifference to the camps, but the same charge could be levelled against sociology. Why has sociology said so little about the suffering and death in the Holocaust? Before this tragedy, sociology seemed to stand mute and inglorious, that is until Bauman wrote *Modernity and Holocaust.*

The genius of this study is to convey a realization that sociology had no resources to characterize these murderous manufactures in the lower depths of modernity save by reference to a deeply unsociological term: evil. The need to resort to this category was deeply unsettling. Its use seemed to arise at a point of paradox in modernity. In its German expression, the technical superiority of bureaucracy (that Weber had endorsed) marked a genius for order and routine, but in these accomplishments that governed what was to be considered as 'normal' lurked something nefarious, something well disguised and something easily domesticated that one thought had been expelled by the light of reason. In facing the Holocaust, sociology had encountered its disciplinary limits. But what is disturbing in Bauman's account is the route through which the matter of evil emerges.

Its more usual route into sociological deliberations can be found in the genesis of modernity, in the idle speculations of the bored *flâneur* who dallied with decadence and found the devil. Not unexpectedly, it might be said that in the fleeting and transient, mirages emerge and these might bear illusory connotations of evil. But in Bauman's case the discovery of evil inverts expectations. It emerges from the quest for order, from the exercise of powers of calculation that exemplify the gifts of modernity sociology most admires. One does not expect to find in the application of Weber's notion of rationalization evil emerging.

The trouble is that the issue of evil has come up on the 'wrong' field and sociology is faced with a test of its moral and humanistic credentials that it cannot seem to pass save by reference to a term that belongs to theology. As the creature of modernity, sociology could not just describe the Holocaust as a refined manufacturing process. The scale, the 'normality' of the operations of the death camps requires reference to another vocabulary, one sufficient to characterize but also to condemn. Facing this peculiar 'accomplishment' of modernity places sociology in retreat from its conventional affirmations of humanism and forces it back into deeper and more transcendent considerations, those proper for theological reflection. Some reference to what is beyond the social, beyond reason and beyond humanity is required as sociology encounters its moral limitations.

In retrospect, the timing of the book's publication in 1989 was peculiarly important. The Berlin Wall had come down; the hegemony of Marxism had collapsed; and as translations of the Frankfurt School, notably of the writings of Adorno and Benjamin were percolating into Anglo-American circles, realizations were dawning that these works contained unexpected and inconvenient amounts of theological reference to Messianic considerations, to naming and to the need for hope. Postmodernity emerged as the umbrella term of the 1990s to characterize the plight of intellectuals whose props of belief in progress and in ideologies that wrapped up all of culture had collapsed. It is to Bauman's credit that he treated this postmodernity not only as a term of a moment, but one whose ramifications required urgent sociological attention. But he also came to realize that something more unsettling was occurring: modernity was liquefying. What was solid had melted in the air. The genesis of this realization can be traced back to *Modernity and the Holocaust* where many of the issues regarding the melting of modernity can be found.

The profound influence of the study is well appraised by Tester who treats it as 'a celebration of the *victory* of morality over utility' (2004: 132). But in the end, the study is less about the Holocaust and more about the dangers posed by a modernity running wild where curiosity is unfettered and the need for mutuality has become marginalized. Sociology is now playing in a culture with no inhibitions or boundaries, with a restless, rootless set of individuals intoxicated with their unfixedness and bedazzled by their limitless prospects of escape. The outcomes are bleak. Weber's worst dreams have come to pass and Bauman chronicles well the worries these generate. As Tester indicates, 'Bauman's sociology focuses on what amounts to the ossification of the human world in relation to humanity and it seeks to uncover from out of the darkness the chances for a revitalisation' (2004: 124). It is this imperative that comes to shape Bauman's expectations for sociology. Certainly, he recognizes that postmodernity offers prospects of enchantment that ameliorate the disenchantment wrought by modernity where the powers of calculation are irresistible. But Bauman is seeking something more for sociology to pursue. His trajectory reflects an insight of Kołakowski that

> [a]fter centuries of the growth of the Enlightenment, we suddenly woke up in a mental and cultural disarray; we are more and more frightened in the face of a world that is losing its religious legacy, and our fear is well justified. The lost myths seem to be replaced less

> by enlightened rationality and more by terrifying secular caricatures or substitutes.
>
> (1997: 106–7)

More than any other major sociologist, Bauman exposes the enduring frailties of the human condition as these are confronted in the circumstances of a liquid modernity incapable of realizing solidarity, mutuality and commitment. He has exposed a fatal irony in sociology: the more it succeeds in its analyses the more it fails. Its domain concern, indeed its intellectual justification, is to find the basis of mutuality as modernity evolves and matures. Sociology thought this could be understood by reference to explanation and calculation; what emerges in Bauman's work is that this mutuality is to be understood by reference to other sources, where its realization can be treated as a gift that is mysterious in its origin. It is one that lies at the root of what it is to be human. In his long march through sociology, Bauman supplies an indispensable witness to this point, but in a way that complements theological insights.

The flaws of the human condition contain the seeds of great tragedy, where man encounters a noble failure in reaching beyond his powers of self-actualization but in so failing is given the grace to discover his redemption. Not to recognize this point is to capitulate to forces of dehumanization whose toxic powers have come to the fore as modernity matures. It is to sink to the level of reflexive modernization and the conceit it presents that failure is culpable and redeemable, being some infelicity of 'pure relationships' ironed out by reference to 'better advice'. In assessing failure, something more enduring, more elevating and enlarging is required. Some reference to what is endemic in the human condition needs to be explored. Many of the elements denoting the tragedy of the human condition can be found in the great dramas played out between God and man that the Swiss Catholic theological Hans Urs von Balthasar has so well explored. These dramas threaten to engulf the hopeless but are surmountable by those filled with hope. Covering the range from fear to fate, from death to evil, these dramas treat human failings by reference to the light and dark of Divinity. In the end, in these tragedies of life and death, love is the only answer for those seeking resolution of their plight. Unexpectedly, Bauman's sociology points towards the form of theology von Balthasar so magisterially laid out in his many writings. This is not to suggest that Bauman orders his sociology in a specific direction to fit into von Balthasar's aesthetic theology. There is more of theology about in an implicit form in Bauman's sociology than many might realize.

Secularity might have felt that it smashed to pieces the theological frame that so hindered the birth of modernity. Oddly, the fragments of that destruction seem to have a curious habit of rising to the surface on the sea of faith and perplexingly it seems the gift of sociology to spot these. They float about ominously, seemingly unaffected by whether the tide is in or out at Dover Beach. A reading of Bauman might suggest that he is good at discerning what is below the surface of this sea, hence why his sociology might be characterized by reference to an implicit theology. Its properties emerge in three specific areas.

First, is his stress on the self-donation to the Other which owes much to the formulations of the Jewish philosopher Emmanuel Lévinas. The second is his realization that mutuality requires a higher form of expression and this is to be found in Victor Turner's concept of 'communitas'. This evokes metaphors not solely of solidarity, but of something higher: communion. Third, Mary Douglas, in her work *Purity and Danger* supplies him with an understanding of 'the social production and effects of ambivalence' (Bauman and Tester 2001: 35–6; Douglas 2002; Tester 2004: 119–20). She is listed as a prime influence on his work. Both Turner and Douglas were Catholics and their religious beliefs had a profound impact on the shaping of their anthropology. It is the last entity that is of crucial significance in attributing an implicit theology to Bauman's sociology. Ambiguity services contradictory ends in his work. In one strand, it trumps reason and perpetuates the need to make choice. But in another way, ambiguity points to an exasperated property of modernity: contingency. It can be spun to realize that fate is one of its properties and as such lies beyond sociological remit to resolve. In this uncertainty, this opening, the issues of an implicit theology emerge.

Bauman is remarkably eclectic in the range of sources used to construct his sociology. He has a breadth and depth of reading that makes any attribution of influence arbitrary. In his writings, one feels the influence of the Polish Catholic philosopher Kołakowski. He too journeyed from the totalitarian claims of Marxism in Poland and is also concerned with responses to exile, not surprisingly as an intellectual refugee like Bauman, not quite fitting on to the landscape of Anglo-American academic culture. Kołakowski also exhibits disenchantment with modernity.

This is expressed in his notion of *horror metaphysicus*. It represents the horror of emptiness, of nothingness, where there is nothing to rescue this state of affairs (Kołakowski 2001a: 22–8; 57–8). Redemption from this plight, cast in terms of Descartes and neo-Platonism (which shaped apophatic theology), leads in a sociological direction and provides an odd complementarity to Bauman. For both Kołakowski and Bauman, the antinomy of Genesis casts a long shadow that provides the backcloth against which are to be set the divisions of human nature. Thus, Kołakowski asserts 'being becomes intelligible within the self-perception of good and evil' (2001a: 103). Two elements stand out at the end of *Metaphysical Horror.*

The first is his emphasis on hermeneutics (also a concern of Bauman) where Kołakowski refers to Gadamar on aesthetics and hermeneutics, but most specifically his citation from Goethe that 'everything is a symbol' (2001a: 126). The second element emerges in his worry over languages, and the need to recast these to articulate the needs of the age. This leads him to ponder that 'more often than not, understanding a new language of philosophy is a matter of spiritual conversion: understanding and believing are indistinguishable. Perhaps the latter even precedes the former' (Kołakowski 2001a: 108). The degree to which symbols are incomplete and offer openings to the indeterminate requires particular languages to realize a fullness of understanding. In a salami culture that delivers 'thick descriptions' in thin slices, the need to attend to the holistic has never been greater. The desire for some transformative experience persists and the searching goes on in unprecedented cultural circumstances. If anything, the ambiguities of life have been accentuated, but ironically, just at the point when the ground of culture seems to have fractured. To reflect the needs of the times, sociology has to think in new ways and Bauman points to these in a language that might seem new, but is old in the ambience from which it is drawn.

To resolve the unfettered individualism which sociology has exposed in the maturation of modernity, Bauman makes some radical inversions of disciplinary assumptions. Thus, he moves away from the stress sociology habitually places on independence and autonomy (one that shapes its vision and defence of identity politics) to an affirmation of the need for dependence. To secure this inversion Bauman reaches into theological realms. Thus, by reference to Cain and in deference to Lévinas, Bauman affirms 'my brother's dependence is what makes me an ethical being. Dependence and ethics stand together'. In a rare theological recognition, he went on to observe that this reiterates 'the hard core of Judeo-Christian teachings which gestated and weaned our common understanding of humanity and civilised being' (Bauman 2000a: 5). The matter of a duty to the Other, to one's brother or one's neighbour is of crucial concern to Bauman (2001: 71–82). It is important to stress, that unlike Bourdieu,

Simmel and Weber, who outgrew their sociology and ventured into careers in politics, poetic reflection and diplomacy, Bauman always kept his feet on the sociological ground. But, in indicating the insufficiency of the discipline to cope with his increasingly pessimistic characterizations of modernity, a worry emerges which Beilharz articulates: 'does sociology have a future? In one perspective, Zygmunt Bauman might be its last man' (2000: vii).

Certainly, there are few sociologists about who loom as possible replacements of Bauman. His reach and span of interests render him peculiarly irreplaceable. But worries over Bauman go further, as whether he has come to be the witness to the incapacity of sociology to break free from the paradigms of modernity cast by Marx, Weber, Durkheim and Simmel and to find new puzzles to secure a radical and complete disciplinary paradigm shift to cope with the consequences of the maturation of modernity that seem limitless but also meaningless. The second worry is that the discipline seems fated, especially in the Unites States to live off the fading dreams of 1968 and never to have the imagination to break free and find another revolution. If Bauman is the last great sociologist in town, it would be truly ironical if the revolutionary basis of his insights into what is to follow modernity, led back to the insights of the discipline it displaced: theology. This reversion might emerge from his concerns with choices whose exercise generates unresolvable dilemmas. The expansion of liquid modernity has brought these to the fore. They relate to its irreconcilable traits: contingency and fate. For sociology, the matter of choice is of inescapable significance.

At the end of *Liquid Modernity*, in an appendix titled 'Afterthought on Writing; On Writing Sociology' (which seems to mimic something of Bourdieu), Bauman (2000b: 216) asserted that

> There is no choice between 'engaged' and 'neutral' ways of doing sociology. A non-committal sociology is an impossibility. Seeking a morally neutral stance among the many brands of sociology practised today, brands stretching all the way from the out-spokenly libertarian to the staunchly communitarian, would be a vain effort.

He concludes by returning to a continuing theme in his writings that 'the job of sociology is to see to it that the choices are genuinely free, and that they remain so, increasingly so for the duration of humanity' (ibid.).

Choices have consequences and Bauman emphasizes this point especially as modernity liquefies. Increasingly, his writings attend to what *should be* the choice and this emerges in his concerns with the vitality of the social bond and the mutuality underpinning it when properties of commitment and trust are in short supply. The individualism and egoism Durkheim deplored was set against hopes for sociology to find new forms of solidarity by reference to the sacred and its transformative powers in ritual. But as Bauman scrutinizes the meltdown of modernity, this form of religion which sociology can endorse, seems insufficient. Something deeper is required. To a degree, Bauman comes to reflect the concerns of the Frankfurt School not so much with mere religion but with hard, deep and demanding theological questions (Mendieta 2004).

These theological concerns were crucial to Benjamin. Indeed, as Turner observed 'Benjamin's importance therefore lies with his presentation of not a sociology, but a theology of modernity' (Turner 1994: 34). Thus, Benjamin noted: 'my thinking is related to theology like a blotter is to ink. It is fully absorbed by it'. It is as if the ink sociology uses to inscribe the particular properties of modernity leaves marks on the blotting paper that only it has the skills of cartography to discern. As Wolin, who cites the above comment suggests, Benjamin felt gloomy; for as his 'trust in the ability of the secular forces of history to lead to a state of reconciliation increasingly waned, he found his historical thinking increasingly in need of theological supplementation' (1989: 224). This supplementation came by means of concerns with allegories, the baroque qualities of modernity, but above all the image of Paul Klee's *Angelus Novus* which came to haunt him.

It is the estrangement from the spiritual that haunts Benjamin, but also Simmel, and perhaps to a lesser extent Weber. In many manifestations, in the symbolism of religious ritual, in what is sought in holistic spirituality, Buci-Glucksmann is right to observe that, since Baudelaire 'angels have never ceased to exercise a kind of invisible guardianship of modernity within the poetic act' (1994: 58). The insecurities of modernity and its cataclysmic properties generated in Benjamin a concern with the Messianic as a Jewish response to exile and displacement (ibid.: 63). Similarly, these properties of dislocation force Bauman to reflect on greater issues and antinomies than the rooted need to consider. As Kołakowski indicates, those exiled have a property of a *felix cupla* where, being torn from 'celestial safety, exposed them to evil, danger, struggles, and suffering and thus laid the necessary condition of human existence. Creativity arose from insecurity, from an exile of a sort, from the experience of homelessness' (1997: 57–8). Perhaps exile accounts for Bauman's capacity to produce a corpus of sociology whose dealings with the maturation of modernity reveal marks of an implicit theology on the blotting paper.

Part of the blindness of sociology to these patterns can be attributed to the short life of the humanist strand of sociology, briefly cultivated in the United States in the 1960s. Oddly, as postmodernity came to the fore, this strand petered out just at the point when it was needed most. But as Coser indicated, this strand drew sociology into a distinctive calling, of characterizing 'the self-interpretation of man'. But such questing can lead sociology in strange directions. As Shils noted some time ago, 'sociological analysis is a continuation in a contemporary idiom of the great efforts of the human mind to render judgement on man's vicissitudes on earth' (cited in Coser 1963: 3). This need to understand human self-interpretation has been expanded to apply to the sociological endeavour itself. Reflexivity is the term that denotes the disciplinary self-awareness of the sociologist who frets over what should be understood. This is not a term Bauman uses but it is one that could be applied to his work where a pincer-like movement can be observed in his sociological diagnosis of modernity as he closes in on the immutable and vulnerable properties of life on earth. Gazing across contemporary sociology, Bauman emerges as singular in the way he takes forward concerns of Durkheim, Simmel and Weber to draw large-scale pictures of the passing moments of modernity in its different and evolving forms.

Some sociologists, and Bauman is one, take on a legendary status in sociology. Clegg recognized this property in Giddens who seemed to have achieved an iconic status in sociology where he could be regarded as a phenomenon (1992). Similar stellar qualities were around Bourdieu who wore the mantle of a public intellectual and by means of the cultural and symbolic capital accruing to his status as a sociologist took to himself the aura of greatness. It is by the superiority of their insights, and their uniqueness and not by their methods, that sociologists achieve stellar reputations that endow them with a mystique, one that affirms the cultic basis of sociology and one that explains why it stands over all other competitors in the humanities (Martin 1974). Bauman is among these, judging by the number of edited collections he has attracted that scrutinize his work. He refracts the times but is never captive to them, moving with awesome application to feel the pulse of the age and to give uncompromising diagnoses of the patient's condition. Insofar as their sociology can be summarized in one word, the word for Bourdieu is resentment, for Goffman siege and for Bauman unsettlement. This word denotes Bauman's disciplinary antennae, his sensitivity to displacement and exile, whose resolution is sought by reference to sociological resources. A very important facet of Bauman is his unwavering loyalty to sociology. Like Simmel, he supplies a pure sociology, not so much in terms of forms and the content of culture, but more in the insights yielded. These invite comparisons with another pure sociologist: Goffman.

Initially, the comparison might seem misplaced, for Bauman's sociology is of the macro and Goffman's decidedly of the micro. Both are Jewish and in some indirect way this background influences their sociological perspective. Each has in common a genius for capturing life as lived on the ground of cosmopolitan culture and to that degree their sociologies have unique powers of analytical penetration. Each produces mirrors of life as lived but framed by sociology in ways only it can refract so well. The genius of their sociology lies less in producing framed refractions of life lived and more in bringing to the fore the price of modernity, where appearances matter, where contingency rules and where endless settings enable the self to scuttle about free but oddly trapped in the freedom. Perhaps too original, like Simmel, each has no heirs. Although inescapably rooted in sociology, they reach outside its conventional resources to coin insights drawn by reference to other disciplines. What they plunder from these disciplines renders sociology less parochial in the insights it yields at their hands. Both share biographical reticence that enhances the mysterious aptness of their insights. Finally, and perhaps oddly, each produces their sociology with no definable sense of place that would give a location to the gestation of their ideas or their application.

Perhaps this masking of the particular in regard to settings facilitates the way their appeal is to the universal, what is of the contingent but above it. As sociologists, what they create emerges from dislocation. Thus, the fixedness of *The Presentation of Self in Everyday Life* (Goffman 1959) was the product of an unfixed life with a number of displacements. The fieldwork was undertaken on the isle of Unst, Scotland; the account was written at a distance in Paris; and infusing the account was a sense of exile from the site, Chicago, where Goffman's sociological imagination was first bestirred. As for Bauman, he is an émigré from Nazi and Communist Poland and his reflexivity is that of a stranger scrutinizing the plights of disconnection in the suburbs of Leeds. As he wrote: '[T]o be in exile means to be out of place; also, needing to be rather elsewhere; also, not having that "elsewhere" where one would rather be' (Bauman 1996: 569). Perhaps both indicate that to understand modernity, the sociologist needs to be in exile within it.

Both Goffman and Bauman share a common fate. As with Simmel, both seem to embody a purity of deliberation that only sociology can distil, yet both seem in revolt against the conventions of the discipline and the tidy methodological orderings research councils seek to preserve. Not quite guardians of the discipline, more poachers, Bauman and Goffman do not quite 'fit' expectations of what it is to be a sociologist. Thus, Goffman's PhD. was passed with reluctance at the University of Chicago, not being deemed sufficiently sociological or respectable in its adherence to conventions of the discipline. Ironically, Goffman was so sociological in his insights as to be misrecognized as one. Only when he was near death did the American Sociological Association recognize his greatness and reluctantly elected him as its President. Similarly, Bauman has never been part of the sociological establishment in the United Kingdom. Conceiving Bauman as having a ghostly presence in the discipline, Blackshaw (2006: 293) rightly asserts:

> All great sociologists stand apart from their time. They are not afraid of leaving the past and operating in some version of the present that is altogether their own. Bauman is that kind of sociologist.

He concludes that Bauman's sociology 'is too good for the discursive formation known as sociology'. His answer to why this should be so appears earlier where he suggests that far from dealing with reality and real lives, Bauman is concerned with the '*fantasy* of human lives *imagined*' (Blackshaw 2006: 304–5). Bauman illustrates well what Nisbet conceived as the logic of discovery and the exercise of a sociology cast in regard to an iconic imagination (2002: 5, 9). This imagination requires reference to a style of expression, an image cast and a sociological landscape of concern uncovered with themes identifiable and particular to an author (Nisbet 2002: 42–67).

To some, this might tilt sociology too much into literature and too far away from the scientific paradigms that supposedly secure its disciplinary hegemony. Yet, as Nisbet noted,

> The great harm of the present consecration of method, including theory construction, is that it persuades students that a small idea abundantly verified is worth more than a large idea still insusceptible to textbook techniques of verification.
>
> (2002: 17)

Bauman stands as a witness against this trend, being very much a sociologist of large ideas that move him in the direction of the poetic metaphors of sociology which Stein delineated some time ago. These metaphors are drawn from a wide range of the humanities. As times and expectations for insights change, so also sociology has to be creative and imaginative in seeking out new metaphors to encapsulate cultural sensibilities. In consequence, as Stein suggests, 'enlarging the metaphoric range of sociological subject matters and thought styles places a new burden on the practitioner' (1963: 181). But what happens if this enlargement requires reference to seemingly discredited sources for new metaphors? These come with expectations and diagnoses that sociology arbitrarily might feel should be discounted. How might sociologists understand Schindler's defence of the contemporary relevance of the French dramatist Paul Claudel? He was deeply worried by the loss of the capacity to make images of heaven. Without these, Schindler suggests that Claudel was convinced that

> without such images, one cannot be said to *hope* in the proper sense. Hope is, after all, a longing of the whole person. The loss of imagination is therefore a crisis of despair.
>
> (2007a: 148)

Metaphors drawn from images of the after-life often carry with them efforts to realize solutions on earth in imaginings, rituals and narratives that belong to theology which has its own solutions to sociological dilemmas. In using metaphors drawn from theology, is sociology captive to its imagination? In an odd way, all these matters come back to issues of choice.

Seeking an implicit theology in Bauman might seem a misguided, if not a bizarre, exercise in sociological proselytism that seems peculiarly insensitive given his Judaism and more importantly his relationship to the Holocaust. But no author owns his texts, for surely they have hermeneutic properties of opening out horizons of understanding as Gadamar well indicated and whose implications Bauman himself has explored. It is not to be suggested that Bauman is a closet Catholic, even though he has been highly sympathetic to John Paul II in ways that stretch beyond their common Polish citizenship (Bauman and Tester 2001: 132). More than any other contemporary sociologist, Bauman invites a theological response to his work.

Those comforted by the benign reading of modernity and culture in one of the charter document of Vatican II, *Gaudium et Spes*, are likely to encounter a shock in reading Bauman. What he produces is a sociology geared to force actors to cope with a modernity that is bleak, dark and dangerous. This is a reading of modernity with no illusions and few comfort stations. Modernity is not conceived as a means of liberation but as a conspiracy of entrapment. Thus, Torevell captures Bauman's worries well that 'modernity has ushered in a new slavery; life is now a lonely pursuit. The inalienable response of the individual is reduced to a lonely voice facing a lonely death' (1995: 151) Bauman's work generates a curious perplexity. Why is it that in regard to contemporary culture, sociology rather than theology seems to produce the richest trove of natural theology (belief in the existence of God by inference and reason rather than revelation)?

Without the solace of faith or the occupation of a long ecclesial tradition, or the rich deposits of cultural, symbolic and religious capital at its disposal, sociologists work in theological darkness, without mandate and, indeed, often in ignorance. If they seek theological relief they do so in ways that seem idiosyncratic to theologians also seeking to read the cultural times aright. In its endeavour to think of the human condition, without ticking theological boxes, the outcome of sociological analyses is to reveal a more brutal side of life in postmodernity and its successor, where present culture seems stuck in a twilight zone, neither of the dark nor the light and where seeing the way ahead is a bit of gamble in the shadows. Perhaps for this reason, Pascal has become a figure of unexpected significance for both Bauman and Bourdieu, though they differ radically in their responses to his insights.

For Bourdieu, Pascal supplies the basis of understanding how bodily knowledge can be harnessed to realize belief. By acting as if believing, the seeker comes to realize its properties. But this acting to become is subverted by Bourdieu. Pascal's wager is adjusted for play with the god of the social (2000: 245). What is sought in this form of play is not faith in God, but powers of consecration and realization where Pascal's metaphor is imperialized to enhance sociology's capacity to disclose the hidden properties of the field and to condemn those who use these to secure advantage.

In *The Art of Life*, Bauman is concerned with the properties of liquid modernity that signify unhappiness. Although not his term, restlessness denotes Bauman's interest in Pascal. Unhappiness emerges because the self is running away from the need to confront the illusions and insignificance of his life. The temptation to cease running, to stand still and to reflect requires strength of character, a resource that is presently in short supply (2008: 36–7). Yet, these issues of restlessness and boredom go deeper than the wishy-washy times of liquid modernity might indicate.

Restlessness has many symptoms, and these can be spiritual, sometimes reflecting a burning sense of the need to find God. As St. Augustine wrote in *The Confessions*:

> When spirits slide away from you they are stripped of their vesture of light and exposed in their native darkness, and then their unhappy restlessness amply proves to us how noble is each rational creature you have made, for nothing less than yourself will suffice to give it any measure of blessed rest, nor indeed can it be its own satisfaction.
>
> (1997: 347)

In a more contemporary setting, López observes that restlessness is not purely about anxiety or the cares of the world, or indeed the fear of death, but that 'it is the indwelling and reciprocity proper to love; that virginal 'yes' to the other that is ever-new and eager to let the other be and to welcome him within oneself' (2007: 187). Restlessness can also be the property of the image of God, as Schindler suggests, one peculiarly disclosed in the setting of postmodernity where the drama of modernity seems to have faded and where we live in '"perpetual rehearsal" in which meaning is endlessly deferred' (2007b: 280).

Boredom is linked to restlessness and Bauman is especially good at articulating the unsettlements that underpin these corrosive effects of liquid modernity. That is, a role articulation is one, he feels, called to undertake on behalf of others. Thus, in sympathy with Bourdieu on the role of the sociologist as a public intellectual engaging with the social forces that threaten to engulf ordinary people, Bauman asserted that 'the logic of sociology leads inescapably to transgression – to the *transcendence* of genuine or putative "objectivity" or research and its interpretation'. To realize this end, sociology takes to itself permission to trespass on boundaries between academic studies (2002: 185). Often this leads sociology on to alien disciplinary terrain such as theology, most especially when the higher and lower facets of the human condition are to be explored.

Such ventures into reflections on human nature and endeavours to mark an ideal type of man are by no means unsociological, Durkheim's *homo duplex* being a case in point. Expressed as antinomies, the social and nature, the sacred and the profane, the body and soul are dualisms the self struggles to reconcile while dimly realizing that these are irreconcilable. What is human is found in the struggle (Cladis 2008: 89–91). Dahrendorf also explored this terrain, but less in a theological sense and more with a view to exposing the limitations of sociology in dealing with its creature: *Homo Sociologicus*. In his account, this creature is the bearer of social roles, necessary constructs set for sociological deliberation. The notion of the role is extended further in part, persona, character and mask (1968: 26). All the time, Dahrendorf expresses exasperation with the price of securing sociological characterizations where limits are to be spurned and 'more' is sought. But this ambition of sociology to spurn limits amplifies the anomic condition Durkheim set the discipline to resolve. It exasperates a sense of melancholy, of sadness that nothing matters, for there are no limits that cannot be overturned and in the limitless universe so created the outcome is dolorous, producing what Jankélévitch ingeniously terms 'the modern face of ancient *acedia*' (2008: 38–9). A theological trait of melancholy finds a secularized return as the reward for the ambitions of modernity so enthusiastically endorsed by sociology. Again a theological metaphor is invoked but not as a rhetorical device but as a diagnosis where the insights of sociology spill over into theology.

The fault-line of sociology, its own disciplinary duplex is to despise what it alone can produce. Dahrendorf goes to the heart of sociology's dilemma over what it creates, pointing to the difficulty that 'society is the alienated persona of the individual, *homo sociologicus*, a shadow that has escaped the man to return as his master' (Dahrendorf 1968: 44). Ironically, in seeking to make an image fit for its regard, sociology invents an actor that is a projection of its disciplinary fantasies. To find what is of human nature is not something which a scientific perspective can answer.

A year earlier than Dahrendorf, Bauman tentatively explored a similar terrain. His target was positivist psychology whose experiments on rats formed a basis for explanations of man. Somehow, sociology and psychology had a common destiny; they occupied similar scientific paradigms (Bauman 1967). Forty years later, worries over this affiliation resurfaced as Bauman sought to understand the basis of happiness, a term of central importance for his exploration of the art of life. These experiments were viewed with repugnance as was his past acceptances of Sartre. The forms of fulfilment Sartre set out in retrospect to Bauman seemed a 'life project', one conceived as a sort of secular pilgrimage (2008: 65–6; 74–5). But in that 1967 essay the matter of choice emerged over which paradigm was sociology to affiliate with. Was it to be with a science where man could learn from the rats, or was another paradigm to be sought, one based on activitism and one endowed with powers of procreation? In the conclusion to that essay, Bauman claimed that 'only the utter imprudence can spur a humanist scientist to dispose of "image of man" as a metaphysical *residium* alien to the spirit of the science and irrelevant to its pursuits'. Even then, he was worried over sociologists 'coronating the "Queen of Sciences" they wish to dethronize'. The outcome he feared was of saturation with 'philosophical' notions that led some to feel 'helpless and disarmed when facing the real choice' (Bauman 1967: 20–1).

By 2008, Bauman had moved on considerably in directions hospitable to theological considerations. Nietzsche and Sartre are spurned in favour of Lévinas. A sociological solution to the ultimate image of man, one at the root of his search for happiness is presented in ways that complement theological insights, most especially those of Christianity. Thus, it is only by giving to the Other and by being for others, that man can find a durable basis for his happiness (Bauman 2008: 122). In asserting the notion of the self finding itself in giving to the Other, Bauman opens out theological windows for sociology to gaze into, for behind these casements love and self-sacrifice are given a fullness of understanding on a scale outside the capacity of the discipline to envisage. Love and its precarious state in liquid modernity formed a particular concern of Bauman (2003).

Always elusive, always desired, sought but seldom found, love sets an image of possibility for the self to find itself. Marked by disinterest rather than interest, love operates without reference to calculation. But in so giving, the self exposes itself to vulnerability, to risks of being spurned or betrayed. As Marx observed, in the context of observations on money, 'if you love without evoking love in return – that is, if your loving as loving does not produce reciprocal love; if through a *living expression* of yourself as a loving person you do not make yourself as a *beloved one,* then your love is impotent – a misfortune' (1975: 326). Thus, to be in love is to be in fulfilment; it is to possess a rare gift, an emotion, a sensibility of the Other that envelops the self and raises it up. It is to escape regulation; it is to transcend the contracts wrought for the often narrow needs of reciprocity. In Christianity and notably in the writings of Paul and John are to be found some of the most beautiful reflections on the nature of love. As a gift, love burns brightly and inexhaustibly. Of all the forms of love, that of God is perhaps the most mysterious, the most fulfilling and the most elusive (1 John 4: 7–21).

Beck and Beck-Gernsheim explored love in terms of fulfilment and as a vitalizing ingredient of life in late modernity in the 1990s. Their account treated the implications of the secularization of love where a new world had been opened up fit for their sociological characterization. In this new order, they observed that 'religion tells us there is a life after death; love says there is a life before death' (1995: 176). Oddly, with the decline of religion, love had increased as a matter of sociological significance. Thus, in their conclusion to the study they suggested, 'we are immodestly and tentatively looking for the meaning of life in a post-Christian modernity society, and our discovery is, quite simply and unsociologically, love' (ibid.: 169). Whatever their caveats, their analysis expressed the hope of a new era of love, one that celebrated autonomy, self-need and identity. The issue of love emerged in another study of the time by Giddens. In *The Transformation of Intimacy*, he sought to characterize 'pure relationships', and that plastic sexuality where the pursuit of mutual satisfaction underlines the need for a restructuring of relationships (1992: 58). These two studies seemed to embody what Bauman deplored in his own work, *Liquid Love* (2003).

In this work, he expressed his deep disenchantment with the outcomes of a world where individualism is realized through 'pure sexuality'. In this world, there are casualties: bonds no longer bind, communitas is for purchase and proximity in virtual form has become the index of the 'real' (Bauman 2003: 46–7; 58–9; 63–5). In short, love in liquefied modernity has become unreal, fleeting and laden with illusions. The antidote to these circumstances leads Bauman in the direction of an implicit theology. Its concerns arise in the context of 'accepting the precept of loving one's neighbour. Not only does the command involve 'a leap of faith'; the precept 'is the birth act of humanity' (Bauman 2003: 78). In dealing with love, Bauman seeks 'the sovereign expression of life', one that manifests itself in 'trust, compassion and mercy' (ibid.: 96).

What worries Bauman is that the liquidizing powers of modernity have moved from 'politics to "life-policies" or have descended from the "macro" to the "micro" level of social cohabitation' (2000b: 7). This downward movement intensifies the demands of social knowing placed on the actor. Ambiguity comes to the fore with changed significance. It represents the need to choose but in settings where fate looms and a sense of fragility threatens to engulf the self. Neither God nor the social provide solace. In liquid modernity, God has melted and the social bond never dries out sufficiently to produce something solid upon which to rely on to get through life. Not surprisingly in this ethos of indeterminacy, fate looms large as the actor comes to a realization of the randomness of events. A strange outcome of these changes in ambiguity is that the fear it generates has been lost (Bauman 2001: 68–9). What *should be* beyond calculation moves in his writings to what *is* beyond regulation and in this way the insecurities of the human condition are brought into focus.

Against this background, it is narratives and tales that count in settings where as Bauman suggests 'sociology is itself a story' (ibid.: 13). This changes the expectations surrounding sociology and the rhetoric it employs. The tale it seeks to tell has to be composed in the unpropitious circumstances of life in liquid modernity, where 'the haunting spectre of insecurity' casts gloom (ibid.: 160). In his response to this gloom, this heightened insecurity, Bauman changes the setting of morality from concerns with reciprocal exchange to the seeking of something more exalted. Thus, he writes with approval of the suggestion of Lévinas that 'the "primal scene" of morality is the realm of "face to face", of the tremendous encounter with the Other as a *Face*' (ibid.: 175).

The face, as Simmel has suggested, is the site for the testing of character, a point Goffman takes forward. Why the testing? Here, one finds a convergence between Bauman and Goffman by reference to the Book of Job. Unsettlement, unease and the vital testing of character in the circumstances of face-to-face encounters suggest a reaching back to Job to understand Goffman's work. Creelan provides an exemplary account of how an implicit theology incorporating Job enables many themes of Goffman's work to be fruitfully understood (1984: 663–95). But Bauman's use of Job goes further, deeper and darker, for his concern is with the unutterable and unimaginable basis of malice, of evil in events, where fate and denial of choice looms (2006: 56–9; 84). This concern with fate again marks a suggestive link between Goffman and Bauman. Fate was an explicit concern of Goffman in his essay 'Where the Action Is'. He was concerned with actions affected by matters of chance, that were denoted as eventful and the consequential (Goffman 1967: 164). In this essay, Goffman anticipated the concerns of virtue ethics by exploring how fate and character were interlinked.

The wager between God and Satan over Job involves testing the conventions upon which virtue is to be recognized. The punishment of Job generates perplexing matter for arbitration. Either Job is innocent and undeserving of his punishment or the ritual apparatus that certifies his claims to virtue is defective. The only proper conclusion is that Job is guilty for it is inconceivable that the rituals are defective – the social consequences of their condemnation are unthinkable. But what is Bauman's own stance towards matters of testing? His responses point to the dark side of modernity, the unfinished businesses of evil and death. It is these concerns that lend a depth to his analyses of the maturation of modernity and are indicative of the concerns of an implicit theology haunting his sociological deliberations.

Increased reference to reflexivity draws out biographical facets involved in fieldwork and these can indicate the way fate arises for those chronicling the lives of others. This was well articulated by Rosaldo as he tried to reconcile his biography to those he studied. In his concern with border crossings between cultures, he stumbled on understandings of his headhunting tribe, the Ilongots, when his own wife had died on fieldwork. This led him to realize the positioned basis of the ethnographer, but above all the provisional basis of his accounts (1993: 7–11). More than many might realize, the persona of the sociologist is implicated in what he seeks to write. This generates a difficulty in regard to Bauman, for on many matters he is a model of biographical reticence. Understanding of his emphases, his values, his insecurities and why he seeks to use his sociology to pursue particular paths elude and in that way Bauman stands oddly outside the expectations of reflexivity. There are some clues as to why issues of human nature loom so large in his sociology.

Realizations of the horrors of his early life and the compromises he had to make to survive can be inferred in an essay by his wife on the betrayals and capitulations to evil that occurred in Poland during WWII in two Jewish ghettoes (Bauman, J. 2003). It was she who challenged Bauman to write a sociological response to the Holocaust.

Lurking behind that dreadful tragedy is the issue of fate. How could it come to pass that in a culture where all could be controlled, fate played such a horrible hand? Whereas other sociologists such Beck and Giddens caught the fear and anxiety of reflexive modernization in the 1990s, Bauman was discerning something deeper, something endemic in modernity itself, things it had not quite expelled. These were fate and fear. These posed metaphysical and sociological dangers and Bauman's background as a Polish Jew gives him good reasons to recognize what those living in English suburbs might not discern. For Bauman,

> Fear is at its most fearsome when it is diffuse, scattered, unclear, unattached, unanchored, free floating with not clear address or cause; when it haunts us with no visible rhyme or reason, when the menace we should be afraid of can be glimpsed everywhere but is nowhere to be seen.
>
> (2006: 2)

Fate and fear converge around the matter of death. It presents itself as *the* fact of life, one which modernity with its much vaunted concern with the empirical seeks to mask, to ignore or to treat as a shameful event, one that unsettles those foolish enough to think they inhabit an eternal present.

Few other processes so mark secularization as the removal of death from the sphere of clerical intervention to medical arenas where scientific miracles are increasingly seen as regulating the end of life. Illich provided a pioneering critique of this medicalization of death and the recasting of its image. Death increasingly became a question of social control rather than Divine intervention and as he observed 'society has become responsible for preventing each man's death: treatment, effective or not, can be made into a duty' (Illich 1975: 141). Medical science might well regulate death, but the end of life still generates deep unsettlements, fears and anxieties that are peculiar to the age.

For Bauman, death keeps reappearing and it comes all the more perplexingly for being uncoupled from worries over eternity (2006: 45). Death seems to have few terrors as the shadows cast by the afterlife fade. As death is secularized and the disposal of the deceased is personalized, Christians become oddly hesitant about proclaiming the Resurrection of the dead (Jupp 2008a: 16–16; Jupp 2008b: 67–81). A curious hesitation about the afterlife has pervaded Catholicism, where only a few magnificently evil might be eligible for hell, virtually all are given passes to heaven, its waiting room, limbo has been closed down and purgatory has emerged as a washing station for the sinfully scruffy who are cleansed and are rapidly dispatched to heaven in the wink of an eye. As always, Anglicans did the decent thing for sinners: they abolished hell altogether (Badham 2008: 101–2). A curious outcome of Bauman's sociology is the way it forces back hard questions on to theologians, about the persistence of evil, about Divine retribution and the need to be more specific about the goods for salvation requisite for life after death.

In *Mortality, Immortality*, Bauman asserts that 'death is the scandal, the ultimate humiliation of reason' (1992: 15). Those who die present an embarrassment, a matter of shame in modernity, something reason will fix but which it cannot (ibid.: 129). Bauman's interest in death follows a clear path in his writings that deference to the god of reason dehumanizes. Death is not a mechanical matter, a physiological failure rather it is where the purpose of life is to be found, for in the fragility of the human condition greatness can unexpectedly shine forth. All the time Bauman returns to the matter of the social bond, that vital and vitalizing concern of both sociology and theology. In mutuality and sacrifice is that bond to be strengthened by the serendipitous donations of strangers to each other. Thus, drawing from Lévinas, Bauman concludes that the readiness to die for an Other 'is the constitutive act of human individuality and uniqueness' (ibid.: 200).

From his study of the Holocaust, something comes to haunt Bauman: the mystery of self-sacrifice of those who risk a life for the stranger (Bauman 1992: 207–10). Some of these were Poles and some were Catholics. Those who converted an 'ethic of responsibility' into an irresponsible act of love, who made the ultimate sacrifice, galvanize Bauman's sociological imagination. These generous fools perplex and fascinate in ways that seem to cause to melt the boundaries that sociology maintains against theology. They also seem to leave sociology lost for the right words. They can be classified as altruistic, benevolent or heroic but these terms hardly suffice to denote acts of supererogation whose impulses are deeply human but also mysterious. Even more perplexing are the circumstances of evil from which these acts spring.

As suggested above, Bauman's sociological encounter with the Holocaust contributed to rehabilitation of the term but in a disquieting way. Certainly, evil is the only term fitting to describe the wickedness of what happened, but difficulty was that it emerged in ways where its prevalence, so pervasive, so routinized could not be recognized. It would seem that modernity enabled evil to exist on scale in ways that secured its misrecognition. The difficulty is that evil comes in a variety of forms as Paoletti has ingeniously explored in relation to Durkheim. But the neutralization of evil, its reduction to a social form, while leaving open the need for piacular and repairs to the tissue of society does not obviate recourse to notions of the malign and the malicious to characterize the Holocaust (Paoletti 2008: 66).

But reducing evil to a social form still renders it ambiguous for sociological decipherment. Bauman's account of the Holocaust brings this ambiguity to the fore, for his insights rest on inverting Durkheim's notion of social evil. It thrives in disorder, in the pathological and destructive. Bauman's confrontation with evil emerges in contrary social circumstances, of order, of construction and a sense of the normal. It is the routinization of evil, where it becomes conventional that is so disquieting in Bauman's appraisal of the Holocaust. Bauman has exposed a strange anomaly: reason endows matters with endless possibilities of transparency, but also it also facilitates the disguise of what *should* be made manifest. It is this ambiguous property of reason and modernity that made the Holocaust uniquely possible. This terrible event was not simply a function of misplaced technological gifts; it was about the disguise of the nefarious uses to which these capacities could be put.

Bauman asserted that 'evil and fear are Siamese twins' (2006: 54). They both relate to the unknown, but also to what seems irresistible, to what cannot be contained because it is presented as 'normal'. It is this capacity to domesticate evil into conventions of normality, of civilized calculation, that undermines the need for redress and resistance to its persistence. Two events, the Holocaust and the civil rights movement in the United States in the mid-1960s, caused sociology to reconsider its habitual disdain of use of the term evil.

In an anticipation of Bauman's approach to the Holocaust, Coser wondered over what in modernity enabled evil to flourish. Drawing on a paper by Everett Hughes (who greatly influenced Goffman) Coser explored the way evil could flourish if it was treated as dirty but necessary work but kept invisible so as to enable good people to live in tranquil circumstances of normality. Moral sensibilities could flourish intact if those delegated to nefarious dirty tasks kept their evil activities out of sight. In many respects, Coser supplies a variation on Goffman's notion of civil inattention, but in this context in relation to evil, where the other is treated as an object and rendered invisible by distance. Oddly, some see evil all too visibly in the normal, while others do not. Coser's comment still applies that 'the sociology of perception, a sociology elucidating why people sometimes look and why they sometimes look away still is to be written' (1969: 104).

In a curious way, Bauman has moved matters of choice back from the free ranging options of self-authenticity existentialism offered to an older theological emphasis: free will. But at this juncture, Bauman seems to reach a sociological limit to understanding. Before these great matters, sociology is mute. As Bauman caustically observes, 'in the face of human choices between good and evil, sociological wisdom was found to have nothing to say' (2008: 96). Excess of concern with human rights, with the blurring of distinctions between culture and religions produces dreams that are doomed to be false, for as Kołakowski wryly suggested 'the Eden of human universality is a paradise lost (1997: 85). For Kołakowski, there has been a dramatic loss of nerve among theologians, who reflect the fear of the Christian world 'of being trapped in an alien enclave within a basically unChristian world'. In response to that fear, Kołakowski adds, 'not surprisingly', 'the concepts of the devil and of original sin seem almost to have vanished' (1997: 79). But as he suggests, and as Bauman would endorse, the game of good and evil never ceases. There is much in Kołakowski's comment that 'reason and the ability to do evil (i.e., freedom) are inseparable; consequently God, by producing rational creatures – human and angelic – had to suffer the inevitable evil results' (1997: 180). But, as he adds, striving against these generates the pursuit of good, which returns to Bauman's concerns with mutuality, with love and hope.

Compared with Giddens or Bourdieu, in his few writings dealing directly with religion, Bauman displays an unusual sympathy to its attractions. Treating fundamentalism as a reasonable response to postmodernity, indeed as its child, Bauman seems to understand well the need for certainty it fulfils as a particular religious style of the age. Thus, he suggests that 'the allure of fundamentalism stems from its promise to emancipate the converted from the agonies of choice' (1998: 58). But this positive response to that which emerges as postmodernity's religion goes further. Earlier in this essay, Bauman referred to Kołakowski's view of religion as 'the awareness of human insufficiency'. The long citation from his work which followed was introduced with the comment: 'in his classic and in my view unsurpassed analysis of the way in which religiosity is gestated by human existential conditions' (Bauman 1998: 74). It was as if Bauman was recognizing the impulses that made for religiosity.

This 'human insufficiency' returns matters to Pascal's wager which Kołakowski expresses as follows: 'briefly: there is a sense in which the basics tenets of faith – God, the union of mind and body, original sin – are absurd and yet the world image which excludes those tenets is even more absurd' (2001b: 203). Now, Kołakowski viewed aspects of Pascal with alarm, not least his view of evil and his relationship to Jansenism (1998). These criticisms of Pascal remind sociologists that their modest appropriations from theology often exclude reference to vast terrains of writings, for instance of the Desert Fathers, innumerable heresies and arcane disputes whose significance lies peripherally to sociological needs. The particular contribution sociology makes to the humanities is the critical appraisal the discipline makes of what happens at the level of the social, its construction, what it manifests and how its products are received.

In Pascal, the needs of theology and sociology converge in ways both Bourdieu and Kołakowski understand. For Bourdieu, Pascal's 'model of the production of belief' entails the rediscovery of 'postures of the body which, being charged with mnemic experiences, are capable of stirring up thoughts, emotions and imagination' (2000: 144). This returns to a decisive point, one Kołakowski notes, that Pascal's wager is not about a proof of God, but a realization that to act in faith 'is much less risky than its refusal'. Kołakowski observes that Pascal 'never tried, as many theologians did, to convert faith into a second rate secular knowledge'. What is of the first rate comes from above and this entails a realization that

> God is not an unknown quantity in some equation we have to solve but a reality which appears to the believer in the act of worship, and no intellectual contrivance, however ingenious, can of its own power prompt us to such acts or to any acts whatever.
>
> (Kołakowski 2001b: 194–5)

This emphasis on acting, so important in terms of free will provides a ticket of entry for sociology into arenas requisite for theological deliberations. Both forms of understanding converge over a common recognition that faith needs grace but also a ground for its fruitful realization. That ground might be Bourdieu's field, or Bauman's garden nurtured by the state, or it might be the soggy bog of liquid modernity, but in whichever case, it is in and through the social that faith is realized. That social ground of possibility might be interwoven with black threads signifying evil, or white threads denoting good, and it might be that sociologists besotted with secularity, even in post forms, are afflicted with blindsight, being unable to name or decipher what the blessed can discern (Flanagan 2007). Again, to follow Pascal, to realize belief is to act *as if* believing and it is from the ground of culture that this leap in trust and understanding is to be made (Flanagan 2008). Sociology might well claim to part of theology, but in this claim is seldom reciprocated or recognized by theologians. It is not that sociological interventions wish away theology; it is that sociology's intervention confound what theologians think it *ought* to say, but does not.

It is slightly embarrassing, therefore, to admit that this reading of an implicit theology into the works of Bauman comes from within sociology, not theology. One of the few theological responses to his work, Ward's *Liquid Church* received a hopeful reception in evangelical circles (2002). It seemed to Ward that Bauman was offering a mandate for liquid, fluid forms of worship as best fitting the needs of the times, as against solid, traditional styles which seemed culturally estranging. But the study almost completely misread Bauman. Far from treating the liquidity of modernity as a mandate to melt social bonds, Bauman was arguing the opposite. He was quite definite, 'that in our liquid modern times we need and desire firm and reliable bonds more than at any other time only exacerbates the anxiety' (2006: 70). The anxiety arises in seeking these bonds, not in demolishing existing ones that give comfort as in traditional rituals and structured forms of worship as in English cathedrals. The liquid, the unfixed and the indefinite are symptoms of modernity in meltdown of common meanings. This reflects a pathological state (to use Durkheim) set not for theological endorsement but for resolution and transcendence. Even more perversely, Ward is offering a sunny-side-up understanding of liquid modernity, one which, as de Groot rightly observed, ignores the dark side of Bauman's whole sociological project. De Groot notes that while religion is marginalized in Bauman's work (though less than might initially seem the case), what it does supply are accounts of 'the desire for ontological security and the search for social solidarity (which) can be associated with the classic functions of religion'. In conclusion, de Groot suggests that what Bauman has supplied is 'an invitation to Christian theology to reconsider its own view of contemporary culture'. In short, 'theology may benefit from Bauman's almost religious plea against a culture of fear, and in favour of community development' (de Groot 2006: 98).

The thrust of Bauman's sociology is to keep matters open, whether by reference to the varying uses of ambiguity in his writings, the vagaries of contingency and fate or fear of the unknown in liquid modernity. In each case the indeterminate preserves the need to make choices. To foreclose this necessity is to de-humanize. What Bauman mourns is the advent of a culture where no distinctions can be made, for the culture presented is a wasteland. This state of emptiness undermines the prospect of making choices. But choices encounter boundaries that are dualistic if not antinomial, such as those between the sacred and the profane. In liquid modernity, where boundaries melt, transgression emerges as an act devoid of a sense of trespass. If something is to be learnt from sociology, it is that limits have their uses, and if so, they need preservation orders stamped on them to signify the values of a moral and social ecology. The need to inhibit transgressions and violations by the morally slovenly preserves culture from dissolving into meaninglessness and the anomic state Durkheim so feared would come to characterize modernity. As Kołakowski noted 'culture *is* taboos or, to put it another way, a culture without taboos is a square circle'. He goes on to assert that, from the tree of knowledge, that so influenced Bauman and Benjamin 'we owe the moral distinction to our participation in taboos' (Kołakowski 2001b: 186–7; Steiner 1967). These require reference to boundaries but also to limits on what can be understood.

Transitions, exiles and boundaries all amplify for Bauman the significance of choice whose exercise affirms the essential properties of humanity and whose defence lies so centrally to his sociological concerns. But sometimes these choices tilt in unexpected and unsociological directions, as for example in the case of religious conversions. When these transitions are pendulum like, from one religious affiliation to another, the sociological vision becomes blurred as it seeks to appraise such mysterious and perplexing movements. The deathbed conversion of Gillian Rose on the 9 December 1995 is very much a case in point.

The famous English Jewish philosopher Rose was baptized on her deathbed by the Anglican Bishop of Coventry before a gathering of grieving perplexed academics attending a conference she herself had organized at the University of Warwick (Shanks 2008: 1–13; 166–74). In his essay on her conversion, Jay reflected on the bafflement and sense of loss he felt as an agnostic academic Jew at the passing of a colleague into Christianity. The reasons for her conversion were unsettling for, as Jay concluded, 'the consolation of philosophy had ultimately proven inadequate to her spiritual needs' (2003: 61). Her conversion could not be characterized as some sentimental 'born again' deathbed departure, the easeful exit of the muddled. It involved a woman with very definite opinions and who was under no discernible constraints to convert. It was an act freely made. Highly intelligent and educated, she must have known that her baptism was a fundamental re-marking and therefore a decision not to be taken lightly. Few others could have better understood the legacy of conversion. It was the will and testament of a woman who had written with forensic insight on the onset of the cancer that was to kill her, and who provided a unique reflexive account of the contradictions of her personal life, her Judaism and the endurance required to confront a fractured world in which some tenable middle was to be found. The baptism was a leap from the conundrums of philosophical conjecture about this world into the other world.

There are many ironies in her life not least that Kołakowski was the supervisor of her doctoral thesis on Adorno. Known for her interest in exploring 'the broken middle', a position Bauman perceives in a more sociological expression in postmodernity, Rose sought solutions to the fractures she relentlessly uncovered. In the brokenness of Anglicanism, not Catholicism, she found a healing. On the fringes of Radical Orthodoxy (a liberal branch of Anglicanism), Rose shared an odd point with its most conspicuous figure, John Milbank. Both wrote withering critiques of sociology from philosophical positions that might be politely classified as 'diffuse'. But for Rose (and also to a greater extent for Milbank) as Jay reflects, 'sociology, the discipline she so sweepingly condemned in her second book, seems to have blithely gone about its business without losing any sleep' (2003: 66).

Something Rose wrote returns matters to Benjamin's blotting paper. Towards the end of the autobiography, Rose expresses her bafflement over what philosophers feel is current choice: 'revealed religion; enlightenment rationalism; and postmodern relativism'. For her, 'it is *the unrevealed religion* which troubles us more than any revealed religion'. It is the latter which

> has hold of us without any evidences, natural or supernatural, without any credos or dogmas, liturgies or services. It is the very religion that makes us protest, 'But I have no religion', the very *protestantism* against modernity that fuels our inner-self-relation.

Ripe, over mature, 'this is an ethic without ethics, a religion without salvation' (Rose 1995: 126–7).

The end of *Love's Work* is sad, as Rose's hopes for an old age in the persona of Miss Marple (the famous detective in the works of Agatha Christie) never came to pass. But her death left a testimony of a choice made: for revealed religion not the *unrevealed religion*.

Concentration on the peripheries of religion, cults and sects in the last two decades of the 20th century has left a yawning gap in sociological understandings of conversions between major religions. Deference to secularity hides such transitions from sociological view. In disciplinary terms, they do not occur, or if they do they are movements of insignificance (Flanagan 2009). This disciplinary neglect of conversion amplifies the significance but also the peculiarities of Rose's conversion and the unresolved issues it has generated that lie as an inconvenient legacy for many.

As Lloyd indicates, she deeply disagreed with Milbank over solutions to secularity and modernity and the stresses it has generated. For Rose, his solution of transcendence was an escape from the violence of a fracturing world. But as Lloyd notes, her theological solution did not involve a return to Judaism (2008: 202). Yet, the RTE (Irish radio) interview, whose transcript Lloyd introduces, deals much with her Jewish identity (2009: 209–11). Even more oddly, she sought solutions in faith and love, but not in hope, that most Christian of virtues (2009: 202–3).

Conversions can be marked by 'tipping' factors, where the convert falls or slides from one religious affiliation into another. When transitions are radical, unexpected and baffling as in the case of Rose, the 'tipping' factors seem ripe for much biographical inspection but in ways that distract attention from a simple theological point: the gift of grace, that joker in the sociological pack. The final set of entries in her notebooks convey a sense of sinking into the clutches of Christianity, a letting go to its comforts, to the words, images and hope of Christ and, for her, the prospect of escape from hell and despair. All the time, she was seeking to reconcile her Judaism with the prospect of a Christian rebirth. That is why she referred to Simone Weil as an angelus bell, calling others into the Church, even though she desisted from being baptized (Rose 1998: 9). The integrity of her philosophical vocation might have caused her to postpone acceptance of hope, perhaps feeling that to capitulate to Christianity might undermine her duty to her tribe and to her need to analyse ruthlessly without theological solace. In her last writings, there is a sense of just letting go to what she always believed but found impossible to affirm. It is not possible to read her final record any other way. How she might have lived as a convert, in what type and form of Christianity is a matter of conjecture, but whatever the case, the act of converting was deliberate. It was not just an assent of the dying, but involved baptism, communion and confirmation. Clearly, this had been thought out and underlined the factual nature of her conversion and how she wanted it to be understood (Rose 1998: 15).

Why bring the conversion of Rose into an essay on the implicit theology, if any of Bauman? Both share a common Polish background and have contrasting, but not deeply religious, attitudes to their Judaism. As indicated above, it is not clear that Rose's choice could be understood by reference to her philosophical career. But in the case of Bauman, the issue of whether he does convert or not is beside the point, rather it is the outcome of the long trajectory of his writings that unexpectedly yields theological reflection.

Bauman's writings are marked by a stony-faced integrity, one that shapes a ruthless analytical gaze at what Weber treated as the inconvenient facts which he behoved sociology to confront. Nothing appears randomly in Bauman's writing. What he writes is what he feels called to express, to put into words even that which might seem inconvenient. In the writing of books, the beginning and the ends are sites of authorial vulnerability. In *The Art of Life* (2008) a realization dawns that what he is seeking is beyond what sociology alone can illuminate. In the conclusion to this work, he feels he can only repeat the words of Seneca cited at the start of the book that '"when it comes to seeing clearly what it is that makes life happy" we "grope for the light"'. Rather sadly, he goes on to add: 'two millennia later ... we don't seem to be much closer to that light than Seneca's contemporaries. We continue groping. This is, ultimately, what the "art of life" is about' (2008: 124). The study is framed by reference to Seneca; the use of the quotation twice is not accidental, but is marked for significance.

If Steiner famously came to endorse a long Holy Saturday at the end of *Real Presences*, then Bauman seems to mark an Advent in this 2008 study, one that presents the seeking of a light. Clearly, Bauman is not seeking the light of reason nor does he look to Nietzsche, who he disdains in one of the most eloquent chapters of *The Art of Life* which ends with the reference to Seneca. It is to the borderlands with theology, in the realms of the spiritual that Bauman moves to seek his sources of illumination. His concerns with love, with giving and sacrifice seem to write a theological expectation into the end days of his sociology. As he seeks for happiness, not of consumerism and what he scathingly describes as 'postmodern cowboys' (2008: 121), he looks for solutions in the Other of Lévinas but in such searching he comes near to the formulation on love of Benedict XVI. In *Deus Caritas Est*:

> Love now becomes concern and care for the other. No longer is it self-seeking, a sinking in the intoxication of happiness; instead it seeks the good of the beloved: it becomes renunciation and it is ready, and even willing, for sacrifice.
>
> (Benedict XVI 2006: 9)

Seneca was a Stoic philosopher, with an interest in drama. His understandings of the art of life and his other writings generated an early Christian appreciative appraisal. In his letter on lack of moral purpose, 'On Tranquillity of Mind', Seneca seems to anticipate the worst of liquid modernity, when he wrote,

> But if we shun all society and, abandoning the human race, live for ourselves alone, this isolation, devoid of any interest, will be followed by a dearth of worthwhile activity. We shall begin to put up some buildings, to pull down others, to push back the sea, to draw waters through unnatural channels, and to squander the time which nature gave us to be used.
>
> (2005: 37)

The need to find how to live morally, to construct what will endure and to secure solidarity are ambitions reflection on which mark humanist traditions. The value of Bauman's work is that he comes to root his sociology in these traditions. He comes to remind the discipline of what it might forget, that even and perhaps most especially in the setting of liquid modernity, fear, fate and evil persist in their powers to unsettle but that choice still prevails of escape, of love and hope, where the better part is to be found in the mire of life. Thus, uniquely, Bauman has managed to reset sociology in a long line of theological reflection, from St. Augustine, to Pascal to Kierkegaard to realize the degree to which the self is a mystery to itself, fated to choose but strangely paralyzed in doing so from its own resources. Dissatisfaction with this state of affairs generates the restlessness mentioned above. But it is easy to confuse an endemic property of humanity with a trait of liquid modernity. The unsettlements occasioned by restlessness can doom the actor to endless escape, to a reluctance to seek roots when exits exist in their plenitude in liquid modernity, but that trait can sow the seeds of possible redemption. Servais marked this well when he wrote of restlessness:

> It is the emotive correlate to the awareness of the imperfect, chaotic, and indeed even nonsensical character of the world in which we live. Thus, it opens up in man the desire for a better order, one capable of resolving this affective tension; it stirs in him the aspiration to find a peace and happiness that lasts.
>
> (2007: 235)

The dalliances of sociology with light and dark might relate to its conventional understandings of illumination and ignorance, but they can also relate to hope rising over the ominous and pointing to a higher universe of meanings. Is it the fate of sociology to conceive of the ultimate meaning of life, as Bauman would suggest, its art, outside the boxes of theology? But setting the art and purpose of life in regard to Seneca is to open the possibilities of employing other texts with which to mark the ends of sociology's journey.

In the end, Bauman seems to suggest that actor hesitates to grasp that light. But is hesitation binding on other sociologists for whom other choices are to be made and other texts to be found that guide their vision of the art of life? For some there is another text with other ambitions that lies on the fringes of sociology, which gives ultimate focus to its analytical activities: 'walk while ye have the light lest darkness come up you: for he that walketh in darkness knoweth not whither he goes. While ye have light, believe in the light, that ye may be the children of light' (John 12: 35–6).

References

Badham, P. (2008), 'Concepts of Heaven and Hell in the Modern Era', in Peter C. Jupp (ed.) *Death Our Future: Christian Theology and Pastoral Practice in Funeral Ministry*, London: Epworth, 93–103.

Bauman, J. (2003), 'Moral Choices in the Age of Gas Chambers', in Peter Wagner and Bo Stråth (eds), *Between Two Wars: Janina and Zygmunt Bauman's Analyses of the Contemporary Human Condition*, Florence: European University Institute Working paper HEC No. 2003/4, 9–21.

Bauman, Z. (1967), 'Image of Man in the Modern Sociology (Some methodological remarks)'. *Polish Sociological Bulletin*, 1: 12–21.

Bauman, Z. (1989), *Modernity and the Holocaust*, Cambridge: Polity.

Bauman, Z. (1992), *Mortality, Immortality and Other Life Strategies*, Stanford: Stanford University Press.

Bauman, Z. (1996), 'Assimilation into Exile: The Jew as a Polish Writer'. *Poetics Today*, 17 (4): 569–97.

Bauman, Z. (1998), 'Postmodern religion?' in Paul Heelas (ed.), *Religion, Modernity and Postmodernity*, Oxford: Blackwell, 55–78.

Bauman, Z. (2000a), 'Am I my brother's keeper?'. *European Journal of Social Work*, 3 (1): 5–11.

Bauman, Z. (2000b), *Liquid Modernity*, Cambridge: Polity.

Bauman, Z. (2001), *The Individualized Society*, Cambridge: Polity.

Bauman, Z. (2002), 'Pierre Bourdieu or the Dialectics of Vita Contemplativa and Vita Activa'. *Revue Internationale de Philosophie*, 2 (220): 179–93.

Bauman, Z. (2003), *Liquid Love: On the Frailty of Human Bonds*, Cambridge: Polity.

Bauman, Z. (2006), *Liquid Fear*, Cambridge: Polity.

Bauman, Z. (2008), *The Art of Life*, Cambridge : Polity.

Bauman, Z. and Keith, T. (2001), *Conversations with Zygmunt Bauman*, Cambridge: Polity.

Beck, U. and Beck–Gernsheim, E. (1995), *The Normal Chaos of Love*, trans. Mark Ritter and Jane Wiebel, Cambridge: Polity.

Beilharz, P. (2000), *Zygmunt Bauman: Dialectic of Modernity*, London: Sage.

Benedict XVI (2006), *Deus Caritas Est*, London: Catholic Truth Society.

Blackshaw, T. (2006), 'Too Good for Sociology'. *Polish Sociological Review*, 3 (155): 293–306.

Bourdieu, P. (2000), *Pascalian Meditations*, trans. Richard Nice, Cambridge: Polity Press.

Buci-Glucksmann, C. (1994), *Baroque Reason: The Aesthetics of Modernity*, trans. Patrick Camiller, London: Sage.

Cladis, M. S. (2008), 'Suffering to Become Human: A Durkheimian Perspective', in W. S. F. Pickering and Massimo Rosati (eds), *Suffering and Evil: The Durkheimian Legacy*, Oxford: Berghahn, 81–100.

Clegg, S. (1992), 'How to become an Internationally Famous British Social Theorist'. *The Sociological Review*, 40 (2): 576–98.

Coser, L. A. (ed.) (1963), 'Introduction', in *Sociology Through Literature*, Englewood Cliffs, N. J.: Prentice-Hall, 2–7.

Coser, L. A. (1969) 'The Visibility of Evil', *Journal of Social Issues*, 25(1): 101–9.

Creelan, P. (1984), 'Vicissitudes of the Sacred: Erving Goffman and the Book of Job'. *Theory and Society*, 13: 663–95.
Dahrendorf, R. (1968), *Essays in the Theory of Society*, London: Routledge & Kegan Paul.
Douglas, M. (2002), *Purity and Danger*, London: Routledge.
De Groot, K. (2006), 'The Church in Liquid Modernity: A Sociological and Theological Exploration of a Liquid Church'. *International Journal for the Study of the Christian Church*, 6 (1): 91–103.
Flanagan, K. (2007), *Sociology in Theology: Reflexivity and Belief*, Basingstoke: Palgrave Macmillan.
Flanagan, K. (2008), 'Sociology into Theology: The Unacceptable Leap'. *Theory, Culture & Society*, 25(7–8): 236–61.
Flanagan, K. (2009), 'Conversion: Heroes and their Sociological Redemption', in Guiseppe Giordan, ed., *Conversion in the Age of Pluralism*, Leiden: Brill, 33–71.
Giddens, A. (1992), *The Transformation of Intimacy: Sexuality, Love & Eroticism in Modern Societies*, Cambridge: Polity.
Goffman, E. (1967), 'Where the Action Is', in *Interaction Ritual*, Harmondsworth: Penguin, 149–270.
Goffman, E. (1959), *The Presentation of Self in Everyday Life*, Harmondsworth: Penguin.
Halsey, A. H. (1987), 'Provincials and Professionals: The British Post-War Sociologists'. *LSE Quarterly*, 1 (1): 43–74.
Illich, I. (1975), *Medical Nemesis: The Expropriation of Health*, London: Calder & Boyars.
Jankélévitch, S. (2008), '*Le Suicide* and Psychological Suffering', in W.S.F. Pickering and Massimo Rosati (eds), *Suffering and Evil: The Durkheimian Legacy*, Oxford: Berghahn, 31–48.
Jay, M. (2003), *Refractions of Violence*, New York: Routledge.
Jupp, P. C. (2008a), 'The Context of Christian Funeral Ministry Today', in Peter C. Jupp, ed., *Death Our Future: Christian Theology and Funeral Practice*, London: Epworth, 7–19.
Jupp, P. C. (2008b), 'Changing Christian Beliefs about the Afterlife', in Peter C. Jupp, (ed.), *Death Our Future: Christian Theology and Funeral Practice*, London: Epworth, 67–81.
Kołakowski, L. (1997), *Modernity on Endless Trial*, Chicago: The University of Chicago Press.
Kołakowski, L. (1998), *God Owes Us Nothing*, Chicago: The University of Chicago Press.
Kołakowski, L. (2001a), *Metaphysical Horror*, Chicago: The University of Chicago Press.
Kołakowski, L. (2001b), *Religion: If There is No God…*, South Bend, Indiana: St. Augustine's Press.
Lloyd, V. (2008), 'Interview with Gillian Rose'. *Theory, Culture & Society*, 25 (7–8): 201–18.
López, A. (2007), 'On Restlessness'. *Communio*, 34 (2): 176–200.
Macmillan, J. (2008), Lecture to commemorate the 30th anniversary of the Sandford St. Martin Trust, *The Daily Telegraph*, 1st October.

Martin, R. (1974), 'Cultic Aspects of Sociology: A Speculative Essay'. *The British Journal of Sociology*, 25 (1): 15–31.
Marx, K. and Engels, F. (1975), *Collected Works*, vol. 3, London: Lawrence & Wishart.
Mendieta, E. (ed.) (2004), *The Frankfurt School on Religion: Key Writings by the Major Thinkers*, New York and London: Routledge.
Nisbet, R. (2002), *Sociology as an Art Form*, New Brunswick: Transaction Publishers.
Paoletti, G. (2008), 'Some concepts of "Evil" in Durkheim's Thought', in W. S. F. Pickering and Massimo Rosati (eds), *Suffering and Evil: The Durkheimian Legacy*, Oxford: Berghahn.
Pickering, W. S. F. and Massimo Rosati (eds) (2008), *Suffering and Evil: The Durkheimian Legacy*, Oxford: Berghahn.
Rose, G. (1995), *Love's Work*, London: Chatto & Windus.
Rose, G. (1998), 'The Final Notebooks of Gillian Rose'. *Women: A Cultural Review*, 9 (1): 6–18.
Rosaldo, R. (1993), *Culture and Truth: The Remaking of Social Analysis*, London: Routledge.
Schindler, D. C. (2007a), 'Why we Need Paul Claudel'. *Communio*, 34 (1): 120–49.
Schindler, D. C. (2007b), 'Restlessness as an Image of God'. *Communio*, 34 (2): 264–91.
Seneca (2005), *Dialogues and Letters*, ed. and trans. C.D.N. Costa, London: Penguin.
Servais, J. (2007), 'Restlessness as an Image of God'. *Communio*, 34 (2): 224–42.
Shanks, A. (2008), *Against Innocence: Gillian Rose's Reception and Gift of Faith*, London: SCM Press.
St. Augustine (1997), *The Confessions*, trans. Maria Boulding O.S.B., London: Hodder & Stoughton.
Stein, M. R. (1963), 'The Poetic Metaphors of Sociology', in Maurice Stein and Arthur Vidich (eds), *Sociology on Trial*, Englewood Cliffs, N.J.: Prentice-Hall, 173–82.
Steiner, F. (1967), *Taboo*, Harmondsworth: Pelican.
Tester, K. (2004), *The Social Thought of Zygmunt Bauman*, Basingstoke: Palgrave Macmillan.
Torevell, D. (1995), 'The Terrorism of Reason in the Thought of Zygmunt Bauman'. *New Blackfriars*, 76 (889): 141–53.
Turner, B. S. (1994), 'Introduction', in Christine Buci–Glucksmann, *Baroque Reason: The Aesthetics of Modernity*, trans. Patrick Camiller, London: Sage, 1–36.
Ward, P. (2002), *Liquid Church*, Cumbria: Paternoster Press.
Wolin, R. (1989), 'Experience and Materialism in Benjamin's *Passagenwerk*', in Gary Smith (ed.), *Benjamin: Philosophy, Aesthetics, History*, Chicago: The University of Chicago Press, 210–27.
Ziegler, J. (2008), 'Shun Idols'. *The Catholic World Report*, 19 (10): 17–20.

7

Event Horizon: Utopia–Dystopia in Bauman's Thought

Mark Featherstone

In this chapter I explore what I call the event horizon of Bauman's analyses of contemporary global society. In theoretical physics the idea of the event horizon describes a boundary, or limit, in space–time that blocks the transmission of light. More or less no light passes through this boundary. As such, the event horizon tends to mark the outer limit of the impossible space–time of the black hole that crushes everything that enters its gravitational field. But how does the notion of the event horizon relate to Bauman's thought? My contention is that an exploration of Bauman's recent works, from *Liquid Modernity* (2000) through *Society Under Siege* (2002) and *Wasted Lives* (2004a) to *Liquid Fear* (2006), reveals a dystopic image of contemporary globalization characterised by enormous poverty, explosive violence and crippling anxieties about the new insecure world we inhabit. In the wake of interpretations of the evolution of modern capitalism, such as those of Saskia Sassen (2006), I believe that it is possible to root Bauman's theory of liquidity in explanations of the rise of what Edward Luttwak (1999) calls turbo capitalism. However, we must be careful in our use of terms which suggest an undialectical theory of the mobility of contemporary society. Consider Paul Virilio's (2005b) work on speed. Virilio's works explain that the coincidence of neoliberal capitalism, finance markets and new media technologies should not lead us to imagine that contemporary society is completely mobile. On the contrary, what we must recognize is that the new light speeds of global capitalism mean that movement, mobility and flows are endlessly reterritorialized in particular spaces, conditioned by violent collisions between incredible wealth and absolute poverty, and fear-stricken off worlds and Dante-esque slums, precisely because such speeds generate their own gravitational fields and produce the type of time-space compressions David Harvey (1991) associates with the condition of postmodernity. Thus it is a mistake to take Bauman's (2000) liquidity thesis to mean that global society is entirely mobile. Instead what we must recognize in the metaphor of liquefaction is a story of flows contained by planetary territory. The faster the flows move, and with the invention of quasi-instantaneous new media technologies their speed pushes light speed, the more time-space seems to collapse towards the utopic–dystopic event horizon of global capitalism situated in what I call black hole cities.

In light of this theory of the territoriality of flows, I want to suggest that Bauman's studies of liquid modernity simultaneously represent the realization of the neoliberal, turbo capitalist, zero gravity utopia, where flows push towards light speed, and the moment when the same condition creates its own gravitational fields, it leads it to collapse in on itself and close towards particular hot spots, or What Davis and Bertrand (2007) call evil paradises. Here, the utopic–dystopic enclosure of liquid modernity brings the violent contradictions of global capitalism to the boil. In this chapter I, therefore, propose to make four key points. First, I suggest that we must understand the time-space dimensions of Bauman's (2000) theory of liquidity in order to fully understand his theory of utopia in contemporary global society. Second, I claim that we must locate the event horizon, or moment when the light speeds of global capitalism collapse towards a particular site or black hole, of Bauman's liquid modernity in the urban hot spots of global conflict, such as the slums of Baghdad, Sao Paulo, or Gaza. My third claim is that Bauman's event horizon, primarily located in the contemporary urban pressure cookers of the global south that threaten to boil over at any moment, represents the utopia–dystopia of contemporary global capitalism. Finally, I reflect upon Bauman's (1976) own utopianism, through an evocation of the works of utopian thinkers such as Adorno (2008), Benjamin (1999) and Deleuze and Guattari (1972, 1984), in order to try to imagine the other side of the event horizon. Although Bauman (1993a) teaches us that it is impossible to throw light beyond the event horizon, and produce a blueprint for an ideal society that would take us beyond the contemporary impasse, precisely because of the apocalyptic status of the urban black holes that characterise utopia–dystopia realized, he also suggests that the greatest mistake we could ever make would be to give up on the lost cause of the utopia that does not immediately fold into its polar opposite, reconcile ourselves to the misery of the global state of second nature and accept the imagination deficit that limits thought beyond the event horizon of contemporary globalization (Bauman, 1976).

But before we embark on this exploration of the social and political physics of Bauman's thought, and the ways in which this theoretical apparatus connects to notions of utopia and dystopia, we must refer to current scholarship on his utopianism and in particular the work of Michael Hviid Jacobsen (Elliott, 2007) and Keith Tester (2004) in order to show that utopia and utopianism holds a particularly important place in works such as *Socialism* (1976), *Modernity and Ambivalence* (1993b) and *Liquid Modernity* (2000). Both Jacobsen and Tester suggest that Bauman conceives humanity as a utopian species, endlessly struggling against fate, and the confines of its animality. Following this view, Tester, in particular, explains Bauman as a utopian writer in the tradition of the early Marx, Bloch and Adorno, who perceives the utopian nature of humanity and writes through this natural tendency to transgression. Jacobsen agrees noting the ubiquitousness of utopia in Bauman's work. In his view, Bauman's work can be seen to revolve around a tripartite historical scheme of medieval religious gamekeeping utopias, where what mattered was the preservation of God's vision for humanity; solid modern gardening utopias, where men started to design their own perfect worlds; and liquid modern hunting utopias, where the individual is everything and what concerns people is their ability to extract eternity from the singular moment. However, before we consider the nature of the liquid modern utopia, which Bauman links to the notion of the permanent present in order to make the startling claim that we are in fact living in utopia (2005), let us think about the idea of utopia in his earlier works.

We know that this utopian element is present in Bauman's early study *Socialism* (1976), which he relates to the idea of active utopia, and his user-friendly work on the value of sociological thought, *Thinking Sociologically* (2001), which emphazises the value of thinking in relational universalistic terms. In both instances Bauman contrasts human imagination, what Tester calls the human ability to 'think forwards', with the equally utopian, but ultimately conservative, tendency to try to build a totally static, timeless, social system. This latter utopian form, which Bauman (2000) links to the first phase of modernity, what he calls solid modernity, is exemplified by the classical utopias–dystopias of Stalinism and Nazism, and appears in texts such as *Modernity and the Holocaust* (1991) and *Modernity and Ambivalence* (1993b). In my view the opposition between these two utopian modes of thought, the conservative tendency to build static self-identical societies and the radical desire to transgress sameness and unity for the sake of the future, which can be seen to run right through Bauman's work, is essential to understanding his wider thought. The problem is, of course, that the relationship between the solid modern utopias–dystopias of Stalinism and Nazism and the mobile, imaginative, utopianism Bauman foregrounds throughout his work but in particular in *Socialism* (1976) is more complex than appearances might first suggest.

Let us consider the complexity of this relationship in order to try to understand the history of utopian thought Bauman works with, before moving on to explore his particular contributions to understandings of utopia–dystopia today. I think the first point to make is that it is not simply that the solid modern Stalinist and Nazi utopias–dystopias privileged stasis and immobility in their conceptions of social order, or totally centred their utopian visions on spatial segregation and temporal closure, because both totalitarianisms were conceived in modern terms and were constructed on the basis of a vision of the human potential to endless movement and development. As Hannah Arendt (1973) shows in her classic work on totalitarianism, both Nazism and Stalinism were confusions of the classical utopian idea inherited from Plato, which imagined a totally stable social order, cut off from the wider world in both spatial and temporal terms, and the modern utopian tendency to endless progress, which undermined the Platonic idea of a stable *telos*, only to bring it back in through a vision of some geographically distant or futuristic place, a spatially secure, post-historical, island of tranquillity rooted in the modern principles of discovery, exploration and progress. Unfortunately, the latter compromise formation, which was introduced by Thomas More (2004) at the birth of modernity in order to secularize the Platonic-Christian notion of some formal, heavenly, otherworldly, utopian place, and civilize the early capitalistic principle of social, political and economic ballistics supported by Thomas Hobbes (2008) which eventually began to crumble before the modern obsession with movement, mobility, and circulation.

By the time the new totalitarianisms emerged, with their confusion of the Platonic motifs of spatial and temporal stability and the modern Hobbesian obsession with movement, mobility and circulation, the principle of the classical utopian form had been reduced to a shell, a state form, which contained the modern tendency set on futuristic, technological, motion. However, to say that the classical utopian notion of a perfectly static, ordered, place was reduced to the formal shell of the new modern totalitarian utopias is not to say that this process of formal containment was not effective in devastating ways. The contrary is true. What the fusion of formal containment and internal movement led to was the collapse of the notion of historical progress, so that despite the modern, enlightenment and concern for human development, the totalitarianisms became obsessed with post-historical change for its own sake, and the projection of this obsession with change into the social system itself, with the result that a new post-human, mechanistic, bureaucratic, vision of utopian evolution took hold in both the Soviet Union and Nazi Germany (Featherstone, 2007). As Bauman explains in various works, including *Modernity and the Holocaust* (1991) and *Modernity and Ambivalence* (1993b), the result of the emergence of this new version of utopia/nism was the creation of two societies with no moral interest in human life, bent on smashing entire populations into some imaginary post-human future, and modelled on some distant pre-/post-historical future where high-tech peasant communes or Aryan empires would strike uncertainty, contingency and difference out of the world.

Thus, we approach the idea of utopia–dystopia, which I want to foreground in this chapter, and the paradox of a good place which is simultaneously a non-place, first because it does not exist as a good place, instead resembling the kind of horrendous parody of a perfect world Zamyatin (1993) captured in his novel *We* and Lang (2005) imagined in his film *Metropolis*, and second because the reality of living under such cold fascistic conditions is better captured by the modern, scientific, idea of space, which exploded the ancient, medieval, idea of place through its insistence on endless motion across cold, geometric, planes defined by the trajectories of abstract bodies. However, I have other reasons for making use of the compound term utopia–dystopia, which will eventually become important for my reading of the later Bauman, related to the ways in which the confusion of the classical utopian form and the modern tendency towards utopianism interacted in the totalitarianism movements. Perhaps the first point to note here is that even though both Nazism and Stalinism housed the modern utopian tendency within the classical utopian form, the latter could never completely contain the former impulse, which is premised on the will to transgression and expansion, within the state form, with the result that the utopian container was endlessly rescaled to match up with the imperial utopianism of the leader, and only qualified by cynical calculations about how far it was possible to expand without completely exhausting the energy of the movement (Featherstone, 2007). In other words, the paranoia of the totalitarians, which caused them to try to evolve a completely homogenous, spatially segregated timeless place by rooting out and eliminating others, was always compromised by the other side of their utopian temper, which is also perfectly symmetrical with psychoanalytic definitions of paranoia, which compelled them to continually expand through space, taking in ever more others, with the result that they had to endlessly rescale and inflate the utopia state container committed to the elimination of otherness.

What we have here, then, is an image of the political psychopathology of the totalitarian movements, which Bauman (1991) talks about in terms of the totally amoral gardening state, and reference to the notion of paranoia, which shows how Stalinism and Nazism confused classical and modern utopianism, on the basis that Freud's (2003) concept of paranoia fuses persecution fantasies that compel the self to attack all others to save his own skin and megalomania that encourages the paranoiac to see himself as central to some globalized conspiracy bent on his destruction. This is how I interpret the solid modern drive to sameness that Bauman excavates in *Modernity and the Holocaust* (1991) and *Modernity and Ambivalence* (1993b). While the will to unity and opposition to otherness that Bauman links to the modern tendency to rationality can be related to the classical utopian urge to contain history, where history is understood as the humanized narrativized effect of time upon place, which in turn may be read through Freud's concept of the persecution complex that leads the psychopath to close in on themselves, the drive to transgress, extend, colonize and assimilate difference that Bauman relates to the modern obsession with progress reflects the utopian tendency to futurity, the Freudian notion of megalomania and the psychopath's desire to globalize their worldview and wipe out traces of otherness. But beyond these two components, which map onto the classical/modern utopian dualism through the equation of persecution and the fear of otherness and megalomania and the tendency to expand and transgress limits until there is nowhere else to expand and the entire world is implicated in the ideological vision of the utopian qua megalomaniac, the other central component of the Freudian concept of paranoia revolves around the way in which the persecution and megalomania complexes fuse to comprise a totally fantastic image of reality or worldview (Featherstone, 2007). Herein resides my other, related, reason for employing the term utopia–dystopia to try to capture Bauman's (1991, 1993b) theory of the way the principle of perfectibility relates to the idea of modernity. That is that the image of utopia, or perhaps dystopia depending on whether one considers a pure state devoid of otherness a dreamworld or catastrophe, hangs over the reality of societies conditioned by utopian ideology in the form of paranoid fantasy in such a way that cannot but expose the dystopic conditions of everyday life.

In my view this dialectical theory of ideology and reality runs right through Bauman's work, taking centre stage in later works such as

Liquid Times (2007b), which contrasts the ideas of utopia and the inferno through reference to Calvino's *Invisible Cities* (1997). However, before we explore the way Bauman employs the notion of utopia–dystopia in his works on contemporary liquid modernity, let us conclude our study of the relationship between utopia and totalitarianism and show how this work impacts upon the latter phase of his thought. Although the ways in which the totalitarianisms of the 20th century blended the classical and modern utopian forms is not worked out in Bauman's works on modernity and self-identical state building, such as *Modernity and the Holocaust* (1991) and *Modernity and Ambivalence* (1993b), which consider the problem of Nazism and Stalinism, I think it is important to understand the confusion between these two forms in the two major really existing utopias–dystopias of the 20th century because such understanding will help us to shed light on what we might call the hidden complexities of Bauman's own thought regarding utopia, socialism, ethics, morality, the post-modern consumer paradise, the black hole of negative globalization and finally the event horizon of critical thought. Beyond the central point, which is that it may be the case that Bauman overstates the solidity of the modern totalitarianisms by limiting the importance of their obsession with movement, thus exaggerating the novelty of his own conception of socialism, I think we also have to consider how the new liquid modern utopia–dystopia, which dominates Bauman's later work, causes problems for his critical project. In order to explore this problem in more detail let me unpack the above complex of terms and concepts by pointing to Bauman's ambivalence in such a way that may enable us to better understand the ways in which he attempts to negotiate the bind between solid modern stability and motion on the one hand and liquid modern movement and constancy on the other hand.

Against the solid modern utopias–dystopias of Stalinism and Nazism, Bauman (1976) champions the humanistic utopianism of socialism, which he presents as a counter-cultural movement to the modern death drive to combine ceaseless motion and the desire to stability, security and safety. But if this is Bauman's utopianism, a utopianism of openness, imagination and critique, he continually runs the risk of repeating the mistake of the Bolsheviks by collapsing the vitalist model of modern utopian progress back into a static ideological form comprising the image of a new utopic–dystopic city where critique is the rule and positive constructions are banned, beyond the initial positive formation of a negative utopia of processual critique and debate (Bauman, 1999). But this bind, which is in many ways comparable to the impasse

Adorno (2008) was continually forced to confront when thinking through the implications of the possible rationalization of the method of negative dialectics, is one Bauman attempts to sidestep through his works on morality and ethics. In several books which followed *Modernity and the Holocaust* (1991), most notably *Postmodern Ethics* (1993a) and *Life in Fragments* (1995), he seeks to evade the possibility of the collapse of his notion of a utopian community of critique, which would supposedly circumvent the solid modern tendency to utopian–dystopian reification, into a tyrannical community of processual critique, negativity and stasis through an ethical politics of otherness focussed on Lévinas' idea of the face-to-face encounter and a Socratic conception of debate and dialogue. In this way Bauman seeks to evade the problem of the collapse, or condensation, of his utopia of critique into a community of negativity devoid of any positive sense of public or common good by turning to Lévinas' (1999) idea of being or living for the other who it is impossible for one to ever really know and making this idea central to a new politics of communication, citizenship and republicanism. The effect of the turn to the other is, therefore, that he is able to resist the fall into a utopian community of processual or rationalized critique on the basis that one must remain forever open to the contingency of the other who is always a mystery.

In order to restate the key point then, it appears that Bauman's (1999) critical community could never close towards the kind of utopia–dystopia which emerged in the 20th century in Stalin's Soviet Union or Hitler's Germany because his conception of the individual is orientated towards the other and his notion of politics relies on the idea that debate between self and other will never become processual because both parties remain bottomless abysses to each other. In his works on ethics Bauman makes use of this thesis to resist the potential problem posed by the possible equation of his support for radical politics based on movement, motion and contingency and socialistic egalitarian community where personal freedom is subordinate to wider equality and the slide into totalitarianism which exemplified exactly this utopian–dystopian confusion of modern progress and medieval community. There are, of course, several problems with the use of the other to prevent the collapse into fascistic community, which Bauman considers and seeks to address in his later works concerned with liquidity and globalization. The central problem with the Lévinasian notion of the utopian, moral, relationship between self and other is that it relies on the concept of the face, the possibility of face-to-face interactions, and the responsibilities these relations bestow upon the stronger party.

As Lévinas was well aware, the limit of the moral face-to-face relationship between self and other is social space or the introduction of social mediation which lifts the burden of responsibility for the other from the self and locates that burden instead in the ethical domain of rules, regulations and laws which transform moral problems into technical, bureaucratic, or processual considerations (Bauman, 1993a).

Given this view of what appears to be unsustainable nature of originary morality, which shows how face-to-face responsibility vanishes before complex social systems shot through with the kind of indifference Georg Simmel (Frisby and Featherstone, 1997) located in the space of the modern capitalist city dominated by money, we must also address Bauman's notion of politics. Again, we confront the same problem. If it is no longer possible to confront the abyss of the other, and establish some kind of moral relationship that precedes rational process, simply because the mediated other is always a surface, how is it possible to maintain a mode of republican citizenship, or a mode of politics based on the defence of a free and open community, and prevent the slide of republicanism into technical, processual, democracy where critique becomes a cliché, being for the other becomes living with the abyssal other in fearful competition, and freedom of expression in public becomes freedom to pursue recognition through fame and conspicuous consumption (Bauman, 2007a). It would be a mistake to say that Bauman was not mindful of these problems because, of course, the shift from his work on morality and ethics to his more recent studies of liquid modernity, globalization and the consumer society turns off and illuminates the difficulty of establishing moral responsibility, pursuing sociological thought and engaging in meaningful politics in the historical or post-historical period we might call the short American century. In terms of utopian politics and sociological critique, I think it is fair to say that the short American century throws up particularly difficult problems in Bauman's work, simply because the dominant mode of social organization today leaves very little room for political resistance or the kind of serious critique he seeks to promote in the name of socialism, the active utopia.

This is a novel problematic. Although confrontations with the European utopias–dystopias of Stalin and Hitler where never easy in practice, the critic knew where he stood, if he could step outside of utopian ideology and confront the paranoid fantasy of the Party from the perspective of the dystopic reality of everyday life. Theoretically speaking the critic of European totalitarianism could critique the Soviet and Nazi utopias–dystopias because they were not totalitarian, or we might say following Bauman globalitarian, enough to completely close down the space of critique. Of course, critique within the totalitarianisms themselves was nigh on impossible, hence the Gulags and Death Camps which concentrated otherness in order to wipe it out, but once outside the system the defector, the dissident, or to refer to Bauman's favourite critical thinker, the exile, could speak about the horrors of the utopia–dystopia from some other place, usually the west or perhaps, to be even more specific, America, the home of freedom of speech and expression. Of course, the irony of America, the home of freedom of speech, and the place where so many of the exiles of totalitarianism, such as Adorno and Horkheimer, eventually landed in order to continue to think critically, is that it has always been the utopian–dystopian place, where utopia is simultaneously good place and no place, of critical thought, simply because it is the consumer paradise where critique is (im)possible. Although social, political, economic and cultural conditions have no doubt changed since Adorno and Horkheimer (1997) critiqued the consumer society, most spectacularly because of the completion of the process of globalization, the central problematic of Americanism remains central to Bauman's later works. In a nutshell this problematic revolves around the question of whether is it still possible to engage in meaningful critique in a globalized social, political and economic culture which encourages critique, but understands expressions of imagination, dissent and 'thinking otherwise' through the mechanisms of the globalized market, rather than through the kind of serious Socratic politics set on the real modification of both self and society.

In my view this issue, the issue of the (im)possibility of critical thought today, is the central focus of Bauman's later works, which concentrate on the concept of liquidity, processes of globalization and the problem of the consuming self. As such, I think that Bauman is well aware that despite the enormous explosion of critical thought in the post–totalitarian post-World War II world, it is in many respects the possibility of serious political critique, rather than commodified consumer critique, that the American century, and the irresistible rise of the American empire, has progressively collapsed, simply by becoming more totalitarian than the European totalitarianisms Arendt wrote about in the 1940s. This statement, the statement of the totalitarianism of American empire, is, of course, enormously provocative, but it is not one that I mean to take hyperbolically. Despite Hiroshima, My Lai, Guantanamo Bay and Abu Ghraib, I do not believe that America is comparable with either the Soviet Union under Stalin or Germany under Hitler in its use of terror to subdue entire populations. What I would claim is that what has happened over the course of the short American century is the completion of the modern process of globalization which was embodied in the utopian–dystopian movements of Stalinism and Nazism, but which had not really come to terms with the social, political, economic and cultural requirements of superpower status and global leadership. In the post-World War II period, following the exposure of Auschwitz and the collapse of the Stalinist utopian–dystopian model, the classical Platonic utopian principle of perfectibility through containment fell into disrepair, and the American version of social, political, economic and cultural organization based on individual self-realisation came to the fore.

Despite Bauman's (2004b) moral objections to this social form, it is hard to imagine that the European model of social organization which found its logical conclusion in the solid modernities of Stalinism and Nazism could have ever globalized as successfully as the American utopia which is rooted in individualism, democracy, capitalism and consumerism. Whereas the European utopias–dystopias sought to contain the utopian impulse to historical improvement within the classical utopian container which had by the 17th century taken on the modern state form, the American social, political, economic and cultural model swerved the problem of imperial governance, which had plagued European utopians long before the totalitarians came onto the scene, by individualizing utopianism within a state form set up to foreground self-realization and projecting the new desiring individual through the channels of the economy that was not restricted to a particular state, but was on the contrary fated to globalize, primarily because the central player of the new American century, the ideal American, the new desiring individual, was at heart a transgressive frontiersman, a prospector and a gambler. In Bauman's work the social and political implications of the history of the short American century and the emergence of this new post-social, post-political, global utopia is worked through in contemporary studies, including *Globalization* (1998), *In Search of Politics* (1999), *Society Under Siege* (2002) and numerous books on liquidity, which explore the effect of the completion of the modern tendency to globalize; the univerzalisation of the American model of society; politics, economy and culture; the new individualized utopia; and centrally the problem of critical thought in a totally administered world without politics.

Centrally, I think that Bauman made the shift from the study of post-modern ethics and Lévinas' conception of morality, which hinged on the post-modern post-totalitarian realization that modern utopian legislation was in fact bankrupt, insofar as it was more likely to produce dystopian nightmare states than perfect worlds, and that the American model of individual self-realization was the way forward, to the concern with globalization and the possibility of critical political thought, when the hollow ideological counter-weight to American capitalism provided by the Soviet Union was finally removed from world maps in the 1990s, because this was when the American empire became truly globalitarian, the new desiring individualism took hold of most networked societies, and the possibility of critical thought outside of commodity exchange was revealed to be problematic in ways which Adorno and Horkheimer could have not foreseen in the 1940s. Driven by the rise of Reaganomics, and Thatcher's rerun of 19th-century laissez-faire capitalism, post-modern, neoliberal capitalism was not new in the early years of the 21st century, but what was new was the lack of an ideological counter-weight to oppose the globalization of capitalism. This process, which took place in the 1990s and has continued through the early years of the 21st century, is what Bauman explores in his various books on globalization and liquidity.

In the new neoliberal utopian model, which no longer had to restrict itself in order to account for the really existing critique of socialism in the way that it had in the 1970s, the classical utopian container which had existed to manage the vicissitudes of human life and stem the nauseating flow of history since Plato wrote his *Republic* (1991) was not important, first because the state was no longer responsible for the political management of the economy that now became totally deterritorialized in Deleuze and Guattari's (1972) sense of the term, and second because the economy, which was now totally reified to the extent where it completely colonized every aspect of human life, does not admit any sense of history, taken to mean the humanization of the nauseating passage of time in narrative, but only recognizes turnover, change and turbulence conceived as creative destruction. But if the notion of the utopian container was largely irrelevant to the new American model of society and politics, what was central to this new mode of social and political organization was the utopian tendency to endless movement, motion and circulation, beyond any positive political ideological form that could impose limits on economic efficiency. Hence the role of the state in the American model Bauman (2000, 2002) considers in so many of his recent books is purely managerialist in nature. In other words, the state is there to facilitate and promote the expansion of the smooth space of the global economy, rather than to fulfil any kind of humanist, social, political, constructive role, even if this involves pursuing the kind of neocolonialism Retort (2005) explains through the concept of military neoliberalism. This is, in many respects, the central point of Bauman's many works on globalization and liquidity that he attempts to address through critical theory and repeated calls for political intervention. But the problem is that these calls for political intervention endlessly crash upon the rocks of what is new and absolutely dystopic about the novel utopia of total mobility: the dissolution of all solid social, political, economic and cultural formations and the emergence of a totally fluid economy of signs that is impossible for humans to pin down, think about in any rational way, or control simply because it moves at light speeds that are beyond the normal human ability to perceive, manage and narrativize change as history.

Hence the utopia–dystopia of liquid modern global capitalism begins to emerge. Beyond the official utopian neoliberal ideology of freedom of movement through high-speed communication made possible by symbolization and virtualization lay the dystopic reality of a system that haseffectively colonized every available space and all available time and has started to collapse in on itself generating anxious anti-social relations, violent confrontations and phobic attempts to create secure places (Bauman, 2002). This is, in my view, how we must understand the social and political physics contained in Bauman's work. If the emergence of modernity in the 17th century signalled the big bang, when medieval stagnation was exploded and Europeans embarked on the expansive project to modernize society, politics, economy and culture, then it may be the case that processes of post-modern globalization, because I think processes of globalization must rely on post-modernism and post-modernity insofar as these terms refer to the cultural turn to symbolization and communication and shifts in modes of production from industrialism to post-industrialism, signal that the modern project has run into its limit and that a process of violent involution has now begun to occur, which will effectively suck human society back through the historical stages of total global mobility through modern nationalism to neomedievalism urbanism and beyond. Back to the future past, then, it may be the case that today the contemporary post-modern neoliberal utopia of flows, conditioned by endless motion, movement and circulation, has started to condense towards a new form of dystopia, which we might capture through Virilio's (2005a) notion of the claustropolis, where the anti-social individual is confronted by the horror of the abyssal other who appears endlessly threatening in close proximity. But unfortunately for Bauman, and other critical theorists, the everyday experience of this neomedieval condition is not enough to provoke the wholesale return to politics and the humanization of the economy because the masses, or to use a more contemporary term, which indicates the new forced mobility of the majority of the populous, the swarm, live in the state of denial characterized by neoliberal utopian ideology that hides the blindingly clear truth of the raging inferno behind the fantasy of the consumer paradise where homo eligens or man choosing is a sovereign subject rather than a miserable, totally disposable commodity (Bauman, 2007a). The existence of the state of denial is problematic because, as Bauman indicates throughout his series of books on liquidity, we occupy the neomedieval urban condition where the other is more or less always an enemy today, but will very likely slide into a catastrophic situation which is far worse in the near future unless we take effective political action (Bauman, 2006). But what could be worse than the contemporary globalized utopia–dystopia?

Perhaps what lay beyond the kind of neomedieval urbanism, which we see played out in contemporary urban war zones, such as Baghdad, Jerusalem and Mumbai, not to mention other schizophrenic metropolises, such as Los Angeles, Johannesburg and Sao Paulo, which embody the liquid modern division between the ultramobile haves and the totally static, ghettoised, have nots, is the kind of black hole, or singularity, that Bauman (2007b) evokes through reference to Eriksen's (2001) tyranny of the moment or more especially Calvino's (1997) notion of the inferno. Whether or not we occupy the inferno now is a matter of debate, whether or not it is still possible to oppose the logic of neoliberal capitalism and produce serious political critique today is not clear, but we must assume that humanity has not yet collapsed back into complete barbarity and the kind of state of nature symbolized by the complete domination of economic metabolism. If this is the case, then it may be that today we stand on the edge of the abyss like Nietzsche's übermensch, and that our next step is essential to our possible futures. Basically, we must decide to either unthinkingly fall or sleepwalk into the inferno or affirm the human ability to control our own fate and remake our world, where world is understood in Arendt's (2005) use of term to mean human civilization. But how can we make this decision today? Who will be our guide? In his various works on ethics, up to his most recent book on self-making (2008), Bauman is keen to tell us that we must embrace our basic human ability to choose. This does not, of course, mean that we have to choose this, that, or the other commodity, but rather that we must make an existential choice to live in a particular way. But how do we know how to live, how do we know how to choose, when we live in a thin consumer culture where everything is commodified, human significance is more or less non-existent and all that matters are economic calculations about relative monetary value?

If we assume that we have not yet plunged into the black hole, where there is absolutely no human culture but only the state of nature, but rather find ourselves somewhere near the event horizon of the violent singularity of global catastrophe, then I think we must search for shards of light to rethink our world. That is to say that I think we must seek out the fragments of human significance able to escape from the logic of commodification, and the black hole of the market, and try to save them for some future reconstruction project that, similar to Walter Benjamin (1999), who engaged in the construction of what the Frankfurt critical theorists called a thought-image of modern consumer capitalism, may enable us to piece together a serious critical theory of post-modern global capitalism and the horrendous post-political situation we currently occupy. We have plenty of material to begin this work. In several works, Bauman (1995, 2007b) suggests that the idea of the furious new utopian form, which transgresses both the ancient-medieval utopia, in that it is not really attached to place, and the modern utopian fusion of place and movement, in that it does not retain any sense of a positive telos, beyond the negative commitment to reproduction and efficiency, was partially captured by both Luxemburg (2003), who imagined a voracious capitalist machine that could only exist by devouring non-capitalist space, and Schumpeter (1962), who wrote about processes of creative destruction and emphasized the violent nature of economic efficiency. However, what these writers could not know, because they were essentially writing before the onset of post-modernism and post-modernity, was that capitalism would completely liquefy the solid formations of modernity on a more or less permanent basis in order to more effectively globalize the post-political principles of economic efficiency that are totally transnational and completely cross-cultural because they do not recognize any human significance whatsoever, beyond the basic truth of animal metabolism and beyond this principle naked human desire. This is the problem of critical utopianism today. How is it possible to effectively critique a globalized, or globalitarian, system that has more or less abolished the space of serious political critique in favour of a new fetishistic, market orientated, brand of radicalism that cannot even begin to challenge the hegemony of mainstream politics, which is entirely conservative in its embrace of neoliberal capitalism?

The problem of critical theory today, then, revolves around the problem of the totalitarian or globalitarian nature of neoliberal capitalism and the omnipotence of the logic of commodification which has effectively colonized the space of critique and critical thought. In order to resist this logic, which I would suggest was not nearly as complete in the early phase of the American consumer society that Adorno and Horkheimer (1997) wrote about, Bauman has sought to make use of classic critical theory methodology by seeking to expose the schism or what Žižek (2006) calls the 'parallax gap' between what the official utopian ideology of neoliberal ideology promises and the dystopic reality of the contemporary world situation which is plain for everybody to see, but difficult for most to understand primarily because, as Žižek (2008) also shows, we occupy a global society where we appreciate subjective acts of violence, but are totally blind to objective, systemic, forms of cruelty. However, the problem with Bauman's version of critical theory, which is evident in his works on the totally commodified liquid consumer society, is that his efforts to write texts adequate to the conditions of this social system, and engage the swarm of men choosing, continually fold back into the logic of commodification, with the effect that his texts appear to be little more than surface descriptions of the state of contemporary global society. Of course, similar to Marx before him, Bauman is aware of the problem of philosophy, most especially in the liquid society where all that matters is speed, which is that there is no time to pour over learned texts requiring knowledge of the history of thought; but the opposite problem which confronts him, and all critical theorists today, is that texts fit for the lightning speeds of the liquid society suffer from the problem of instant obsolescence. The choice of the contemporary critical theorist is, therefore, a stark one. He must choose between writing heavy, solid, modern learned studies of our contemporary liquid condition, which may not engage the totally mobile swarm, but will contribute to the thick cultural knowledge that humanity has constructed over the past two millennia, but that the neoliberal culture industry of instant obsolescence is currently in the process of deconstructing in the favour of the paradoxical notion of fast culture, or producing enormous quantities of light, liquid, modern commentaries, or thought-images, on the ultraviolence of the neoliberal globalitarian system, with the hope of engaging the swarm, and overwhelming the same system's culture industry through basic excess of critique.

The risk of the former strategy is that it is simply outmoded in its view of the durability of thick human culture, whereas the problem of the latter mode of critique resides in the fantastic nature of the idea that the critical theorist can somehow stay one step ahead of the new, globalized, culture industry and the logics of commodification and instant obsolescence and flood the market with the quantity of critical commentary necessary to effectively engage the swarm caught up in the ideology of consumerism. I would suggest that this latter approach, which Bauman has taken in his effort to critically engage the neoliberal culture industry, is truly utopian in its effort to speed up critique to the extent that it can tackle free market ideology, and effectively expose the gap between the capitalist dream world of fulfilment through commodities and the catastrophe of human misery necessary to produce this fantasy life. That is to say that beyond Bauman's (2003a, 2008) view that resistance to the contemporary capitalist inferno cannot be programmatic, but must instead turn off contingent human decisions, I consider him a utopian writer primarily because of his post-modern approach to critical theory. But what does this approach require in practice? How does it manifest itself in Bauman's work? Essentially, Bauman's post-modern version of critical theory requires him to engage in endless negativity, in much the same way that Adorno (2008) sought to simultaneously critique the culture industry and evade the slide into the construction of some new positive totalitarian utopian vision, but what is new about his contemporary version of critical theory is that it is post-Derridean and post-Deleuzean in its formulation of what it means to practice negative dialectics. Given this historical philosophical legacy, Bauman's version of critical negativity is setup to endlessly transgress or deconstruct the logic of consumer capitalism which insists on the production of fast culture that is here and today gone tomorrow and stay one step ahead of this furious machine. This is why Bauman's texts work on the basis of the post-modern principle of movement, which encourages the reader to speed through his critical construction, and may be understood through Deleuzean (1984) motifs, such as the cut, break and schiz, which show how he privileges the unitary effect of the post-modern thought-image able to move at lightning speeds over the solid modern principle of architectural construction, which manifests itself in critical texts in the form of the slow, methodological, organization of argumentation and evidence.

Thus I believe that we must understand Bauman's contemporary works, which seek to address the problem of liquidity, globalization and the consumer society, through Deleuzean (1984) notions, such as the rhizome, which can simultaneously show how individual texts work, and how those individual texts contribute to the overall thought-image, or desiring machine, of what we may call Bauman-text. However, regardless of the philosophical pedigree of Bauman's approach to critical theory, it is not clear how effectively it works, where the term 'works' refers to Deleuze and Guattari's (1984) view that what matters about a text or assemblage is not what it means or does not mean, but whether or not it works. Clearly, on one level Bauman-text works, because there is little doubt that Bauman has constructed a critical machine that is endlessly productive. However, what is less clear is whether Bauman-text evades the problem which plagued Adorno's method of negative dialectics, which was that it seemed fated to produce a self-identical critical machine, or more especially Deleuze and Guattari's (1984) schizophrenic machine, which was that their critical, transgressive, assemblage simply could not escape the paranoid-schizophrenic logic of post-modern consumer capitalism. In the case of Deleuze and Guattari's schizophrenic, transgressive, desiring machine, which primarily shot through *Anti-Oedipus* (1972) and *A Thousand Plateaus* (1984), it is possible to suggest that the critical energy of the 1968 generation, which their schizo-analytic methodology employed to oppose market totalitarianism ended up simply contributing to the productive capacity of capitalist war machine that evolved through the 1980s to the 1990s and into the first decade of the 21st century. I think that we must ask whether Bauman-text is any different in this respect. How far is it possible to say that the endless negativity of Bauman-text, which Bauman employs to try to resist the vertiginous logic of black hole consumer capitalism, is effective in the face of the monstrous machine he talks about through the notion of negative globalization, the mode of thoughtless globalized capitalism that simply works?

Regardless of how we answer this question, I think that what is clear is that the problem Bauman addresses in his contemporary works, the problem of critical thought in the totally commodified world, is *the* problem of contemporary social theory. We have seen how Bauman arrived at this problematic. From his critiques of the European totalitarianisms, with their confusions of the utopian principles of movement and stability, which relied on the idealization of the utopia of socialism, through the ethical works on the asocial nature of post-modern society, which solved the potential problem of totalitarian socialism by foregrounding the importance of being for the other, but threw up the problems of the effect of the economic colonization of social relations, the rise of being with the other and asocial tolerance, and the closure of critical space through the globalization of capitalism and the expansion of the culture industry, we have seen how Bauman reached the point of confronting neoliberal liquid modern capitalism. Related to this story we have also considered Bauman's response to the horror of the contemporary world situation that resides in the simultaneous existence of the neoliberal utopia of flows, which has started to collapse back towards a black hole of singularity of enclosure, immobility and paranoia, and a dystopia of ultraviolent social relations that he seeks to capture through reference to Calvino's (1997) idea of the inferno. That we continue to live with the total transparency of the latter condition and behave as though it somehow does not exist is testament to the power of the neoliberal consumer utopia, which promises to deliver individuals a better world, and the same ideological structure's naturalization of inequality, which leads us to ignore objective forms of violence, and concentrate our attention on terrible acts that we can understand through subjective terms of reference (Žižek, 2008). It is this ideological structure that Bauman's works attempt to critique.

But in a world where there is no real room for serious critical thought, the attempt to expose the parallax gap between the fantastic utopia of neoliberal capitalism and the horrendous dystopia of the same system can only work if the critical theorist is willing to stand on the edge of the abyss, to space walk on the event horizon, which separates the voracious black hole of post-human capitalist chaos from the humanistic universe of illumination, understanding and civilization, and run the risk of falling into the bottomless void of pre-/post-human insignificance. In Bauman's case we have seen that the cost of straddling the event horizon, which separates the black hole of neoliberal capitalism from the universe of illumination, understanding and critical thought, is that his works are continually in flight or on the run from the monstrous logic of commodification which seeks to destroy human significance the moment it is born. Against this post-human machine, it is difficult to sustain serious critical thought. I think that Bauman's later works show that this is the case simply because they are so clearly caught on the boundary between commodity and critique, where commodity represents the pseudo-transgressive principle internal to the capitalist system and critique reflects the impossible utopian desire to step outside of that globalized system that has no other or outside. What, then, can we take from Bauman's critical theory of neoliberal capitalism that has more or less totally colonized the space of critique? In my view, we must take Bauman's (2007b) use of Calvino seriously and try to save what is worth saving from the inferno of contemporary capitalism and the monstrous machine that commodifies all critique. We must save Bauman's work for its critical potential, capture the shards of light that escape the logic of the black hole and pass through to the other side of the event horizon, and construct a new form of dire utopianism on the basis of the kind of constructive methodology Benjamin employed in his *Arcades Project* (1999). Perhaps this is what utopianism means today? That is to say that we must recognize the risk involved in critical theory, understand that it is not possible to completely escape the logic of commodity capitalism, and salvage the weak messianism of the fragment to build a new utopian machine, or assemblage, to oppose the post-human neoliberal machine. If this is, in fact, the best way to 'think forwards' in the contemporary world, then it may be the case that Bauman-text is one of the best resources we have for constructing such a utopian machine.

References

Adorno, T. W. (2008), *Lectures on Negative Dialectics: Fragments of a Lecture Course – 1965 / 1966*. Cambridge: Polity.

Adorno, T. W. and Horkheimer, M. (1997), *Dialectic of Enlightenment*. London: Verso.

Arendt, H. (1973), *The Origins of Totalitarianism*. London: Harvest.

Arendt, H. (2005), *The Promise of Politics*. New York: Schocken.

Bauman, Z. (1976), *Socialism: The Active Utopia*. London: George Allen and Unwin.

Bauman, Z. (1991), *Modernity and the Holocaust*. Cambridge: Polity.

Bauman, Z. (1993a), *Postmodern Ethics*. Oxford: Blackwell.

Bauman, Z. (1993b), *Modernity and Ambivalence*. Cambridge: Polity.

Bauman, Z. (1995), *Life in Fragments: Essays in Postmodern Moralities*. Oxford: Blackwell.

Bauman, Z. (1998), *Globalization: The Human Consequences*. Cambridge: Polity.

Bauman, Z. (1999), *In Search of Politics*. Cambridge: Polity.

Bauman, Z. (2000), *Liquid Modernity*. Cambridge: Polity.

Bauman, Z. and May, T. (2001), *Thinking Sociologically*. Oxford: Blackwell.

Bauman, Z. (2002), *Society Under Siege*. Cambridge: Polity.

Bauman, Z. (2004a), *Wasted Lives: Modernity and its Outcasts*. Cambridge: Polity.

Bauman, Z. (2004b), *Europe: An Unfinished Adventure*. Cambridge: Polity.

Bauman, Z. (2005), *Living in Utopia*. Ralph Milliband Public Lecture, London School of Economics. 27 October 2005. Available online at: http://www.lse.ac.uk/collections/LSEPublicLecturesAndEvents/pdf/20051027–Bauman2.pdf

Bauman, Z. (2006), *Liquid Fear*. Cambridge: Polity.

Bauman, Z. (2007a), *Consuming Life*. Cambridge: Polity.

Bauman, Z. (2007b), *Liquid Times: Living in an Age of Uncertainty*. Cambridge: Polity.

Bauman, Z. (2008), *The Art of Life*. Cambridge: Polity.

Benjamin, W. (1999), *The Arcades Project*. Cambridge, Mass: Harvard University Press.

Calvino, I. (1997), *Invisible Cities*. London: Vintage.

Davis, M. and Bertrand M. D. (eds) (2007) *Evil Paradises: Dreamworlds of Neoliberalism*. New York: New Press.

Deleuze, G. and Guattari, F. (1972), *Anti-Oedipus: Capitalism and Schizophrenia: Volume I*. London: Athlone.

Deleuze, G. and Guattari, F. (1984), *A Thousand Plateaus: Capitalism and Schizophrenia: Volume II*. Minneapolis: University of Minnesota Press.
Elliott, A. (ed.) (2007), *The Contemporary Bauman*. London: Routledge.
Eriksen, T. H. (2001), *The Tyranny of the Moment: Fast and Slow Time in the Information Age*. London: Pluto.
Featherstone, M. (1997), *Tocqueville's Virus: Utopia and Dystopia in Western Social and Political Thought*. London: Routledge.
Freud, S. (2003), *The Schreber Case*. London: Penguin.
Harvey, D. (1991), *The Condition of Postmodernity: An Enquiry into the Origins of Cultural Change*. Oxford: Blackwell.
Hobbes, T. (2008), *Leviathan*. London: Penguin.
Lang, F. (2005), *Metropolis*. Eureka Entertainment.
Lévinas, I. (1999), *Totality and Infinity: An Essay of Exteriority*. Pittsburgh, PA: Duquesne University Press.
Luttwak, E. (1999), *Turbo Capitalism: Winners and Losers in the Global Economy*. London: Weidenfeld and Nicolson.
Luxemburg, R. (2003), *The Accumulation of Capital*. London: Routledge.
More, T. (2004), *Utopia*. London: Penguin.
Plato (1991), *The Republic of Plato*. New York: Basic Books.
Retort. (2005), *Afflicted Powers: Capital and Spectacle in a New Age of War*. London: Verso.
Sassen, S. (2006), *Territory, Authority, Rights: From Medieval to Global Assemblages*. Princeton: Princeton University Press.
Schumpeter, J. (1962), *Capitalism, Socialism, Democracy*. London: Harper.
Simmel, G. 'The Metropolis and Mental Life' in Frisby, D. and Featherstone, M. (eds) (1999) *Simmel on Culture: Selected Writings*. London: Sage, 174–86.
Tester, K. (2004), *The Social Thought of Zygmunt Bauman*. Basingstoke: Palgrave Macmillan.
Virilio, P. (2005a), *City of Panic*. Oxford: Berg.
Virilio, P. (2005b), *Negative Horizon: An Essay in Dromoscopy*. London: Continuum.
Zamyatin, Y. (1993), *We*. London: Penguin.
Žižek, S. (2006), *The Parallax View*. Cambridge, Mass: MIT Press.
Žižek, S. (2008), *Violence*. London: Profile.

8

Totalitarian Bureaucracy and Bauman's Sociological Imagination: In Defence of the Ivory Tower

Paul Taylor

> The purpose of the various investigations of the present study is not to add to specialist knowledge and to enrich certain marginal preoccupations of social scientists, but to open up the findings of the specialists to the general use of social science, to interpret them in a way that shows their relevance to the main themes of sociological inquiry, to feed them back into the mainstream of our discipline.
>
> (Bauman 2008: xiii [italicized in original])

> Proletarians of all countries refused to follow Marx's call, but there seems to be a well-entrenched and thriving International of establishment lovers.
>
> (Bauman and Tester 2001: 27)

This year marks the anniversary of two classic sociological texts. It is the fiftieth anniversary of the original publication date of C. Wright Mills' *The Sociological Imagination* (1959), and the 20th anniversary of Zygmunt Bauman's *Modernity and the Holocaust* (1989). In the first of the above quotations (a point that could just as easily have come from Mills) – Bauman states his book's key contribution to, and further demand for, sustained reflexivity, not just in sociology, but in social science more generally. This chapter argues that the joint anniversary of these works is a particularly appropriate time to re-emphasize the continued relevance of their profoundly critical analyses to the current state of academia in which reflexivity is honoured more in the breach than the observance despite the reasonable assumption that it should form an integral aspect of genuinely intellectual enquiry. These two works share a critique of the Ivory Tower's shortcomings embodied in both their explicit content and their inspiring mode of delivery of that content. Thus, using a combination of style and substance, they argue and illustrate, by strong example, a range of methodological and conceptual gaps that social science needs to address. In this chapter, a close reading is given of Mills and Bauman's texts. In particular, it is argued that Bauman's interrogation of the Holocaust's true historical meaning encapsulates the best aspects of a truly sociological imagination – or what Arendt defines as 'the power of narratives to release new meanings', 'thinking without a banister', 'enlarged thought' and 'training the imagination to go visiting' (Arendt cited in Taylor, Barr and Steele 2002: 48).

The unifying theme of Mills and Bauman's work is their call for sociology to fulfil its own potential, a call that appears from today's academic climate to remain largely unanswered and hence still very much pertinent to the role of the Ivory Tower. In an interview (Bauman and Tester 2001), Bauman vividly recounts the forces of intellectual conformism routinely arrayed against Mills at the time they met in Warsaw in the late 1950s:

> At that time Mills baiting was a favourite pastime among the most distinguished members of American academe: there were no expedients, however dishonest, which the ringleaders of the hue-and-cry would consider below their dignity and to which they would not stoop. Mills, after all, was a thorn in the flesh of the thoroughly conformist sociological establishment, having assaulted, one by one, every single one of its sacred cows. He was deviance incarnate, the critic of the American creed among its preachers and admirers ... Mills was a sort of Typhoid Mary. Less controversial figures, like Paul Lazarfeld ... were greeted with unpolluted enthusiasm.
>
> (Bauman and Tester 2001: 27)

Mills scorned those establishment lackeys he called 'cheerful robots' and was amused when Bauman and others complained that the First Secretary of the Polish United Workers Party, Władysław Gomułka, was going on radio to criticize an academic colleague. Mills suggested to Bauman: 'How lucky you are and happy you must be – the leader of the country responding to philosophical tracts! No one at the top pays any attention to what I am doing' (ibid.: 28). Despite this playful envy, however, a shared quality of Mills and Bauman's work is their sustained critique of those academics who are either incapable or unwilling to provoke the establishment in the first place. By contrast, in keeping with Mills and Bauman's emphasis upon the innately imbricated nature of micro and macro environments, the reader of this chapter is also invited to exercise their own sociological imagination to apply the themes discussed here to their own experiences within the Ivory Tower.

At an apocryphal and personal level, many readers may be familiar with what appears to be a precisely inverse relationship between the nature of an academic's specialist theoretical expertise and their actual behaviour in practice. Thus, it is not unusual for sociologists with detailed knowledge of Weber to create their own personalized iron cages of rationality when in positions of authority themselves, nor for communications specialists to exhibit extremely poor communicational skills etc. Beyond the casual empiricism of such individual experiences, however, academia as a whole today presents systematic, deeply institutionalized examples of similarly unreflexive and uncritical attitudes at a profession-wide level: 'In the very institution that prides itself on its reasonableness, there is a continuing falling short of what it might be' (Barnett 2003: 14). Hence, social scientists who should be best equipped to understand and challenge the bureaucratic mentality have participated as enthusiastically as any others in various behemothic processes providing plenty of evidence that Mills' concerns about social science's tunnel vision have been borne out (see Taylor 2003 and 2008). A key theme in both Mills and Bauman's work is this apparent disjuncture between the individual's intellectual and moral resources and the betrayal of those personal qualities when that individual becomes an agent within a large, complex social system. Thus, in the first paragraph of *The Sociological Imagination*, Mills points to this tension between micro and macro environments: 'Nowadays men often feel that their private lives are a series of traps ... And the more aware they become, however vaguely, of ambitions and of threats which transcend their immediate locales, the more trapped they seem to feel' (Mills 2000 [1959]: 3). Similarly, throughout *Modernity and the Holocaust*, Bauman frequently emphasizes the paradoxically essential normality of those individuals responsible for some of history's most heinous mass political acts and thereby echoes Hannah Arendt's unsettling description of Adolf Eichmann as 'terribly and *terrifyingly normal*' (Arendt 1994a: 276).

To the extent that the sociological imagination does still exist, it frequently assumes a perverted form as, in either unedifyingly quiescent or proactive ways, academics have sought ever more ingenious ways to connive at their own oppression. This startling failure of the sociological imagination can be viewed as an intellectual variation of the specific psychoanalytical concept of *perversion*. As so vividly illustrated by Karl Kraus's pithy observation: 'There is no more unfortunate being under the sun than a fetishist, who yearns for a woman's shoe and has to make do with a whole woman' (Kraus 1977: 225); perversion is typically associated with sexual aberration. In psychoanalytical theory, however, the notion of a pervert is a pathological condition that goes beyond the sexual connotation. Instead, it refers to an excessive reliance upon rules and structures dominant in any area of human endeavour. Without using the same precise term,[1] it is ultimately the perverted reason of a social science that had become distorted by institutional and social factors that C. Wright Mills critiqued so forcefully 50 years ago. Similarly, Bauman's approach to the Holocaust allows a sustained analysis of what would otherwise appear to be an oxymoronic perversion – the irrational ends of excessive rationality.

Steering magisterially between Mills's Scylla and Charbydis of abstracted empiricism and grand theory, Bauman's work is of particular significance for the manner in which he forensically delineates both the nature of Holocaust's perverse logic and the paradox that the most infamous episode in humankind's cruelty was not perpetrated by the bloodthirsty killers witnessed in other genocides. Rather, the Shoah occurred via bureaucrats who undergirded the subsequent horror by acting as the personification of calmness as they oversaw processes that can be considered highly 'reasonable' if one can momentarily divorce the notion of efficiency from the victims upon whom it was applied with such inhuman *sang froid*. Bauman's sociological imagination is such that he avoids the fault of other writers who dwell upon the inhuman aspect of this process of abstraction to use it as an alibi with which to avoid uncovering its unacknowledged links to our everyday bureaucratic processes and mentality. Instead, he focuses directly upon the reasons lying behind Mills' repeated claim that modern life is marked by a disjuncture between the individual's subjective experience and the macro-level structures that circumscribe it. Bauman refuses to quarantine off considered analysis of the Holocaust's implications for everyday life because of its atypically horrific nature. He combines a specific history of the horrendous suffering under the Nazi regime with an incisive account of the features of its war machine that are generalizable to our own time.

Despite the obscenity of the event, for Bauman, the Holocaust becomes the ultimate warning of the dangers that accompany a loss of reflexivity both at the level of the individual and society at large – and how these two levels influence each other. For some, the mere use of the Holocaust for wider illustrative purposes is deeply problematic. However, implicit in Bauman's account is the belief that the Holocaust is diminished, not by sociologically imaginative analysis, but rather by its unimaginative reduction to an uncritical *myth* – the creation of 'what goes without saying' as Barthes defines the term or as Arendt puts it, the need to avoid 'interpreting history by commonplaces' (Arendt 1994a: viii). The Holocaust frequently acts as a sort of Medusa's face that paralyzes social scientific interrogation of the complex relationship that existed between the all-too-real mass murder and the abstract reasoning that lay behind the process-driven nature of the killing. While horrific killing sprees have been an innate part of human history, it was the quality of systematic abstraction that gave the Holocaust its uniquely industrial quality. Bauman provides us with the intellectual equivalent of Athena's polished shield so that we can finally behead the Gorgon of the Holocaust's terror that continues to inhibit our imagination.

The myopia of social science – Abstracted empiricism and grand theory

> These pictures ... represent only an extreme manifestation of a tendency which may be discovered in all bureaucracies, however benign and innocuous the tasks in which they are currently engaged. I suggest that the discussion of the dehumanizing tendency, rather than being focused on its most sensational and vile, but fortunately uncommon, manifestations, ought to concentrate on the more universal, and for this reason potentially more dangerous, manifestations.
>
> (Bauman 1989: 102)

The Holocaust is commonly considered as the most unarguably unproblematic example of extreme and exceptional evil in human history. However, Bauman points out above that the emblematic pictures seared on our collective consciousness of emaciated Jewish corpses and whole communities being transported to their deaths risk blinding us to the less dramatic but no less real lessons to be learnt. Bauman demonstrates his sociological imagination in the way in which he makes us reassess our commonly held, almost sacrosanct, beliefs about the Shoah. He does this not by diminishing in any shape or form the extent of the tragedy suffered by the millions of victims, but by insisting upon its continued relevance to contemporary life. Bauman is clear in his counter-intuitive claim that, rather than emphasizing thankfully rare historical outbreaks of extreme violence, our focus should in fact be placed upon the potentially *more dangerous* potential of the everyday bureaucratic processes that surround us. Mills and Bauman are united in their criticism of sociology as a discipline that persistently fails to deliver on its intellectual duties – the tracing of the complex interrelations between the micro and macro levels of society.

In the following excerpt, Mills denigrates the tautologically inhibited nature of much of the sociological work that does tend to take place:

> In abstracted empiricism, what to verify often does not seem to be taken as a serious issue. How to verify is almost automatically provided by the terms in which the problem is stated: these feed into correlational and other statistical procedures. In fact, the dogmatic requirement for such verification often seems the sole concern, and hence limits or even determines the Concepts used and the problems taken up by those committed to this microscopic style.
>
> (Mills 2000 [1959]: 125)

He targets his critique at *grand theory* which refers to the ungrounded and overly speculative – '... conceptions have indeed become Concepts' [Mills 2000 [1959]: 23] – and *abstracted empiricism* (excessively grounded, aconceptual fact gathering in which, 'methods have become Methodology' [ibid.: 24]). The combined effect shares with totalitarian modes of thought; 'the curious contradiction between ... avowed cynical "realism" and their conspicuous disdain of the whole texture of reality' (Arendt 1994a: viii). This failure of social science to address what should be its substantive concerns partakes of the same mode (albeit at an immensely lower level) the Nazi apparatchiks' failure to confront the evil essence of the processing procedures they were helping to run. Moral insensitivity buttressed by bureaucratic structures is their common quality. The comparison between the bureaucracies of our daily lives and those of the Third Reich risks censure because of the huge disparity of their actual consequences, but Bauman's insistence is that a basic ethical indifference to substantive concerns informs *all* bureaucratic mindsets largely irrespective of the ultimate ends to which they are applied.

Fifty years ago, Mills identified a deficit in moral fortitude and imagination among academics that demonstrated Arendt's disdain for the whole texture of reality: 'Many practitioners of social science ... abdicate the intellectual and political tasks of social analysis; others no doubt are simply not up to the role for which they are nevertheless being cast ... they seem almost deliberately to have brought forth old ruses and developed new timidities' (Mills 2000 [1959]: 21–2). Academic timidity takes two main forms:

(1) A reluctance to apply intellectual reflexivity to academic's own practices

For example, while various forms of postmodernist thought have had a huge impact within academia, they have seldom been used to improve academics' own position within the purportedly empowering, deterritorializing modes of being enabled by a combination of new technologies and related social formations, instead, paraphrasing Mills' original description of US democracy, universities are 'generally intellectual mainly in form and in the rhetoric of expectation' (Mills 2000 [1959]: 188). Worse than this, the rise of postmodern thought's popularity has accompanied largely unchecked trends to deprofessionalize and increase the role of heteronomous pressures in undermining academic autonomy. Thus, the functional language of skills and training is employed by academics themselves (tellingly in the UK under the auspices of the Government's Department for Innovation, Universities and Skills – with little demurral from academics, universities are now considered as part of a triumvirate of functional considerations). Pedagogic relationships have also been replaced by technocratic learning outcomes, the calculus of student credits delivered etc. and as Mills points out in relation to the 'human engineers' of early audience research, this represents a disturbingly defining internalization of heteronomous values: 'To use these slogans as a statement of "what one is about" is to accept a bureaucratic role even when one is not enacting it' (Mills 2000 [1959]: 115).

While the traditional liberal notion of education included an essential element of personal development (*bildung*) or, 'the ancient sense of clarifying one's knowledge of self' (Mills 2000 [1959]: 186), this is increasingly difficult when those in the role of educators have so thoroughly and uncritically implicated themselves in what Castoriadis refers to as 'imaginary significations' (Castoriadis 1997) and Foucault termed 'discursive formations' (Foucault 1972), or, as Mills puts it, 'We may ... speak of "common values" when a great proportion of the members of an institutional order have taken over that order's legitimations, when such legitimations are the terms in which obedience is successfully claimed, or at least *complacency secured*' (Mills 2000 [1959]: 38–9 [emphasis added]). Perhaps the single best example of this process of securing complacency is provided by the now ubiquitous terms 'excellence' and 'quality' to the extent that 'The account of quality and the implicit framing of Higher Education take in each other's washing: they form a discursive compact *and* it is a discursive compact that brooks no dissent' (Barnett 2003: 95). Contemporary academia provides plenty of examples of the effects of dissent's absence. The profession's sleepwalk into new speech rules has underlay the evolution of achievement-based criteria to task terms (Barnett 1990: 7) and research *projects* routinely subject to external management and supervision now increasingly supplant sustained autonomous scholarship. In such a context, academics suffer from a contagion of 'insistent *blankness*' (Barnett 2003: 19 [italics in original]) and find that 'Rationality is not absent but is only the servant of imagination' (Taylor, Barr and Steele 2002: 46).

(2) The limited nature of the methods and content of those academic studies that do take place.

The sociological imagination is important because it provides what both abstracted empiricism and grand theory lack, namely the previously mentioned ability to consider both the micro and macro rather than dwell excessively and limitedly in the realm of just one: 'the capacity to shift from one perspective to another ... the capacity to range from the most impersonal and remote transformations to the most intimate features of the human self – and to see the relations between the two' (Mills 2000 [1959]: 7), a dual perspective that Žižek (2006) terms the *parallax view*. What distinguishes Bauman and Mills from their less imaginative counterparts is their willingness to engage with the problems of theorizing the lived experience of 'liquid modernity's' uncertain flux rather than succumb to the dominant social science tendency to hide its disciplinary insecurities behind a wall of falsely confident empirical methods. Over-emphasizing the science aspect of the term social *science*, the field risks aping scientific rigour and correctness at the expense of social ambiguity and truth while refusing to consider adequately Arendt's texture of reality: 'methodological inhibition stands parallel to the fetishism of the concept' (Mills 2000 [1959]: 50). The loss of the most basic critical independence by the academic profession is illustrated by the dominance of tautological modes of enquiry designed to condone rather than challenge the status quo – Bauman's thriving 'International of establishment lovers'. For example, various forms of research based upon cultural populism, such as active audience theory, serve to celebrate the glints off the bars of the gilded cage with disturbing implications for the state of democratic plurality:

> It is a significant measure of the impotence of liberal democracy that it must increasingly use its social sciences not directly on democracy's

> own problems, but tangentially and indirectly; it must pick up the crumbs from private business research on such problems as how to gauge audience reaction so as to put together synthetic radio programs and movies.
>
> (Lynd cited in Mills 2000 [1959]: 115)

In theory, the conducting of such research is part of a diverse palate of approaches but this overlooks the insidious manner with which the sociological imagination becomes colonized so that heteronomously derived values are internalized and undermine autonomous academic values: 'Those who promote and practice this style of research readily assume the political perspective of their bureaucratic clients and chieftains. To assume the perspective is often in due course to accept it' (ibid.: 101) – scholars have been supplanted by 'executives of the mind' (ibid.: 103). The über-executive of the mind is the figure of the 'academic statesman' caustically defined as someone for whom '[a]s long as he lives, he'll be the most eminent man in his field; two weeks after he dies, no one will remember him' (Mills 2000 [1959]: 109).

When academics are both methodologically driven and socially in hock to their paymasters, they lose both their intellectual and moral autonomy/authority. Mills is consistent to his own normative standard by which he argues that sociological imagination should trace the links between the individual and their broader social environment: 'The individual social scientist tends to become involved in those many trends of modern society that make the individual a part of a functionally rational bureaucracy … social science itself often tends to become a functionally rational machine' (Mills 2000 [1959]: 180). The emphasis Mills and Bauman place upon the sociological imagination is thus an important resource with which to attempt to get outside the whale as Orwell might put it.

Imagining the unimaginable – getting outside the whale of social science

> Cultural criticism finds itself faced with the final stage of the dialectic of culture and barbarism. To write poetry after Auschwitz is barbaric. And this corrodes even the knowledge of why it has become impossible to write poetry today. Absolute reification, which presupposed intellectual progress as one of its elements, is now preparing to absorb the mind entirely. Critical intelligence cannot be equal to this challenge as long as it confines itself to self-satisfied contemplation.
>
> (Adorno 1983 [1949]: 34)

> Our metaphysical faculty is paralyzed because actual events have shattered the basis on which speculative metaphysical thought could be reconciled with experience. Once again, the dialectical motif of quantity recoiling into quality scores an unspeakable triumph ... Perennial suffering has as much right to expression as a tortured man has to scream; hence it may have been wrong to say that after Auschwitz you could no longer write poems.
>
> (Adorno 1973: 362)

Adorno's much-cited phrase of the challenge posed by the brute facticity of the Holocaust to poetry (and by extension all artistic and sociological imagination) has been fundamentally misinterpreted and subsequently blithely repeated as a dictum that is mistakenly seen to encapsulate a blanket rejection of artistic endeavour (see Hofmann 2005). The above two excerpts provide a mere hint of the much more complex aesthetic dialectic at stake in Adorno's work than is typically recognized through their misleadingly selective quotation. A fully contextualized reading demonstrates the eloquence of Adorno's problematization of the jarring encounter between the limits of our imagination and the horror of the Holocaust. The sentence 'To write poetry after Auschwitz is barbaric' has typically been privileged through repetition at the expense of the qualifying meaning of its textual location both within its original essay and Adorno's later work. The immediately subsequent sentence 'And this corrodes even the knowledge of why it has become impossible to write poetry today' makes a much more complex and paradoxical point than can be appreciated from merely the bald statement created by the tendency to create a dictum by either running together or citing together in edited form two otherwise crucially separated sentences in the following manner: 'To write poetry after Auschwitz is barbaric ... it has become impossible to write poetry today.'

As Hofmann (2005) explores in detail, hugely significant meaning is lost in this crude juxtaposition. For example, the full version alludes to the danger that focusing upon barbarous qualities risks undermining (corroding) our ability to then think through the implications and relationship of that barbarity to our conventionally non-barbarous lives (for example, Bauman's sustained argument that the barbarism of the Holocaust acts like Banquo's ghost at modernity's feast). This is what is meant by the point made at the beginning of this chapter that the Shoah's horror should not act as an alibi for a failure in our intellectual duty to analyse the full range of its ongoing social implications for today's world. 'Self-satisfied contemplation' is an acerbically succinct summary of the thought for which Bauman's sociological imagination is an exemplary antidote and Mills similarly encapsulates in his cogent summary of intellectual conformism – 'complacency secured'.

In relation to Adorno's response to the horrors of Auschwitz, the redemptive power of *Modernity and the Holocaust* stems from the way in which Bauman applies his sociological imagination to produce a series of cogently argued, iconoclastic assertions and paradoxes.

He asserts,

- The true concern of the Holocaust does not relate to fears about the breakdown of civilization, but rather that the Holocaust signifies an underacknowledged aspect of modernity's inherent potential: 'It towers high above the past genocidal episodes in the same way as the modern industrial plant towers above the craftsman's cottage workshop, or the modern industrial farm, with its tractors, combines and pesticides, towers above the peasant farmstead with its horse, hoe and hand-weeding' (ibid.: 89).
- Rationality is not the unalloyed good we are sometimes led to believe. Uncritical, unreflexive belief in the power of reason fails to take into account the importance of the context in which that reason is to be applied: 'under sharply assymetrical power conditions, rationality of the ruled is, to say the least, a mixed blessing' (ibid.: 149).
- The insufficiently contextualized misapplication of reason creates a bureaucratic swamp defined as 'a kind of ingenious system so constructed that however the objects immersed into it move, their movements always add to the "sucking power" of the system' (ibid.: 157).
- It is not the Holocaust we struggle to understand but Western Civilization itself.
- 'The unimaginable ought to be imagined' – contrary to conventional assumptions of the profound effect of the Holocaust on our historical consciousness, Bauman argues that the Shoah has changed little if anything in our understanding of its root causes and our ability to prevent it happening again.
- Instead of being a unique, atypical event, the Holocaust shares common features with today's pervasive atmosphere of uncritical conformity: 'the situation of the individual in the modern state is in principle roughly equivalent to the situation of the prisoner in Auschwitz: either act in accord with the prevailing standards of conduct enforced by those in authority, or risk whatever consequences they may wish to impose' (ibid.: 86).

- Conscience and the superego are not eliminated within bureaucratic structures, but they are redeployed in a perverted fashion so that 'Superego shifts from an evaluation of the goodness or badness of the acts to an assessment of how well or poorly one is functioning in the authority system' (ibid.: 160).

His analysis also throws up a series of provocative paradoxes:

- Our willingness to recognize and portray the apparently unprecedented nature of such an evil event may actually serve to undermine its true historical significance and continued relevance for our own times. A subtle form of Holocaust denial risks being caused by the best of intentions – for example, the desire to keep it in the historical spotlight. This is because 'more often than not it is allowed on the public stage in a sanitized and hence ultimately demobilizing and comforting form' (Bauman 1989: ix).
- The very discipline – sociology – that should be most equipped to address the Holocaust as a social phenomenon has proved largely incapable of responding to the challenge.
- Rational processes pursued as neutral categories can produce profoundly irrational, non-neutral, immoral outcomes: 'The inherent moral indifference of the principles of rationality was thereby pushed to the extreme and exploited in full' (ibid.: 143).
- The same technology and instrumental reason that have caused modernity's problems are presented as the solution for the problems they have caused.
- The ethically-informed attempts of those who wish to slow down the onward march of bureaucracy is not only viewed indifferently, but receives the closest bureaucratic systems can come to forming their own moral opinions – vehement censure and marginalization.
- The unprecedented lethal destructiveness of the Holocaust was only possible due to the promotion of calm, bureaucratic behaviour *not* psychotic blood lust.

The sense of unease that stems from a close reading of Bauman is the cumulative resonance the reader perceives between the Nazi's chosen means for genocide and essential features of our nominally neutral social systems. For Bauman, the Holocaust represents a sociological laboratory in which to explore some of the dark inherent potentiality of society that because it rarely surfaces tends to be dismissed as atypically unique, but which is concept of unique normality aims to restore to sociological focus: 'The Holocaust has exposed and examined such attributes of our society as are not revealed, and hence are not empirically accessible, in "non-laboratory" conditions ... *I propose to treat the Holocaust as a rare, yet significant and reliable, test of hidden possibilities of modern society*' (Bauman 1989: 12 [italics in original]). Bauman thus cites Stillman and Pfaff's observation that 'We may wish to deny the connection, but Buchenwald was of our West as much as Detroit's River Rouge – we cannot deny Buchenwald as a casual aberration of a Western world essentially sane' (cited in Bauman 1989: 9). He is also unambiguous in his identification of the crucial role played by bureaucracy: '*the very idea of the* Endlösung *was an outcome of the bureaucratic culture*' (ibid.: 15 [italics in original]).

The dark heart of bureaucracy

> To a degree much too high for comfort ... Except for the moral repulsiveness of its goal (or, to be precise, the gigantic scale of the moral odium), the activity did not differ in any formal sense (the only sense that can be expressed in the language of bureaucracy) from all other organized activities designed, monitored and supervised by 'ordinary' administrative and economic sections.
>
> (Bauman 1989: 14)

In the Holocaust, there were two main modes by which the extirpation of moral values lay the ground for the subsequent attempted extermination of a whole people: technology and bureaucracy. While technology facilitates and provides the sufficient conditions for this leap from the elimination of ethics to the elimination of people, it is bureaucracy that provides the necessary organizational conditions for such a disturbing abdication of the most basic human values of decency. Because of the previously cited typical elevation of the Holocaust to a uniquely privileged position in the annals of human depravity, there is perhaps an understandable reluctance to appear to make facetious comparisons that could be interpreted as demeaning the suffering of its victims. However, Bauman is clear in his identification of the bureaucratic elements of Nazism with the same essential features of *any* complex technological social system in which technical systems-derived values are allowed to supplant extra-systemically derived countervailing values.

Bauman cites Max Weber's characterization of bureaucracy's 'objective' status as one which is dependent upon processes that proceed purely on the basis of their calculability and 'without regard for persons' (ibid.: 14).

It is this nominally value-free 'objective' quality that is a crucial point to be considered when assessing common features between otherwise drastically different ends. What makes the Holocaust 'uniquely normal' for Bauman is this very feature of banal matter-of-fact methods in such close juxtaposition with almost inconceivably depraved purposes. The uncomfortable truth this common feature then opens up is the extent to which all bureaucratic processes in contemporary life share at least some small part of the Nazi-perfected elimination of human values. Bauman is adamant in his claim that tracing these links is not just intellectually justifiable but a necessary testament to their full historical and contemporary significance: 'There is nothing in this description that warrants questioning the bureaucratic definition of the Holocaust as either a simple travesty of truth or a manifestation of a particularly monstrous form of cynicism' (ibid.: 14).

The Shoah occurred in its perversely efficient form *because of*, not despite, modern processes based upon rationality. Bauman argues that a mistake consistently made by those who wish to uphold threatened values is the notion that reason alone is sufficient condition to improve the situation. Bauman's warning is that if the rules of the game have been rigged in advance because of assymetric power conditions, then, in practice, the application of reason just bogs the victim down further within the swamp of ultimate ends beyond the individual's rational control. From this insight, can be deduced two further particular factors at work to undermine, in a cumulative fashion, social and cultural values vulnerable to colonization by heteronomous factors so that victims find themselves rationally co-operating with their own highly rationalized victimization:

(1) *Ghettoization* – all actions within a pre-enscribed arena become objectively functional for the external authority's oppressive purposes and designs. For example, 'Freely held' elections were important to the Nazi overseers to create the appearance of Jewish autonomy. The extent to which such processes that merely facilitate predetermined outcomes qualify as authentically 'free' is open to serious doubt because victims' rational choices, while appearing rational, are only so in terms of the superimposed framework within which they are allowed to operate: 'the bureaucracy that conducts a "targeted" policy and retains the exclusive right to conduct it, is fully competent to set the parameters for its victims' behaviour and thus able to enlist the victims' own rational motives among the resources it can deploy in the pursuit of its task' (Bauman 1989: 123).

This co-optation of the victim's own rationality creates 'the experience of constant activity within the framework of overwhelming fatality' (Arendt 1994b: 331). Familiarity with such fatality is perhaps familiar to academics, who despite good performances in university league tables, ruefully regret the time expended in misguided complicity when performance is not met with proportionate economic rewards.

Victims' disappointment with bureaucratic outcomes, however, can still be an integral part of its mode of operation rather than a threat to its smooth functioning as long as some (albeit vaguely defined) hope of better outcomes is still offered for certain exceptions:

> The opportunities to add authority to the rule through fighting for exemptions (and in the end reinforcing the rule by deploying it as an entitlement to seek individual privileges) were ample and varied … benevolent ruling took attention away from the much more sweeping rule from which it provided an exception. Whoever saw in the ruling a personal chance could claim the benefits only while simultaneously accepting the assumption that warranted both the general rule and the exceptions.
>
> (Ibid.: 131)

Gullibility towards benevolent rulings is exacerbated by a loss of community values with which to challenge the essential validity of the ruling and to criticize the ultimately ersatz quality of that benevolence. In reality, victims only succeed in conniving at their own oppression to an extent that constitutes an important element of the Holocaust's unprecedented aura of tragedy. For example, Bauman cites deeply disturbing examples of *Judenräte* leaders who, tangled up in a 'rational' calculus of survival costs, surrendered large numbers of their communities in a vain attempt to avoid yet worse in terms of bald numbers, but failing to realize the depths and consequences of the moral and practical capitulation this represented for their Nazi persecutors. In the environment of the ghetto such attitudes created a series of essential reductions: Jewish community leaders were reduced to self-justifying 'survival brokers' capable of explaining the calculated sacrifice of others with craven admissions, 'Yes, it is my duty to foul my hands' (ibid.: 142); rationality was reduced to cooperation; and 'the awesome identity of imminent fate' (ibid.: 133) was reduced to a myopic fixation upon short term gains. Attitudes which have more than passing significance in the context of today's academic fellow-travellers with university bureaucracies.

(2) The removal of the *distance and spontaneity* necessary for independent critical thought – 'moral evaluation is something external to the action itself' (Bauman 1989: 18). While bureaucracy provides a process-driven framework, its specifically totalitarian application derives from its ability to inveigle its way into prior community structures and values. Bauman thus describes how 'the total subjection of a population to an unconstrained will of their captors was achieved not through destruction, but by reinforcing the communal structure and integrative role played by native elites' (Bauman 1989: 122), while Arendt similarly points out that totalitarian tendencies as the name implies relate to total domination: 'totalitarian bureaucracy "intruded upon the private individual and his inner life with equal brutality"' (Arendt 1994b: 245). Because bureaucracy displaces and systematically overlooks value-based judgement criteria, its ammorality of method creates environments in which immorality of purpose can then prosper. Bureaucracy works as a process that can co-ordinate the actions of otherwise moral people for *any* purposes including immoral ones and it does this through the evacuation of non-abstract, grounded, community-based judgements. What normally stops such a pervasion of ammorality is the existence of what Bauman calls '*non-political power resources and institutions of social self-management*' (Bauman 1989: xiii [italics in original]).

Academics without conviction

> They have studied problems of abstracted empiricism; but only within the curiously self-imposed limitations of their arbitrary epistemology have they stated their questions and answers ... they are possessed by the methodological inhibition ... in these studies the details are piled up with insufficient attention to form; indeed, often there is no form except that provided by typesetters and bookbinders. The details, no matter how numerous, do not convince us of anything worth having convictions about.
>
> (Mills 2000 [1959]: 55)

> ... the curious passion for the mannerism of the non-committed.
>
> (Ibid: 79)

The etiolation of community values is facilitated when a group such as academics internalize the functionality of means as an end in itself based upon 'the *meticulous functional division of labour*'.

'the *substitution of technical for a moral responsibility*' (Bauman 1989: 98 [italics in original]). The removal of spontaneity/discretion and moral responsibility added to functional specialization has the combined effect of increasing the sense of individuals' distance from the direct consequences of their actions within a complex system: 'communal mechanisms of social regulation have all but disappeared and local communities ceased to be self-sufficient and self-reliant ... the void tends to be filled by new ... supra-communal forces' (ibid.: 112). It is these supra-communal forces that now dominate today's academic discourse in the new speech rules described previously and the ubiquitously looming presence of various external quangos and funding council structures. Bauman talks of 'The silencing of morality' (ibid.: 29) and a loss of our 'universe of obligation' (ibid.: 27) that results from 'Moral sleeping pills' (ibid.: 26) while similarly, Mills refers to the 'Blind Drift' (Mills 2000 [1959]: 169) created by 'Rationality without reason' (ibid.: 170).

Although nefarious purposes may well be the ultimate driving force lying behind these technical processes, a key element of bureaucracy's harmful impact is the extent to which moral agents caught up in the day-to-day functioning of systems may further those nefarious ends unwittingly but highly effectively and with their own sense of rectitude still very much intact. Because of factors such as uncritical institutional loyalty: 'actors' moral drives may be deployed for morally abject purposes, without sapping the ethical propriety of intercourse within that area of proximity which the moral drive covers' (Bauman 1989: 195). As a result of all the processes for creating distance between action and outcome previously described in detail, morality itself becomes a quality subject to translation into functional imperatives. The development of alternative sources of morality is further pre-empted by additional modes of reification:

(1) The 'schismogenetic chains' described by Gregory Bateson (1973: 41–2) – authority breeds submission in an exponentially expanding, self-referential cycle
(2) 'Carefully circumscribed parochiality' (Bauman 1989: 211) – in the context of academia, the disciplinary perversion of narrow intellectual foci due to the widespread instrumentalization of research.
(3) The elimination of teleological categories – 'the relegation of values to the realm of subjectivity' (Bauman 1989: 10). Traditional academic values look increasingly anachronistic and off the pace from the perspective of new managerial discourse.

The combined effect of this imbrication of systemic processes, and the cultural norms so produced, creates what Bauman pace Milgram terms an 'agentic state' – effectively, the rise of heteronomous rather than autonomous thought. In such a state, the usual notion of responsibility becomes 'free-floating': to the extent that '*the organization as a whole is an instrument to obliterate responsibility*' (ibid.: 163 [italics in original]). From this state of play arises Bauman's previously cited notion of the uniquely normal – horrendous acts are suddenly within the capabilities of previously unsuspected candidates, not because of an undetected inherent proclivity for evil, but because normal social and personal modes of regulation are, as Bauman puts it, obliterated.

For Arendt (1994b), the total nature of totalitarianism is not about domination per se but making people superfluous, it is not about the indoctrination of opinions but the preventing their formation ahead of time. The living dead in the death camps lost control even over their own deaths. Total victims are thereby created even before they reach the scaffold. Likewise, while the example of the Ivory Tower is much less serious (but, at the same time, not inconsequential), new academics are not so much browbeaten over time, as their autonomy is pre-emptively lost. Paraphrasing Adorno, they belong to the bureaucracy even before they join it. Commonsense and truth are then free to be supplanted by super-sense where 'nothing matters but consistency' (Arendt 1994b: 458) and the pseudo-reality thus created begins to offer its own bureaucratically textured compensation to the extent that 'totalitarian regimes hold the power to demonstrate the relativity of success and failure, and to show how a loss in substance can become a gain in organization' and then factuality itself becomes dependent upon the totalitarian world that created the initial fiction (ibid.: 385). Hence, in terms of externally situated labyrinthine auditing regimes, universities make sustained attempts to meet the requirements of the defining terms of the model irrespective of their significance for the reality of life on the chalkface. In this climate, the distinction between truth and falsehood becomes blurred and fact dissolves into bland statements of corporate purpose in ever more glossy brochures.

Arendt vividly expresses how this appears to the loyal party member: 'they know that when they are told that only Moscow has a subway, the real meaning of the statement is that all subways should be destroyed, and are not unduly surprised when they discover the subway in Paris' (ibid.: 385). Likewise, the 'German people were perfectly aware ... that the famous Nazi slogan of "guns or butter" actually meant "butter through guns"' (ibid.: 410). Just as academics today, in their heart of hearts, realize that the choice between quality regimes or the death of universities actually means the death of universities through quality regimes. The overall result of these effects is an institutionalized cynicism and bad faith, what Mannoni succinctly expresses as *'je sais bien mais quand même'* (Mannoni 1966). Arendt's crucial notion of the resulting creation of a pseudo-texture of reality comes from the reassuring repetitions of the over-arching system. Alternative views and values are defined and processed out of existence. In Mills' terms an unreflexive and unimaginative sociology defines when it thinks it is describing. It appears that academics are in need of Arendt's previously cited identification of 'the power of narratives to release new meanings' and thereby learn to be more critical sensitive to the defining abilities of fictional representations whether they be literary or bureaucratic.

The sociological imagination revisited and the theme of appropriate shame introduced – taking the literary dog for a walk

> If, without knowing his own voice, he should not find any public, but speaks solely for some record kept by no one, then I suppose we have to admit that he is a true manufacturer of the standardized prose: an autonomous sound in a great empty hall. It is all rather frightening, as in a Kafka novel, and it ought to be: we have been talking about the edge of reason.
>
> (Mills 2000 [1959]: 221)

> Kafka's genius was to eroticize bureaucracy, the nonerotic entity if ever there was one ... What can be more 'divine' than the traumatic encounter with the bureaucracy at its craziest ... It is in such encounters that we get a glimpse of another order beyond mere earthly everyday reality. Like God, bureaucracy is simultaneously all-powerful and impenetrable, capricious, omnipresent and invisible.
>
> (Žižek 2006: 115–16)

The kynic tradition of the Greek philosopher Diogenes the Kynic (from the Greek for dog – *kyon*) offers a form of the non-bureaucratized spontaneity Bauman desires. Diogenes achieved notoriety in ancient

Athenian society for his shockingly active disengagement with conventional behaviour including public acts of masturbation and defecation. Less extreme kynic episodes relevant to dealing with bureaucracy included his famous interaction with Alexander the Great, who upon asking Diogenes (sitting in his barrel) what he could do for him, met with the reply 'stand out of my light'. Additional instances such as publicly begging from statue (in order to practice disappointment) demonstrate a healthy recalcitrant desire to problematize the previously discussed tendency of bureaucracy to evacuate substantive meaning. Thus we are told that the reason he left his homeland of Sinope for Athens in the first place was due to the accusation that he had adulterated the coinage (*paracharaxai* to *nomisma*): an accusation of wider significance in that

> if monetary forgery undermines the government by stripping it of its economic power, play devalues the concept of truth, the currency of intellectual rulers ... the phrase *paracharaxai* to *nomisma* ... is a pun based on the homonymity of *nomisma*, which originally signified anything sanctioned by law or convention and only through a subsequent extension was applied to money as legal tender.
>
> (Steiner 2000: 41)

The semantic importance of this adulteration is the way in which Diogenes is able to undermine all pre-conceived standards and institutionally driven notions of truth and use imagination to recreate the sense of playful autonomy expunged by bureaucratic systems. Žižek (1989) cites Pascal's observation that one may not believe in religion but the moment one kneels down and partakes in its ceremonies, one begins to believe nevertheless. Likewise, academic submission to corporate modes of thinking creates its own *cynically* accommodationist modes of behaviour.

Similarly, in the very first sentence of Hašek's rebelliously kynic novel *The Good Soldier Švejk*, we are told that after leaving the army certified as an imbecile, Švejk made living dealing in 'ugly, mongrel monstrosities whose pedigrees he forged' (Hašek 1973 [1921–3]: 3). An important strand of Peter Sloterdijk's *Critique of Cynical Reason* (1988) is his tracing of how the resistance of the *kynic* is subordinated in the modern world to the manipulative acts of the *cynic* of which the bureaucratic mindset is a typical example. Even if only as models existing in the pages of fiction, characters such as Švejk and *Catch 22*'s Yossarian keep the kynic flame alive. In this context, the stubbornly powerful resonance of Kafka's work for contemporary life resides in the manner with which he is able to vividly express the dystopian costs in terms of human dignity when the Law functions with indifference. In *The Castle*, for example, we see in discombobulatingly imaginative detail Bauman and Arendt's notion of totalitarianism's ability to transubstantiate reason into fate. Kafka's work thus inimitably answers Mills and Bauman's call for an imagination that bridges the micro and the macro. Thus, beyond the inchoate guilt and powerless revulsion felt by the individual, Kafka repeatedly uses the evocative image of canine submissiveness (the shift from the kynic to the cynic) to highlight a wider group notion of shame.

Kafka's story 'In the Penal Colony' relates how 'the condemned man looked so like a submissive dog that one might have thought he could be left to run free on the surrounding hills and would only need to be whistled for when the execution was due to begin' (Kafka 2005b [1949]: 140). Sternstein argues that most Kafka critics concentrate upon his work's depiction of individual guilt and fail to take into account adequately the performative, public aspect of shame that he presents: 'A truly radical reading of Kafka, then, must underscore the equally important (if not more important) interest in the performance of a collective shame. "In the Penal Colony" ... is a document of shame written upon the body politic' (Sternstein 2001: 318). Yet more memorably, in the final lines of *Der Prozess* (*The Trial*) Josef K. mourns the nature of his servile death: 'Like a dog!', he said. It was as if the shame of it would outlive him (Kafka 1980 [1925]: 254). By stark contrast, Bauman points out that in the face of Nazism a 'remarkable thing about the surrender is that however painful it might have felt at the beginning, it tends to travel from shame to pride. Those who surrender become accomplices of the crime, and deal appropriately with the cognitive dissonance the complicity generates' (Bauman 1989: 128). This is perhaps the darkest legacy of the current academic climate. Whereas Kafka's characters still battle to assert their authority, academics tend to exhibit what Arendt identified as simultaneous gullibility and cynicism. Gullible enough to be led initially by falsehood, even when 'they were given irrefutable proof of their falsehood, they would take refuge in cynicism; instead of deserting the leaders who had lied to them, they would protest that they had known all along that the statement was a lie and would admire the leaders for their superior tactical cleverness' (Arendt 1994b: 382).

Conclusion – Reintroducing shame and recklessness to the Ivory Tower

> Evil can do its dirty work, hoping that most people most of the time will refrain from doing rash, reckless things – and resisting evil is rash and reckless.
>
> (Bauman 1989: 206)

> [O]nly the liberating feeling of shame may help to recover the moral significance of the awesome historical experience and thus to help exorcise the spectre of the Holocaust, which to this day haunts human conscience ... only when feeling ashamed for one's weakness can one finally shatter the mental prison which has outlived its builders and its guards.
>
> (Ibid.: 205)

While it may be an overstatement to describe conditions within the Ivory Tower as evil, they do seem to fit Mill's observation that such is the failure of the sociological imagination that 'newer beginnings are ambiguous to the point of moral stasis' (Mills 2000 [1959]: 4). It is a sad indictment of the Ivory Tower that Bauman can legitimately claim that the Holocaust tells us more about sociology than vice versa. There is an intellectual blind spot at the heart of sociology/social science – it has become incapable of extending its imaginative resources and reflexivity and so fuels the limited form of rationality upon which both bureaucratic processes and bureaucratized disciplines are predisposed to function. This accounts for the excessively technological/instrumentalized form of reason that social science now frequently presents as the solution rather than the symptom of the problem. For example, the way in which digital citizenship offers a point and click polity as the answer to a disenchanted and excessively disconnected electorate.

Bauman's endorsement of the rash and reckless as a countervailing value system with which to confront etiolated moral environments still resonates with the need for academics enframed within complex, highly functionalized and differentiated, educational establishments to develop more of the imaginative, non-conformist resources also described by Mills. Imagination, rashness and recklessness, are all examples of the sort of non-instrumental qualities vulnerable to the bureaucratic mentality of 'complacency secured' but with which '[t]heir capacity for astonishment is made lively again' (Mills 2000 [1959]: 8). A prerequisite before such necessary imagination can be applied, however, is a sufficiently developed sense of shame to help us recognize its appropriateness – a sense we have seen in literature but sadly lacking in our own shameless times. On the final page of *The Sociological Imagination* Mills remains true to his unashamed commitment to value-driven enquiry in opposition to the 'deadly indifference' (Mills 2000 [1959]: 191) with which Bauman so chasteningly engages. Mills makes this plea: 'Above all, do not give up your moral and political autonomy by accepting in somebody else's terms the illiberal practicality of the bureaucratic ethos or the liberal practicality of the moral scatter' (ibid.: 226).

Otherwise proudly moral academics nevertheless seem fully capable of succumbing to the moral scatter and illiberal practicality. As just one commonplace example, they see no contradiction in such now commonplace acts as the marketing of courses for the financial rather than pedagogical gain of their institutions and 'customers'. Bauman's *Modernity and the Holocaust* constitutes a profound admonition about the devastating social consequences that attend the displacement of reason's moral context by ethical distantiation and abstraction as does Arendt's concluding warning in *The Origins of Totalitarianism* about the danger of 'organized loneliness'. The warnings encountered in these pages should remind us of the importance of regaining our true academic collegiality and attempting to overturn the worst excesses of our bureaucratic internalizations. The Ivory Tower is frequently used as a pejorative dismissal of the intellectual life, in these liquid times we should be so lucky to have such a solid bulwark against the tides of unreason.

Notes

1. Mills did, however, explicitly state that, at the time he was writing, psychoanalysis had been underutilized: for example, 'Unfortunately, psychoanalysis has not become a firm and integral part of academic research' (Mills 2000: 160).

References

Adorno, T. (1973 [1949]), *Negative Dialectics*. London: Routledge.
Adorno, T. (1983), *Prisms*. Cambridge MA: MIT Press.
Arendt, H. (1994a), *Eichmann in Jerusalem*. London: Penguin.
Arendt, H. (1994b [1951]), *The Origins of Totalitarianism*. New York: Harvest Books.

Barnett, R. (1990), *The Idea of Higher Education.* Buckingham: Open University Press.

Barnett, R. (2003), *Beyond All Reason: Living with Ideology in the University.* Buckingham: Open University Press.

Bateson, G. (1973), *Steps to An Ecology of Mind.* Frogmore: Paladin.

Bauman, Z. (1989), *Modernity and the Holocaust.* Cambridge: Polity Press.

Bauman, Z. and Tester, K. (2001), *Conversations With Zygmunt Bauman.* Oxford: Blackwell.

Castoriadis, C. (1997), *World in Fragments: Writings on Politics, Society, Psychoanalysis, and the Imagination.* Stanford, CA: Stanford University Press.

Foucault, M. (1972), *The Archaeology of Knowledge,* Trans. by A.M. Sheridan Smith. London: Tavistock Publications Ltd.

Hašek, J. (1973), *The Good Soldier Švejk.* London: Penguin.

Heller, J. (1994), *Catch 22* London, Vintage.

Hofmann, K. (2005), 'Poetry after Auschwitz – Adorno's Dictum'. *German Life and Letters,* vol 58; no. 2, 182–94.

Kafka, F. (1980 [1925]), *The Trial.* London: Picador.

Kafka, F. (2005b), *The Complete Short Stories.* London: Vintage.

Kraus, K. (1977), *No Compromise: Selected Writings of Karl Kraus.* New York: Ungar Publishing.

Mannoni, O. (1966), 'The Deconstruction of Myself: Je sais bien mais quand même'. *Race,* vol 7.

Mills, C. W. (2000 [1959]), *The Sociological Imagination.* Oxford: Oxford University Press.

Sloterdijk, P. (1988), *Critique of Cynical Reason.*

Steiner, P. (2000), *The Deserts of Bohemia: Czech Fiction and Its Social Context.* New York: Cornell University Press.

Sternstein, M. (2001), 'Laughter, Gesture, and Flesh: Kafka's *In the Penal Colony*'. *Modernism/modernity,* vol. 8, no. 2, 315–23.

Taylor, P. A. (2003), 'Humboldt's Rift: Managerialism in Education and Complicit Intellectuals'. *European Political Science,* vol 3.1

Taylor, P. A. (2008), 'Perverted Research and the Political Imagination – the Trial of the Good Scholar Švejk'. *European Political Science,* 7(3), 335–51.

Taylor, R., Barr, J. and Steele, T. (2002), *For a Radical Higher Education: After Postmodernism.* Buckingham: Open University Press.

Žižek, S. (1989), *The Sublime Object of Ideology.* London: Verso.

Žižek, S. (2006), *The Parallax View.* London: MIT Press.

9
Resistance Towards Ethics

Tom Campbell and Chris Till

Zygmunt Bauman's work has reinvigorated sociological interest in ethical questions. Ethics has been at the core of his work for at least the past two decades and he has convincingly positioned ethics and morality as central issues for sociology in our globalized world and liquid modern times. We consider Bauman's decision to prioritize ethics over ontology, to be critical to the understanding of his works' strengths and failings. Through a reading of Emmanuel Lévinas, Bauman wishes to unsettle the traditional prioritizing of the question of how the world *is* with the question of how the world *ought* to be.

In this chapter we shall outline how Bauman came to be concerned with positioning ethics as primary after his work on the Holocaust and his diagnosis of a postmodern world. Moreover, we aim to throw some light upon how his recent work on *Liquid Modernity* (Bauman, 2000) has impacted upon this. We draw similarities between Bauman's position on the rationality that underpinned modernity and the study of the emergence of biopolitics that has been elaborated by many writers since Michel Foucault. We suggest that the classification process has been distinctly modern as it has utilized the assumption of similarity as its point of departure. We then problematize similarity through a discussion of difference wherein we side with Bauman's axiom that we must assume difference rather than similarity. We then engage with Bauman's move to dethrone ontology with ethics and explore the sociological and political consequences of this. Through a deployment of Gilles Deleuze's work on ontology and Judith Revel's work on Foucault's ontology we offer a position that promotes resistance as ontology and this places the promotion of justice as fundamental. We thus argue for the primacy of ontology over ethics.

From modern to postmodern ethics

Bauman's two-pronged engagement with Lévinas (Bauman, 1993; 1995; 1998) and the Holocaust (Bauman, 1989; 1991) led to a questioning of the moral worth of ethical rules. For Bauman, such rules rather than promoting moral conduct in fact encouraged us to not worry about the impact of our actions as all we need to do in order to be moral is to follow the accepted rules. This explained the possibility of an event such as the holocaust as individuals can personally justify their actions even if they find them distasteful as it is deemed inherently right to follow the rules and accept orders. Individuals were able to compartmentalize their actions, ignoring the context within which these actions take place. Lévinas provided for Bauman a way of thinking about morality that prioritizes individual interactions over the impersonal ethical rules that make it possible for individuals to put aside their feelings. In works such as *Entre Nous* (1998), Lévinas proposes the primacy of the face in moral interactions; he suggests that we make moral decisions based on micro-interactions and that these are more important than following prescribed rules. Such ethical rules are necessarily one-size-fits-all and are unable to take into consideration every possible context as they must legislate for what is generally right most of the time. But in order to have any legitimacy they must be deployed as if they are always right all the time, they must be universal, otherwise they would be constantly broken. The lack of the universal applicability of laws is evident in the countless successful challenges to punishments meted out to particular individuals. The morality proposed by Lévinas is always contextual and is self-sacrificial as it originates from an unconditional concern for the other. If we start from a position of being-for-the-other we cannot prioritize the following rules over the well-being of an individual whom we come face-to-face with as we must always be concerned with them, totally and without restrictions. Bauman uses Lévinas to formulate an optimistic theory of morality in what the former saw as a radical possibility for a new potentially more moral era of postmodernity.

In *Postmodern Ethics* (1993), Bauman suggests that the questioning of the universality of truth, and by proxy, universal laws underlines the skepticism symptomatic of postmodern thinking and may provide the possibility for a new more moral world. The reverence of supralocal ethical laws did not prevent, and for Bauman, enabled such atrocities as the Holocaust. The argument he formulated in *Modernity and the Holocaust* (Bauman, 1989) claims that it was modernity itself and all of its great achievements – the efficiency of bureaucratic institutions; the cold effective nature of scientific rationality; the microscopic nature of taxonomic knowledge and the effectiveness of disciplinary technologies – that enabled such widespread and overt extermination to take place. Suspicion towards the iron-like ethical laws which formed an intrinsic part of modernity may, Bauman suggests, leave space for morality to be established on a more contingent level, in the form of a moral engagement with the other on a one-to-one, case-by-case basis – specificity contra universality. But as Crone (2008: 68) demonstrates, such a situation did not emerge; instead we find ourselves in a world which Bauman describes in his latest works *Consuming Life* (2007) and *The Art of Life* (2008a). In this Liquid Modern world we now primarily engage with one another on an aesthetic rather than a moral level.

It is thus straightforward to suggest that Bauman's turn to ethics was a direct result of his concern that the rationality that guided European society and sociology had remained unchanged since the Holocaust. The final challenge of *Modernity and the Holocaust* was that we should stop acting as though the Holocaust did not happen and his turn to ethics was a direct result of this. But what would Bauman's postmodern ethics look like? They would need to develop away from the socially constructed, objectively existing ethics of rules and laws. Postmodern ethics would develop out of a pre-social morality and allow the naturally occurring moral impulse of human beings to flourish. They would be contingent and subjective, only concerned with the other in front of us. It would be impossible to develop transcultural or transhistorical laws out of this moral impulse. The natural moral impulse that emerges when we are faced with another face had been denied by modernity, instead encouraging us to follow arbitrary rules. In the postmodern distrust for universal laws Bauman saw the possibility for us to be constantly concerned with morality.

Bauman objects to the kind of disciplinary ethical rules instituted throughout modernity because they prescribe certain actions rather than encouraging just behaviour that is actively participated in. But is Bauman's insistence on moral actions as other-directed prescriptive in a different way? Is being-for-the-other always better? Certainly it could be a paternalistic and unsolicited form of moral action as we are required to always be for the other regardless of whether they are for us and of whether they want us to be. Is being-for-the-other anthropocentric because it privileges being-for-the-*other* over being-in-the-*world* or being-in-*time*? The disastrous consequences of an anthropocentric ethics are clearly evident to us (the environment).

An ethics which considers only our relation to the other and not our relation to the world seems like an archaic and inappropriate solution for the contemporary world. Could the other include animals, plants or the environment in general? It most likely could, although for Lévinas the signifying of the face is at the heart of morality which may seem to preclude non-human, or at least non-sentient beings. Perhaps this is why Bauman tends to concentrate on a morality of proximity rather than the face. Before addressing these issues we wish to embellish on our reading of Bauman's approach to ethics by considering his theory in relation to the immense increase in classification that took place over the 19th and 20th centuries which provides us with a pertinent context for the lack of moral engagement made possible by modern ethics.

Classification

> I mistrust all systematists and avoid them. The will to system is a lack of integrity.
>
> (Nietzsche, 1998: 9)

Classification is congruent with the kinds of modern ethics that Bauman found to be problematic, it may encourage complacency by suggesting that there is a proper way to deal with people and once one has the skills and knowledge to match up a certain classification with an associated course of action there is little else to worry about. Danger derives from the fact that these classifications typically proceed from a clinical rationality which assumes similarity rather than difference.

Classifications are useful for easy communication and for directing people to relevant support networks or research programmes; they are a useful tool for sorting people and the management of populations and individuals. Furthermore, 'Classification allows one to be arbitrary' (Halmi, 1983: 22), to bracket out some factors as irrelevant, for the task at hand. The activity of classification, is, and we mean this in a Heideggerian sense, essentially a revealment of 'things'. It allows us to perceive ourselves and others through a particular lens which in turn allows people to live their lives, and their lives to be acted upon in, in a particular fashion. Classifying is also a process of situating a thing in a cosmology, to position an individual within a context. This process of classifying is neither necessarily positive nor negative and if it were left to be a continuous process of differentiation, it may be able to fulfil Bauman's wish of prioritizing difference, but as has been demonstrated:

> Modern culture – in Bauman's view – is both heterophobic and morally indifferent, and as such will be well disposed to any means that proposes the extirpation of difference.
>
> (Hughes, 2002: 576)

When used for the purposes of binding some together and making strangers of others, or of encouraging the outsiders to make themselves less strange, classifications can be a tool with which to eradicate difference. By applying a certain lens to the world that reveals some to be healthy, morally upright or reasonable people, such people are presented as not needing intervention or correction. The people who are revealed as problematic are highlighted for further action to be taken. If one wants to avoid becoming a member of this latter group, and part of the waste of modernity, then they must present themselves as normal. The concept of normality is a peculiarly modern one that Ian Hacking (1990) and Lennard Davis (1995) have dated to the early 19th century. The development of statistical methods, and their need for classifications instigated a dramatic increase in the amount of available classifications that were applied to people. The statistical norm came to be synonymous with moral uprightness and was connected with a hegemony that promoted moderation and 'middleness' as espoused by the middle classes. We see the emergence of *l'homme moyen* as an important moment in the ascension of similarity, as normality and similarity were here utilized as the central technologies in the articulation of a particular strategy of government which has since been identified by critics as biopolitics (Hacking, 1990).

Similarity has been equated with goodness: moral, political and utilitarian. It is used to unite people for political struggles and by the same token it divides. Similarity requires an Other, a negative form of difference to give the cry to unite force, and power – if sameness is good then difference is negative. Similarity is however fabricated; it is difference which is primordial and omnipresent. Classifications are of course fabrications themselves – social constructions. They are not, as some social constructionists contend, negative, but neutral categories that allow for access to support, strategies for managing populations. The classification is merely a tool, a technology for articulating power. Our concern is the privileging of similarity over difference, where sameness is seen as a good unifying factor and difference as negative.

We thus assert the ontological and ethical primacy of difference, and following Bauman, call for 'difference rather than similarity'. Our diagnosis of the rise of biopolitics and its use of the concept of similarity and the tool of classification is similar but not analogous to Bauman's analysis of modernity, the consequences of the differences between our two approaches will now be expounded through a discussion of our differing treatments of ethics and ontology.

The primacy of ontology

Bauman's critique of modernity and of the ethical rules that developed with it rests upon an engagement with a central philosophical tenet, that of the primacy of ontology. Following Lévinas, Bauman suggests we should think in terms of being-for-the-other rather than being-in-the-world because he considers that it is better; not because it is more accurate or more useful, simply because it is better (Bauman, 1993: 75). This, quite clearly, is necessarily a value judgement: Being-for-the-other is less likely to provide the conditions for the kind of detachment from the other necessary for events such as the Holocaust to occur. This prioritizing of ethics, rather than ontology, is necessarily anti-empirical; we may think that being-in-the-world is a more accurate way of describing our existence but the value of an ethics of the other for enabling a more just world is compelling. What is the value of being-for-the-other over being-in-the-world, surely the latter already has a significant moral component. If we exist in the world, rather than as a disembodied, Cartesian consciousness, then we must surely take account of others and the world; as can be seen in the ecological readings of some of Heidegger's work (Holland, 1999). In Bauman's liquid modern world the contingency of truth is a given; we have realized that truth was always fluid and contextual, so there is now little value in pursuing a path to find the most accurate representation of the world as this is not possible anyway. Morality, however, is pre-social so, unlike ethics, is not a social construction that was assumed to exist objectively by the moderns.

Bauman's position is not a wholesale rejection of ontology, but a challenge to its primacy:

> It is the whole realm of ontology that is 'bracketed away'; not denied or put into question, but 'suspended' for the time we explore the sense of morality.
>
> (Bauman, 1998: 16)

Is Bauman suggesting that ontology and morality cannot be considered at the same time? Not necessarily, just that ontology has to be suspended if we want morality to be the main guiding force behind our thinking. Ontology will otherwise assert its primacy, by defining the intellectual milieu; by making issues such as being, time and space the beginning of any intellectual problem. We would accept that too much consideration for what *is* may cloud one's judgement of what *ought* to be, and *vice versa*. So, for Bauman the debate comes down to what one considers to be more important and for him it is the *ought*, or morality. Nietzsche (1974a; 1974b; 1990), and latterly Foucault (Foucault, 1989; 1991; 1998; 2002; 2006) and Deleuze (2004; 2005; and with Guattari 1984; 1988), encouraged a constant distrust for truth and moral values: they must always be questioned no matter how strongly attached to them we are. If something has attained the status of truth, it has only to be able to do this by articulating numerous technologies of power. Nietzche's distrust for morals is in fact a *hyper*-morality. One must be concerned with every single action one makes, as Foucault so beautifully stated:

> My point is not that everything is bad, but that everything is dangerous, which is not exactly the same as bad. If everything is dangerous, then we always have something to do. So my position leads not to apathy but to a hyper– and pessimistic activism.
>
> (Foucault, 1983: 231–2)

This perpetual questioning of one's actions in relation to one's life as a work of art is a maxim that Bauman builds on in his most recent book *The Art of Life* (Bauman, 2008a). Foucault's position would entail an endless ethical questioning of one's actions; would an unwavering total concern for the other, that Bauman proposes, result in the same ethical strategy? Although, Foucault's form of questioning would not necessarily be moral on Bauman's terms, if morality necessarily prioritizes the other because the moral questioning involved in Foucault's work could conceivably be individualistic. It could be suggested that Foucault's ethical position entails no immediate concern for the other, as one is only concerned with living their own life. However, if one is deeply concerned about one's own life as a work of art, they are doomed to live with the consequences of their actions for all eternity *ala* Nietzsche's (1968: 544–50; 1969: 232–8; 1974b: 273–4) eternal return; thus one would not want to live with the guilt of having mistreated someone.

Bauman claims that morality is prior to ontology, *for* is before *with*. But this does not mean that ethics is more fundamental than ontology or that it is chronologically prior, as these are ontological not moral concerns. It is ontology, which brings concerns such as chronology to bear on thought.

> The 'before' of morality is instituted not by the absence of ontology, but by its demotion and dethroning. The moral self comes into its own through its ability to rise above being, through its defiance of being.
>
> (Bauman, 1993: 72)

Ontology is not useful for answering ethical questions; questions resulting from ontological concerns will be asked but ethical problems precede them and therefore define the space in which the ontological questions are subsequently asked. The primacy of morality is difficult to conceptualize because of our indebtedness to ontology as the very foundation of all thought. But morality is, for Bauman, the chance to reject ontology, the world as it is, truth or the hierarchy imposed by ontology at the top of which it places itself. There is no ground or foundation to morality (Bauman, 1993: 73) and it is this that entices us; it is, like all things Liquid Modern, constantly shifting and ungraspable. Morality is before being in a non-ontological sense, because ontologically there is nothing before being, it is only in a moral sense that it is before being, morality is before because it is better (Bauman, 1993: 75). Morality is better because ontology cannot be good, it merely *is*:

> one cannot derive the 'ought' from the 'is'; one cannot argue values starting from the facts. Facts are neither good nor bad; true facts are neutral and must remain neutral to stay true; 'facts of the matter' do not include evaluations...Whoever starts from ontology does not embark on founding morality.
>
> (Bauman, 1993: 71)

Perhaps the most fundamental reason here for morality's superiority to ontology is its potential for the acceptance of difference. A subjective, contextual, *pre-social* approach to ethical questions, one that is not concerned with the production of universal laws, but takes the peculiarity of moral situations for granted and responds to a specific local situation rather than looking to abstract ethical laws.

We see Bauman's challenge to the primacy of ontology as analogous with Elias' (see for example Elias, 1978: 37–8, 41, 51, 60; 1987) challenge to the primacy of philosophy as a discipline, as the queen of the sciences. One of Norbert Elias' (Kilminster, 2007: 13) many important contributions to the discipline of sociology was to resuscitate a distrust and scepticism towards the primacy of the discipline of philosophy and the way that the subject has thus inadvertently and overtly framed many intellectual problems and research projects. Elias thus aims to strip away the residue of philosophical and natural science upon sociology. Concepts are thus reconstituted in an appropriately sociological idiom, and the direction of foundational research questions is reconsidered and re-established from sociological starting points. In this re-evaluation of the very nature of the discipline it is not hard to imagine the spectre of Heidegger looming behind the young Elias, as both projects appear to be concerned with a radical reconsideration of the nature of philosophy. Elias appears to go a few steps further than Heidegger and recent scholarship has shown this to be a distinct possibility (Kilminster, 2007: 19). While Bauman challenges the primacy of philosophy's principal concept, ontology, in a sense he is substituting one metaphysical concept for another. He does not overcome philosophy to the extent that Elias did because he does not reformulate philosophical questions in another form, that of the sociological. Bauman's moral questions are not sociological in the sense that Elias' work is. Bauman's (1993: 43) conception of the moral impulse is, he claims, pre-social. In his discussion of this issue Keith Tester (2004: 144–5) suggests that Bauman really means that morality is *pre-societal* rather than *pre-social*. This makes sense, as it is the 'objective' character of ethical rules that Bauman is concerned about.

This, paradoxically, could be where Bauman's strength lies. To produce a sociological theory of morality that is relatively detached from the social world in which it is produced, in Elias' terms, would require ontological engagement which would be counter to Bauman's project. He is attempting something potentially more radical than Elias' *sociological* overcoming of philosophy. While Elias rigorously created sociological concepts, he did not fundamentally challenge philosophy's master concept, ontology. Elias creates a sociological, conceptual apparatus which he hopes has very little philosophical residue but this analytical framework is built upon a philosophical foundation. This is perhaps because, unlike Bauman, he is unwilling to produce a contra-factual (Crone, 2008: 69) theory, to reject ontology. Elias is firmly rooted in a tradition that perceives sociology as a scientific discipline in the pursuit of objective truth. This is of course a particular approach to objectivism in the sense that knowledge can gain 'relative independence *vis-à-vis* specific individuals and groups, though, of course not *vis-à-vis* men altogether' (Elias, 1972: 124). Alternatively, Bauman seems willing to discard truth in favour of morality. He makes a considered decision, informed by his position that an *ought* cannot be developed out of an *is* to be more concerned with morality than ontology. He is more concerned with intensifying our concern for the other, than convincing the reader that the argument presented is true. Bauman's approach to ethics can, therefore, be seen as a more radical challenge to philosophy than Elias'. The latter attempted to overcome philosophy by demonstrating how sociology can answer philosophical questions more completely than philosophy can, but Bauman challenged the very core of philosophy, ontology. This, we see as an empowering step that gives us the space to build on Bauman's challenge and suggest that rather than suspending ontology to allow a clarity of moral consideration; perhaps we can see Bauman's ethical position as one that is resistant in a similar fashion to such Nietzschean thinkers as Foucault and Deleuze. In the following section we will begin to describe how we have formulated our concept of resistance through a synthesis of various strands of Bauman's thought.

Disobedience

Bauman is not simply a questioner but a creator of new ways of seeing social relations and offering the possibility of not-yet-existing social relations. While we feel that Tester (2004: 20) is correct to emphasize the importance of the concept of possibility in Bauman's work, we suggest that the concept of resistance, born out of a synthetic reading of various different strands of his thought, demonstrates an important link between Bauman and a *overcoming* Nietzschean tradition that positions as central the affirmation of human, all too human, possibility. Bauman's position is very much one of attempting to open up human possibility but it is equally one of resistance. This can be seen in a number of key themes in his thought and through its connection to his approach to ethics which takes a central role in his work. His concept of possibility is seen as a 'refusal to be constrained within the limits of the "is"' (Tester, 2004: 20). The *is* here refers to that which exists, as the *is* is synonymous with being and the science of being, ontology, and is only concerned with what exists in the world. Tester sees possibility as a guiding thread in Bauman's work as it is this faith that things can be different to how they are, that there are alternative ways of conceiving things and of doing things that drives his sociological imagination.

Possibility is, therefore, a resistance to accepting existing ways of understanding the limits of human action. Tester (2004: 18) emphasizes the importance of 'possibility' and Bauman uses the metaphor of the sociologist knocking down walls that would constrain human possibility. This can be interpreted as a resistance towards the limiting of possibilities. The possibilities allowed by the destruction of such limits are framed by their construction and as such direct how we see the possibilities that their destruction enables. We see in Bauman a resistance to the restrictions of human possibility typified in the administration of classifications.

We feel that Bauman, and Tester, does not emphasize how such possibility is produced through a resistance to the *is*, the production of new possibilities in the form of identities or social groups are usually enabled through a resistance to being understood in conventional terms. Bauman's position on possibility can only be understood through his belief in the primacy of ethics over ontology, already discussed in detail in this chapter. Just because something does not yet exist, it should not stop us from striving for it. While critics never tire of diagnosing Bauman as pessimistic, he seems to have an unrelenting faith that something else, something better, is always possible. Tester (2004: 39–40) has characterized Bauman as a disobedient thinker and the latter's indebtedness to the Polish sociologist Ossowski emphasizes his desire to challenge the *status quo* (Davis, 2008: 14–16). It is perhaps this tendency that draws him to the work of Georg Simmel who he admired for his fragmentary style that is difficult to systematize (Bauman, 2008b: 235). This disobedient mindset leads us to privilege the activity of resistance, as a theme in Bauman's writing.

Like Nietzsche, Bauman's (1976) characterization of socialism as an *active utopia*, also highlights his antipathy towards systematizing as it is here that he proposes that socialism is unrealizable on a state level and can, and should, only be used as a critical tool for challenging state governance. Born out of a desire for justice, socialism for Bauman is resistance to social engineering born out of a desire for justice. What we identify in these strands of Bauman's thought is an encouragement to resist conventional thinking and more controversially by not allowing one's thinking to be limited by what already exists. In the following section we will demonstrate how these themes are present in Bauman's treatment of the concept of *difference* and how these, in conjunction with a consideration of the primacy of resistance that can be found in the work of Foucault and Deleuze, and specifically Judith Revel's reading of them, can help us to reformulate our understanding of Bauman as a resistant thinker.

Difference

One of Bauman's most important contributions to ethical, and sociological thought, is that 'We are not bound to each other by similarity, but by difference, and in contingency' (Beilharz, 2000: 125). The violent eradication of difference in the holocaust and it's seemingly banal equivalent in the rationalities which guided many bureaucratic institutions led Bauman to a distrust of similarity as a basis for solidarity. Attempts to find a common base for human being in which to build solidarity will inevitably be exclusive. Difference is always present and primary. Similarity is but the repetition of difference; 'Repetition [...] consists in conceiving the same on the basis of the different' (Deleuze, 2004: 51). Power positions itself as primary, as does ontology yet 'power is action over action: thus it always comes second – logically, ontologically and chronologically' (Revel, 2008: 37). We, like Revel, see difference and resistance as synonymous, and consider these to be prior to ethics and fall under the auspice of ontology. It is through a reading of power that we can see this.

> The transitivity of power is the necessity for it to apply itself to something that is, from the beginning, heterogeneous. In this sense, power nourishes itself on its other, upon which it is dependent.
>
> (Revel, 2008: 38)

Power can only reproduce, it cannot invent. It is, therefore, secondary to difference. Power requires difference in order for it to have something to act upon; power cannot create but only reproduce. The production of a classification is an act of resistance by producing something new and resisting existing knowledge but the reproduction of the classification is purely an articulation of power. The use of medical classifications to order populations and to normalize people are examples of relations of power being invoked in the service of government. Foucault demonstrates in detail the ways in which power works through classificatory systems to act on populations and to normalize (Foucault, 1998; 2002; 2003; 2004; 2006; 2007). Rationalities of government articulate relations of power to reproduce that which was initially produced by resistance. Through the deployment of these relations of power the values that guide the rationality of government may be reproduced upon bodies.

Medical classifications, such as *homosexuality*, may have initially been constituted to restrict and manage homosexual acts, but in fact were used by homosexual women and men to a form a site of resistance routed in identity politics (Hansen, 1992). When such classifications are used in order to divide, segment and organize a population into categories such as normal and abnormal, there is an articulation of power; these attempts to conduct the conduct of others should be considered to be dangerous. Of course the art of classification is a dangerous one, with the activities of segmenting and organizing the population and changing how populations viewed themselves and are viewed by those concerned with conducting conduct. This danger appears to us to be exacerbated when the activity of classifying, is guided by a rationality where normality is seen to be good and desirable, and abnormality to be negative and undesirable. The activity of classifying thus engraves a moral worth onto body.

We, like Revel, consider resistance as ontology. Being is resistance, and resistance is everywhere. Resistance is prior to power and to domination. Resistance produces the difference that Bauman discusses and the constant proliferation of classifications that Foucault's researches have so often documented, are one of these forms of resistance. The invention of new ideas, new ways of being and new concepts should be understood as resistance, as the invention of a new idea requires resistance against the intellectual status quo. Resistance here should be read as almost analogous to Deleuze's conception of difference and creation in *Difference and Repetition* (2004). Almost analogous as unlike Deleuze's conception of being/difference/creation, which has recently been criticized by Peter Hallward (2006: 164) for leaving little hope for political action, beyond the creation of new ideas; resistance, however, implies a struggle against dominant power, not just creation for creation's sake as Hallward's treatment of Deleuze suggests, but creation to invoke social change. Resistance against injustice. To resist injustice is to be ethical. Ethics derives from resistance, and as we have learnt from Revel, resistance is ontologically and chronologically primary. We wish to turn to the difference between ontology and ethics: the resistance between ontology and ethics rather than prioritizing one or having one 'dethrone' the other. This is because both ontology and ethics are processual rather than static and the relationship between them, and the boundaries between them, should be seen as liquid, always moving and difficult to contain. The relationship between ontology and ethics is one of resistance.

Bauman wants to prioritize ethics, because it is 'better'; but how can we judge where ontology ends and ethics begins. For Deleuze (2004) what ontology describes is a continuous process of differentiation of the universal substance of being to which everything is reducible. Deleuze's position is ontological but can it also encompass ethics in its similarities to Bauman's seeing difference as fundamental? Similarly, for Heidegger, ontology and difference are the same thing; questioning and scepticism are already present in the being ontology tries to describe; 'questioning is the piety of thought' (Heidegger, 1977: 35). Deleuze describes Heidegger's ontology: 'We regard as fundamental this "correspondence" between difference and questioning, between ontological difference and the being in question' (Deleuze, 2004: 79). And, similarly to Deleuze, Bauman sees difference as primordial:

> [E]verywhere where humans live, the perpetual rebirth and reincarnation of the world is what all and any human mode of being-in-the-world consists of.
>
> (Bauman, 2004: 11)

Creation in Bauman's thought is resistance to the tyranny of the actual, something as yet unknown, and something better is always *possible*. Ethics is resistance to injustice, and if resistance is ontologically and chronologically primary, then in a sense ethics, as a component of resistance, is primary. We affirm the difference between ethics and ontology. The difference between the two is what is irreconcilable between ontology and ethics: the irreconcilable space.

The consequences of Deleuze's ontology for politics are that political action should be the creation of new possibilities for thought. For us, this seems unfortunately like the ideology of capitalism in our liquid modern times, as endlessly creating new possibilities and new ways of living appears to be somewhat similar to the rationale of producing new commodities to be consumed. As a juxtaposition to this, the possibilities for resistance as ontology have been summed up by Foucault; there is always something to do and we are thus left in a state of hyper and pessimistic activism (1983: 231–32) as there will always be injustice in the world. Furthermore, even in contexts were there does not seem to be injustice, we should still question and resist. As Nietzsche (1990) and those who have followed him (for example Deleuze, 2005: 55) have shown, facts often turn out to be values and moral judgements are revealed in places previously considered to be objective. There will always be the injustice we have yet to realize is unjust.

Conclusion

This chapter has proposed that the rationality that guides processes of classification, be they bureaucratic, medical or scientific is informed by an assumption of similarity. This in turn has been equated with moral, political and aesthetic goodness. Difference, has been imbued with negative associations of abnormality, outsiderness and in some cases immorality. The activity of classifying is typically guided by these moral assumptions, and this exacerbates the danger present in the aforementioned actions. The danger here is that bodies are engraved with moral values, which are naturalized and left unquestioned. We explored Bauman's dethroning of ontology and exploration of the primacy of ethics as a potential strategy for affirming difference over similarity. However we were left unconvinced, by what we saw as the unsociological implications of his position. By reading the developments in his ethical thinking and through a consideration of medicine and medical classification we highlight some of our concerns with it. Through its collision with modern ethics, the neutral process of classification had dangerous consequences as an effective method of normalizing populations. It is a fear of the eradication of difference that led Bauman to reject the primacy of ontology and to propose a radically different approach to moral issues, one that starts from moral concerns rather than deriving them from ontological observations. Bauman optimistically suggested that there was a possibility for moral engagement away from disciplinary rules that were now possible in a postmodern world less enamoured with universal laws. This early optimism would later be rejected in favour of a turn towards a form of legislation that will encourage justice. This move towards legislation brings out our concerns with Bauman's conception of ethics which seems to have utopian undertones. His critique of ontology, which lies at the centre of his ethical theory, however, excites us and we take tentative steps towards our own position. That is to say, while in disagreement on the value of prioritizing ethics, we share similar attitudes towards the importance of justice and the contingency of truth.

We have proposed a position which draws heavily upon the ontology of Deleuze (ontology is the creation of difference) and Revel's reading of Foucault's ontology (resistance is ontology). We, like Revel, assert that resistance is ontology; we affirm that difference is resistance, but resistance is not necessarily difference. Resistance is prior to power, and difference is prior to similarity. We, like Revel, prefer difference to similarity, but for ontological rather than ethical reasons. The ontological primacy of resistance means that resistance against injustice is ontologically fundamental. In Bauman's hands, disobedience and ethics are exemplars of resistance. Ethics is encompassed within our conception of resistance as ontology. We are thus following Bauman's call at the end of *Modernity and the Holocaust* to revaluate the rationality that guides sociology, but in our opinion we, unlike Bauman, do this by developing a sociological ontology rather than take recourse to the primacy of philosophical ethics – where the moral party of the two appears to be strangely outside of history, outside of society and outside of power relations.

References

Bauman, Z. (1976), *Socialism: The Active Utopia*. London, Allen & Unwin.

Bauman, Z. (1989), *Modernity and the Holocaust*. Cambridge, Polity.

Bauman, Z. (1991), *Modernity and Ambivalence*. Cambridge, Polity.

Bauman, Z. (1993), *Postmodern Ethics*. Oxford, Blackwell.

Bauman, Z. (1995), *Life in Fragments: Essays in Postmodern Morality*. Oxford, Blackwell.

Bauman, Z. (1998), 'What Prospects of Morality in Times of Uncertainty?' *Theory, Culture and Society*, 15 (1): 11–22.

Bauman, Z. (2000), *Liquid Modernity*. Cambridge, Polity.

Bauman, Z. (2004), *Europe: An Unfinished Adventure*. Cambridge, Polity.

Bauman, Z. (2007), *Consuming Life*. Cambridge, Polity.

Bauman, Z. (2008a), *The Art of Life*. Cambridge, Polity.

Bauman, Z. (2008b), Bauman on Bauman – Pro Domo Sua. *The Sociology of Zygmunt Bauman: Challenges and Critique*. M. H. Jacobsen and P. Poder. Aldershot, Ashgate, 231–40.

Beilharz, P. (2000), *Zygmunt Bauman: Dialectic of Modernity*. London, Sage.

Crone, M. (2008), Bauman on Ethics – Intimate Ethics for a Global World. *The Sociology of Zygmunt Bauman: Challenges and Critique*. M. H. Jacobsen and P. Poder. Aldershot, Ashgate, 231–40.

Davis, L. (1995), *Enforcing Normalcy: Disability, Deafness and the Body*. London, Verso.

Davis, M. (2008), *Freedom and Consumerism: A Critique of Zygmunt's Bauman's Sociology* Aldershot, Ashgate.

Deleuze, G. (2004), *Difference and Repetition*. London, Continuum.

Deleuze, G. (2005), *Nietzsche and Philosophy*. London, Continuum.

Deleuze, G and F. Guattari (1984), *Anti-Oedipus: Capitalism and Schizophrenia*. London, Athlone Press.

Deleuze, G and F. Guattari (1988), *A Thousand Plateaus: Capitalism and Schizophrenia*. London, Athlone.

Elias, N. (1972), 'Theory of Science and History of Science: Comments on a recent discussion'. *Economy and Society*, 1 (2): 117–33.

Elias, N. (1978), *What is Sociology?* New York, Columbia University Press.

Elias, N. (1987), *Involvement and Detachment*. Oxford, Blackwell.

Foucault, M. (1983), 'On the Genealogy of Ethics: An Overview of Work in Progress'. *Michel Foucault: Beyond Structuralism and Hermeneutics*: H. L. Dreyfus and P. Rabinow. The University of Chicago Press, 229–52.

Foucault, M. (1989), *The Birth of the Clinic. An Archaeology of Medical Perception*. London, Routledge.

Foucault, M. (1991), *Discipline and Punish: The Birth of the Prison*. London, Penguin.

Foucault, M. (1998), *The Will to Knowledge: The History of Sexuality Volume 1*. London, Penguin.

Foucault, M. (2002), *The Order of Things: An Archaeology of the Human Sciences*. London, Routledge.

Foucault, M. (2003), *Abnormal: Lectures at the Collège de France, 1974–1975*. London, Penguin.
Foucault, M. (2004), *Society Must be Defended: Lectures at the Collège de France 1975–76*. London, Penguin.
Foucault, M. (2006), *History of Madness*. London, Routledge.
Foucault, M. (2007), *Security, Territory, Population: Lectures at the Collège de France 1978–1979*. Basingstoke, Palgrave Macmillan.
Hacking, I. (1990), *The Taming of Chance*. Cambridge, Cambridge University Press.
Hallward, P. (2006), *Out of this World: Deleuze and the Philosophy of Creation*. London, Verso.
Halmi, K. A. (1983), 'Classification of Eating Disorders', *International Journal of Eating Disorders*, 2 (4): 21–6.
Hansen, B. (1992), 'American Physicians' "Discovery" of Homosexuals, 1880–1900: A new Diagnosis in a Changing Society'. *Framing Disease: Studies in Cultural History. C. E. Rosenberg and J. Golden*. New Jersey, Rutgers University Press, 104–33.
Heidegger, M. (1977), *The Question Concerning Technology. The Question Concerning Technology and Other Essays*. M. Heidegger. London, Harper and Row, 13–35.
Holland, N. J. (1999), 'Rethinking Ecology in the Western Philosophical Tradition: Heidegger and/on Aristotle'. *Continental Philosophy Review*, 32 (4): 409–20.
Hughes, B. (2002), 'Bauman's Strangers: Impairment and the Invalidation of Disabled People in Modern and Post–Modern Cultures'. *Disability and Society*, 17 (5): 571–84.
Kilminster, R. (2007), *Norbert Elias: Post-Philosophical Sociology*. London, Routledge.
Lévinas, E. (1998), *Entre Nous*. London, Continuum.
Nietzsche, F. (1968), *The Will To Power*. Vintage, New York.
Nietzsche, F. (1969), *Thus Spoke Zarathustra: A Book for Everyone and No One*. Harmondsworth, Penguin.
Nietzsche, F. (1974a), *Beyond Good and Evil. A Prelude to a Philosophy of the Future*. Penguin, Harmondsworth.
Nietzsche, F. (1974b), *The Gay Science: With a Prelude in Rhymes and an Appendix of Songs*. New York, Vintage books.
Nietzsche, F. (1990), *The Genealogy of Morals: An Attack*. London, Anchor Books Doubleday.
Nietzsche, F. (1998), *Twilight of the Idols or How to Philosophize with a Hammer*. Oxford, Oxford University Press.
Revel, J. (2008), 'The Materiality of the Immaterial: Foucault, against the Return of Idealisms and New Vitalisms'. *Radical Philosophy*, 149: 33–8.
Tester, K. (2004), *The Social Thought of Zygmunt Bauman*. Palgrave Macmillan, Basingstoke.

10
What's in the Post?

John O'Neill

We shall not gain much from starting with definitions of postmodernism as either a period or counter concept – it is too late for such starts. Any essay on postmodernity remains a satellite of modernity which is itself a comet envisioned at a distance from the medieval world and the ancient cosmos. So, I shall begin by pinning up the following:

Theses on Postmodernism

(1) No attempt to *epater la bourgeoisie* can satisfy its capacity for shock, violence and deception.
(2) Novelty is the new conformity, yet.
(3) The return to history is rather an escape from history.
(4) The norms of subjectivity and pleasure are conscriptions of repressive jouissance; at the same time as …
(5) The open history of fashion and style is the end of all histories mirrored in our own.
(6) Fashion rewrites the body, assigns its moods, movements, and manageability in order to distract us from the corpse of politics.

(O'Neill, 1995: 15)

The exaggeration in such rhetorical devices is due to their loss of narrative strength in cultural criticism when disembedded from tradition or translation between the discursive and practical economies of the life-world's arts and sciences. Let us therefore explore our modernity as our embrace of corrigible knowledge driven by the desire to lean only upon ourselves in matters of politics, morals and science. Having placed nature in our mind, so to speak, we are determined to bring it within the moral history of our self-civilizing institutions. By the same token, we believe we have removed ourselves from nature's law of survival through sacrificial excess, seismic catastrophe and wholesale obsolescence which have ruled planetary and pre-historic time. We aspire to set ourselves a smaller watch within a more self-loving creation. We have ritualized our births and deaths and moralized our murders, thefts and gifts. We have declared ourselves a thinking and moral universe and taken upon our divided conscience its commitments towards good and evil, truth and falsity. We have set humanity the task of becoming human. We have set civilized history the larger task of leaving no one outside of this utopian project (O'Neill, 2004). Yet we may have driven out the idols of the marketplace in favour of a market of ideas whose own idol is the market itself. In short, we have recommitted our faith to the impersonal laws of economy both in God's house and our own. In exchange we have imposed upon ourselves a severe pedagogy of falsifiability in matters of science and of failure in matters of economy. These are the twin pillars of our morality. They define the spirit both of our protestantism and our capitalism. These in turn have shaped our left and right parliamentarianism that sustains the covenants and contests through which we understand ourselves.

We may speak in two ways about the ruling ideas of a modern society. We may regard them as rules that we discover to operate upon us like the laws of nature whose observance enables our practices while limiting our phantasies. Or else, we may find in the laws of nature and history a permanent struggle between the pleasure principle and the reality principle, between metaphysical scarcity and phantastic abundance. In either case, our cultural narrative supports us in the belief that the way things are and the way we desire them to be are not entirely divorced. Bauman's perspective upon this cultural project is haunted by its defeats, its self-appointed disappointments and its fall into the homogenous time of journalism ruled by the uniformity of events in 'now time' (*jetzeit*) that collapse the story they claim to unfold (Elliott, 2007). Everyday experience is ruled by *metonymy*, that is, by accidental and random associations rather than by *synecdoche*, or necessary and essential relations. The paradox of the inarticulateness of the age of communication derives from the materiality and facticity of its representation of a world whose sense is suspended between meaningfulness and non-sense. Communicative chatter never embarks upon any narrative quest because its maps are no longer marked with places of hidden treasure. Put another way, modernity has unleashed appearances from essences, just as industrialism sank feudal corporate relations in the exchange values of a global market. Of course, metaphysical scarcity continued to rule the material realm of production and the labouring body. But industrialism also unleashed a realm of cornucopian consumption and a body of limitless desire. Hence, modernity has wavered between surrendering its idealism to its materialism and refurbishing its rational/ethical ideals to constrain its materialism in the name of social justice. But these alternatives no longer appear to be of equal strength, or as necessary elements contributing to the vitality of a larger collective history. The two orders of idealism and materialism, or of economy and politics, when viewed in terms of their incredible death toll, appear to have stalled Benjamin's angel of modernity, (Jacobsen, 2003).

The extraordinary accumulation of Bauman's work demands that one confront the central thesis which haunts it – namely, that *postmodernity is modernity without illusions* (Elliott, 2007: 8). The spectre raised from the grave is whether cultural criticism can responsibly escape the history of its own histories of our becoming human. However, rather than play upon the contradictions in a science of utopia or even a utopian science, I want to explore what is *normative* in the future of a human future. This question is what motivates Husserl's reflections on the crisis of European rationality:

> We have also become aware in the most general way ... that human philosophizing and its results in the whole of man's existence means anything but merely private or otherwise limited cultural goals. In *our* philosophizing, then – how can we avoid it? – we are *functionaries of mankind*. The quite personal responsibility of our own true being as philosophers, our inner personal vocation, bears within itself at the same time the responsibility for the true being of mankind; the latter is, necessarily, being toward a *telos* and can only come to realization, *if at all*, through philosophy – through *us, if* we are philosophers in all seriousness. Is there, in this existential 'if', a way out? If not, what should we, who *believe*, do in order to *be able* to believe? We cannot seriously continue our previous philosophizing; it lets us hope only for philosophies, never for philosophy.
>
> (Husserl, 1970: 17, my emphasis)

I propose, then, to elicit the prayer (*pro nobis*) with which Husserl underwrites the *telos* of civilized thought as I find it in the millennial poetics of Vico (1970), Joyce (1968) and Calvino (1988) who will not suffer any loss of hope or exhaustion in reason's utopian reach. We are coming to our topic. Our topic is desire. But we are not yet there. We are approaching desire through an extraordinarily roundabout route.

This detour is meant to bring us back to *our desire for a theory of desire*. The truth of desire may be *utopian*. Yet we seem to be caught in a regression. That is to say, it may take a long time to discover our desire, truth, justice and love. Of course, there are voices to seduce us with the claim that we never need an origin of desire. We are told that desire is recognized in the instant or through the very insistence of its objects. Yet against this view of the evanescence of desire, a story can be told of desire's endless resistance.

The confusion of tongues at work in cultural criticism may well be an effect of the failure of both its legislative and interpretative functions. In the aftermath of (post)modernity, intellectuals and ideologists now scramble over one another to claim their self-sorted portion of truth and justice. By now, the tropes of 'posting' modernism threaten to exhaust critics determined to maintain their own speed, lightness and liquidity – even the dogged Bauman himself!

> There are many signs that the traditional role (performed or aspired), portrayed by the metaphor of 'legislators', is being gradually replaced by the role best captured by the metaphor of 'interpreters'. Is this, however, an irrevocable transformation, or a momentary loss of nerve?
>
> (Bauman, 1987: 125)

Bauman's question wounds intellectual pride as much as it dissipates its moral ambition and governance. It betrays a figure wracked/wrecked by his own embrace of the law of the loss of law which results in an endless flood of interpretation. To resist the metastasis of meaning's loss of meaning, only the 'theorist' still seeks health by running ever faster. Forwards, or backward? That is the question:

> How can one argue the case for or against a form of life, for or against a version of truth, when one feels that one's argument cannot any more legislate, that there are powers behind the plural forms of life and plural versions of truth which would not be made inferior, and hence would not surrender to the argument of their inferiority?
>
> (Bauman 1987: 141)

As I see it, the postmodern death of high culture – its self-abnegation, its swooning before the lights and liquidity of communicative excess, its delirious ride upon the waves of superficiality in fashion and the arts – represents the latest *trahison des clercs*. Of course, one might regard postculturalism as a move to redistribute cultural capital – except that it is university culture and an elite discourse within an already elite institution. Thus its effects are authoritarian since its strategy of 'forgetting' the canon means that students can achieve no orientation except from criticism, style or top of the pops pronouncements. The need to be in fashion is driven by the terror of being out of fashion; hence the cultural groupies, concerts, conferences that are the ersatz equivalents of churches, party meetings and sporting venues. The spectacle and the talk, the pratfall, fill the void of authority. What has 'posted' modernity is the market. It sells autonomy, rationality, choice and sovereignty. 'Late' capitalism is our mirror-image. In it we exchange democracy for the demotic supplements of the same – with a remainder for the inassimilable waste on our streets, in our prisons, camps and cyberspace. Yet, how are 'we' to pronounce such laws without imprisoning ourselves, albeit in the thinker's comfortable cell? And what is left of cultural theory once it rides the dizzy metaphors of capitalist time-space, liquidity and speed? Here speculation becomes doubly spectacular. We have gambled against ourselves while constructing glass towers to reflect everything we have lost – a corporate Babel where language holds to no centre. Reflecting our reduced polytheism, the glass corporation miniaturizes us with its welcome, its disposability, its accommodation of our wants generated on its behalf.

I think it is necessary, therefore, to pull back from Bauman's conclusion to resist, if only for a moment, its seductive signature – its fall into its own 'signage'. Let us ask instead, what would enable us to project the cultural survival of the social sciences as a necessary part of ourselves? May we not conceive of literature and poetry as evidence of our ability to survive the histories in which we overwhelm ourselves? Like Vico, Joyce and Italo Calvino, in his *Six Memos For the Next Millennium* (1988), let us regard 'ourstory' as evidence of our struggle against destruction and despair, as a light seen from the future towards a past which becomes our present/future? Our guarantee that we are not the aliens of the universe is that it is a universe of communicative bodies destined for poetry, science and literature (O'Neill, 1989). Metaphysics is therefore not a study of nature but of the history of human imagination. Poetry precedes ontology: it inaugurates a theatre of the senses, passions and thought, to catch the flux of experience in the throw of language: 'Signatures of all things I am here to read, seaspawn and seawrack, the nearing tide, that busty boot' (Joyce, 1968: 57) The power of literature lies in its ability to *save time*, that is, to redeem our singular experience, catching it in the unbearable lightness of the word. Narrativity exemplifies the relativity of real time and story-time;

it praises the mind's temporality, or its *quickness*, as Calvino (1988) prefers it. *Agility* and *brevity* are also essential to our humanity if we are to pull out of the flux of events an eternally necessary moment of experience. Thus our stories are a vital response to our awesome origins; they are a self-shaping recollective practice that binds nature to culture:

> Were I to choose an auspicious image for the new millennium, I would choose that one: the sudden agile leap of the poet–philosopher who raised himself above the weight of the world, showing that with all his *gravity* he has the secret of *lightness*, and that what many consider to be the vitality of the time–noisy, aggressive, revving and roaring–belongs to the realm of death, like a cemetery for old cars.
>
> (Calvino, 1988: 12, my emphasis)

Social scientists are fascinated with futurology because it empowers the sociological word. Now Calvino assigns a millennial power to the values in the word (s) – Lightness (*Leggerezza*), Quickness (*Rapidita*), Exactitude (*Esattezza*), Visibility (*Visibilita*) and Multiplicity (*Molteplicita*). These words represent a constellation of literary, scientific and anthropological values which shift into another without hierarchy or erasure. Like hunting, art and science proceed from traces quickly patterned and re-patterned for individual and collective survival. Thus the fable, nature and the city represent different levels of structure and history, of invariance and agitation, whose moral value we must preserve in the arts of the next century. Commercial communication, however, does not favour the values of exactitude, clarity of image or precision of thought. This is because it confounds variety and uncertainty with immensity and infinity. There is little that is pleasant in the modern pursuit of pleasure and sensation because they are unsheltered from anxiety and horror. Thus contemporary science and folk fiction colonize our galactic imagination with keloids and cyborgs that are the metamorphs of a political technology of global alienation. Such fiction does not extend our moral imagination. We are now unable to assign the mythic force of cosmogony either to science or fiction because we have confounded the universe with cultural globalization. In the process we have undermined our communicative need for a cosmological model or a mythological framework in which the forces of chaos and order are not opposed but held together in a crystalline structure of internal agitation and external invariance, of root and arborescence.

Our everyday encounters lack the time to take their time, to look and to be looked upon; we are the traffic in which we cannot bear to slow down along the highways we have built to bypass the invisible cities of the imagination and the lake waters of another soul. Yet when Mr. Palomar does decide to take his time, to return the world's gaze – he dies ... *memento mori!* What civilizes us is our capacity for structure, measure, memorable imagery and narrativity. What endangers us is a commercial culture which degrades language, image and vitality because its prefabricated images weaken our capacity for evoking absent things, of writing upon the shifting sands and half-lit seabed. The atomic swerve (*clinamen*), the cell, the mollusk shell, the exterior signs of interior life, all pull the cosmos towards humanity, communication and the two adventures of knowledge and love. The burden of our arts and sciences is to lift the weight of sorrow, to lighten suffering and to sustain the mind's capacity for complexity, polyphony and metamorphosis. Our collective story is one of resistance, of hope and of endurance. Thus our arts and sciences civilize the word. They displace the barbarism of intellect without compassion and they affirm the millennial chorus of humanity. The cosmicomical dance and seaspawn song of the self-lit signs woven from anxiety and art are Calvino's message to and from all things barely born and yet to be born in the crevice of time. In the historical struggle for justice, Calvino sides with Ovid's metamorphism which like Marx's choice of the Epicurean swerve (*clinamen*) over Democritean atomism which shifts the fixed world into a world conformable to passion. Thus the poet/philosopher/scientist knows two things: the *weight* of things/ their *lightness* and the soul's *gravity*/its *subtlety*. The two economies of *lightness and gravity* work off one another, connecting macrocosm and microcosm, welding melancholy and humour.

In the same vein, Fredric Jameson (1981) has argued that every genre of thought (myth, literature, science) has to be grasped as a psycho-historical master-narrative (*the political unconscious*) which properly interpreted is Marxism. Here Jameson's particular strength lies in his will to carry the burden of dialectical switching between the secularization and re-enchantment of the life-world and its modern vocation, while seeking to avoid Weberian pessimism as well as Nietzschean cynicism. He does so, fully conscious that the age of religion has passed, tempting us to embrace an 'aestheticized' religion, an imaginary or hallucinated community in an age that is neither religious nor social. How, then can Marxism exempt itself from such sentimentalism? The answer is that Marxism and religion may be embraced as necessary elements in a *marital square* in which history and collectivity join individual and community action and understanding against passivity and ignorance that dispossess the community and exploit it in favour of its masters:

> Only Marxism can give us an adequate account of the essential mystery of the cultural past, which, like Tiresias drinking the blood, is momentarily returned to life and warmth and allowed once more to speak, and to deliver its long forgotten message in surroundings utterly alien to it. This mystery can be re-enacted only if the human adventure is one; only thus – and not through … antiquarianism or the projections of the modernists – can we glimpse the vital claims upon us of such long-dead issues as the seasonal alternation of the economy of a primitive tribe, the passionate disputes about the nature of the trinity … only if they are retold within the unity of a single great collective story … Marxism, the collective struggle to arrest a realm of Freedom from a realm of Necessity … it is in detecting traces of the uninterrupted narrative, in restoring to the surface of the text the repressed and buried reality of this fundamental history, that the doctrine of a political unconscious finds its function and its necessity.
>
> (Jameson, 1981: 19–20)

The stages along the way, so to speak, require that nature never falls outside of the romance in which it responds to our desires in figures of good and evil, of wildness and civilization through which we in turn educate our imagination, as Northrop Frye would say. In the same vein, Vico and Marx insisted upon the archaeological continuity between past and present hermeneutics in recognition of the social debt which capitalism represses (as the basis of its political unconscious) but which socialism recognizes as its humanist *point d'honneur.* From this standpoint, the Marxist critique of reification and fragmentation is not simply an exercise in dialectical epistemology. It represents an ethical rejection of every possessive appropriation of values and relationships that breaks off, interrupts and represses the recognition of exchange, intergenerationality and collective debt. Here what is difficult is to weigh the practices of equality that reduce civic exclusion with the respect for what in each of us is a remainder of character and circumstance that tests our fellow love in our indifference to difference, expressed through social policies (health, housing, education, employment) legislated on behalf of the 'least advantaged' among us (Rawls, 1971; O'Neill, 2004) rather than in those random acts of love or beauty called for on bumper stickers.

Yet the problem of historical agency remains the agonizing issue at the heart of Bauman's lifelong work. He asks himself for whom and why does he continue to write? How are the two sides of left writing and reading connected? Is his considerable stream of work, he wonders, simply an act of desperation or of unbroken hope ... is it akin to Adorno's 'message in a bottle'?

> [In Adorno] ... the message in a bottle is a testimony to the transience of frustration and the duration of hope, to the indestructibility of possibilities and the frailty of adversities that bar them from implementation...
>
> Perhaps I scribble messages destined for a bottle. Bottle messages have no preselected addressees (if they had, there would be no need of consigning them to the waves), but I trust the messages to seek and find, after the pattern of 'smart missiles', their targets: to select, among the individual sailors whom our liquid-modern society has burdened with the task of seeking and finding solutions to the problems with which it confronts them, such sailors who might be eager to open the bottles and absorb the messages inside them.
>
> (Jacobsen and Tester, 2007: 310–12).

While one may admire such stoic conceit, one must nevertheless resist its unbearable self-enclosure and paradoxical call upon its readers to begin where everything ends. I believe that Bauman's bottle has no addressee – anymore than television or the news media which cannot think for itself (O'Neill, 2002) but to which he claims to have shifted for company. Perhaps here I might enter a friendly caution.

TV health warning

(1) There is never anything on TV – if there were, the system would break down;
(2) Since all of life is on TV, you can expect to have already seen it;
(3) TV is part of the family – it babysits its mind;
(4) TV is not free – you must donate your time to it;
(5) No one knows whether TV is real.

(O'Neill, 2002: 183).

Critical thought cannot be separated from a better place – far less likened to a 'message in a bottle' which is more the story of thought's hope in Theophrastus' experimental oceanography rather than a desperate toss in the sea. Our two knowledges of the world and of the soul can never be entirely separated. Nor can they ever be reduced to a note tossed into the sea once sang by Homer nor Joyce's river babble. In any case, what must not be forsaken as the frame of all civilized life is its intergenerational narrative of life and death in which no one is ever born or dies 'once' because our births and deaths are never lost in the story of humanity that serves against all excommunication. So it is with what I have called *wild sociology* (O'Neill, 1975) whose birth in Durkheim and Weber owes as much to prayer – society is God, society is spirit – as to the method of its fathers. In this, sociology is tied to singing itself as much as the world it furnishes. We are ourselves and our circumstances: this is the natural light of wild sociology which embraces the convergence of science and poetry. The panorama of our beliefs, needs and values is not given to unsituated perspectives because it is through and through circumstantial, embraced in ancestral patterns of need, friends and family, instrument and advice. So, too, our moods, our resignation, our hopes and brooding memories are the substance of metaphor and relevance, as well as plain talk, vice and unfulfilled virtue forged from the conversable uses and sufficiencies of our daily living: in lifting, folding, sowing and cutting; in hauling, shipping, mining, weaving and baking; in reading, writing, praying and singing; in burying, marrying, mothering; and learning in fields, factories, schools and churches that circle our being, our joys and sorrows – all in their endless epiphany:

> Many things then come out in the repeating that make a history of each one for any one who always listens to them. Many things come out of each one and as one listens to them listens to all the repeating in them, always this comes to be clear about them, the history of them of the bottom nature in them, the nature or natures mixed up in them to make the whole of them anyway it mixes up in them. Sometime then there will be a history of every one.
>
> When you come to feel the whole of anyone from the beginning to the ending, all the kind of repeating there is in them, the different ways at different times repeating comes out of them, all the kinds of things and mixtures in each one, anyone can see then by looking hard at any one living near them that a history of every one must be a long one. A history of any one must be a long one, slowly it comes out from them from their beginning to their ending, slowly you can see it in them the nature and the mixtures in them, slowly everything comes out from each one in the kind of repeating each one does in the different parts and kinds of living they have in them,

slowly then the history of them comes out from them, slowly then any one who looks well at any one will have the history of the whole of that one. Slowly the history of each one comes out of each one. Sometime then there will be a history of everyone. Mostly every history will be a long one. Slowly it comes out of each one, slowly any one who looks at them gets the history of each part of the living of any one in the history of the whole of each one that sometime there will be of every one.

(Stein, 1934: 128)

References

Bauman, Z. (1987), *Legislators and Interpreters*. Cambridge: Polity Press.

Calvino, I. (1988), *Six Memos For The Next Millennium*. Translated by Patrick Creagh. Cambridge: Harvard University Press.

Elliott, A. (ed.) (2007), *The Contemporary Bauman*. New York: Routledge.

Husserl, E. (1970), *Crisis of European Sciences and Transcendental Phenomenology*. Evanston: Northwest University Press.

Jacobsen, M. H. and Keith T. (2007), 'Sociology, Nostalgia, Utopia and Morality: A Conversation with Zygmunt Bauman'. *European Journal of Social Theory*, 10 (2): 305–25.

Jacobsen, E. (2003), *Metaphysics of the Profane: the Political Theology of Walter Benjamin and Gershom Scholem*. New York: Columbia University Press.

Jameson, F. (1981), *The Political Unconscious: Narrative as a Socially Symbolic Act*. Ithaca: Cornell University Press.

Joyce, J. (1968), *Ulysses*. Harmondsworth: Penguin.

O'Neill, J. (1975), *Making Sense Together: An Introduction to Wild Sociology*. London: Heinemann Educational Books Limited.

——— (1989), *The Communicative Body: Studies in Communicative Philosophy, Politics and Sociology*. Evanston: Northwestern University Press.

——— (1995), *The Poverty of Postmodernism*. London and New York: Routledge.

——— (2002), *Plato's Cave: Television and its Discontents*. Cresskill, NJ: Hampton Press, Inc.

——— (2004), *Civic Capitalism: The State Of Childhood*. Toronto: University Of Toronto Press.

Rawls, J. (1971), *A Theory of Justice*. Cambridge, Massachusetts: The Belknap Press of Harvard University Press.

Stein, G. (1934), *The Making of Americans*. New York: Harcourt, Brace and Co.

Vico, G. (1970), *The New Science of Giambattista Vico*. Trans. G. Bergin and Max H. Fisch. Ithaca, NY. Cornell University Press.

Conclusion: The Triple Challenge

Zygmunt Bauman

Like the Holy Trinity known from the Scriptures, the challenge which humanity is currently facing and which, once complemented by the responses it may eventually evoke or fail to evoke, is bound to shape the future of the planet, is triple yet *triune* ('three in one', or 'both three and one at the same time'). It is made of three parts: interregnum, uncertainty and institutional disparity; yet each part conditions the other two, while being inseparable from them.

Interregnum

Sometime in the late 20s or early 30s of the last century, Antonio Gramsci recorded in one of the many notebooks he filled during his long incarceration in the Turin prison:[1] 'The crisis consists precisely in the fact that the old is dying and the new cannot be born; in this interregnum a great variety of morbid symptoms appear.'

The term 'interregnum' was originally used to denote a time-gap separating the death of one royal sovereign from the enthronement of the successor: these used to be the main occasions on which the past generations experienced (and customarily expected) a rupture in the otherwise monotonous continuity of government, law and social order. Roman law put an official stamp on such understanding of the term (and its referent) when accompanying *interregnum* with proclamation of *justitium*, that is (as Giorgio Agamben reminded us in his 2003 study of the *Lo stato di eccezione*) an admittedly temporary suspension of laws heretofore binding (presumably in anticipation of new and different laws being possibly proclaimed). Gramsci however infused the concept of 'interregnum' with a new meaning, embracing wider spectrum of the socio–political–legal order, while simultaneously reaching deeper into the sociocultural condition. Or rather (taking a leaf from Lenin's memorable definition of the 'revolutionary situation' as a condition in which the rulers no longer *can* rule while the ruled no longer *wish* to be ruled), Gramsci detached the idea of 'interregnum' from its habitual association with the interlude of (routine) transmission of hereditary or electable power, and attached to the extraordinary situations in which the extant legal frame of social order loses its grip and can hold no longer, whereas a new frame, made to the measure of newly emerged conditions responsible for making the old frame useless, is still at the designing stage, has not yet been fully assembled or not strong enough to be put in its place.

I propose (following recent Keith Tester's suggestion[2]) to recognize the present-day planetary condition as a case of interregnum. Indeed, just as Gramsci postulated, 'the old is dying'. The old order founded until recently on a similarly 'triune' principle of territory, state and nation as the key to the planetary distribution of sovereignty, and on power wedded seemingly forever to the politics of the territorial nation state as its sole operating agency, is by now dying. Sovereignty is no longer glued to either of the elements of the triune principle and entities; at the utmost, it is tied to them but loosely and in portions much reduced in size and contents. The allegedly unbreakable marriage of power and politics is, on the other hand, ending in separation with a prospect of divorce.

Sovereignty is nowadays, so to speak, unanchored and free floating. Criteria of its allocation tend to be hotly contested, while the customary sequence of the principle of allocation and its application is in a great number of cases reversed (that is, that principle tends to be retrospectively articulated in the aftermath of the allocating decision, or deduced from the already accomplished state of affairs). Nation states find themselves sharing the conflict-ridden and quarrelsome company of actual, aspiring or pretending, but always pugnaciously competitive sovereign, subjects, with entities successfully evading the application of the heretofore binding triune principle of allocation, and all too often explicitly ignoring or stealthily sapping and impairing its designated objects. Ever rising number of competitors for sovereignty outgrow already, even if not singly then surely severally, the power of an average nation state (multinational financial, industrial and trade companies account now, according to John Gray,[3] 'for about a third of world output and two-thirds of world trade'). Sovereignty, that right to decide the laws as well as exceptions to their application, and the power to render both decisions binding and effective, is for any given territory and any given aspect of life-setting scattered between multiplicity of centres – and for that reason eminently questionable and open to contest; while no decision-making agency is able to plea full (that is unconstrained, indivisible and unshared) sovereignty, let alone to claim it credibly and effectively.

Uncertainty

Risk, says Ulrich Beck, the pioneer of its contemporary exploration and still its leading and most proficient theorist,[4] from the beginning of modernity 'amalgamates knowledge with non-knowing within the semantic horizon of probability'. 'The history of science dates the birth of the probability calculus, the first attempt to bring the unpredictable under control – developed in the correspondence between Pierre Fermat and Blaise Pascal – to the year 1651.' Since then, through the category of risk, 'the arrogant assumption of controllability', Beck adds, 'can increase in influence'.

With the benefit of retrospect, from the perspective of the admittedly liquidized sequel to the compulsively liquidizing yet solidity-obsessed early modernity, we may say that the category of risk was an attempt to reconcile the two pillars of modern consciousness – the awareness of contingency and randomness of the world on one hand, and the 'we can'– type confidence on the other. More exactly, the category of 'risk' was an attempt to salvage the second, despite the obtrusive, resented and feared company, from the first. The category of 'risk' promised that even if the natural setting as well as the human-made additions to that setting are bound to stop short from unconditional regularity and so away from the ideal of full predictability, humans may still come quite close to the condition of certainty through gathering and storing knowledge and flexing its practical, technological arm. The category of 'risk' did not promise foolproof security from dangers: but it promised the ability to *calculate their probability and likely volume* – and so, obliquely, the possibility of calculating and applying the optimal distribution of resources meant to render the intended undertakings effective and successful.

Even if not explicitly, the semantics of 'risk' needed to assume, axiomatically, a 'structured' ('structuring': manipulation and the resulting differentiation of probabilities), essentially rule-abiding environment: a universe in which the probabilities of events are predetermined, can be scrutinized, made known and assessed. But however far may the 'calculation of risk' stop from a flawless and infallible certainty, and thus from the prospects of pre-determining the future, its distance may seem small and insignificant in comparison with the unbridgeable categorical abyss separating 'semantic horizon of probability' (and so also the hoped-for risk calculation) from the premonition of uncertainty saturating and haunting contemporary liquid-modern consciousness. As John Gray pointed out already a dozen years ago,[5] 'the governments of sovereign states do not know in advance how markets will react ... National governments in the 1990s are flying blind'. Gray does not expect the future to usher into a markedly different condition; like in the past, we may expect 'a succession of contingencies, catastrophes and occasional lapses into peace and civilization'[6] – all of them, let me add, unexpected, unpredictable, and more often than not catching their victims as well as their beneficiaries unawares and unprepared...

It seems ever more likely that the discovery and announcement of the centrality of 'risk horizon' in modern mentality followed the eternal habit of the Owl of Minerva, known to spread its wings at the end of the day and just before the nightfall; or the yet more common proclivity of objects, as noted by Heidegger, to be transported from the state of 'hiding in the light', of staying immersed in the obscure condition of *zuhanden*, to the dazzling visibility of *vorhanden* no earlier than they go bust, fall out of routine or otherwise frustrate the (only half-conscious and tacit, as a rule) expectations; in other words, things become known thanks to their disappearance or shocking change. Indeed, we have become acutely conscious of the awesome role which the categories of 'risk', 'risk calculation' and 'risk taking' played in our modern history, only at the moment when the term 'risk' lost much of its former utility and called to be used (as Jacques Derrida would suggest) *sous rature*, having turned (to use Beck's own vocabulary) into a 'zombie concept'. When, in other words, the time has arrived to replace the concept of *Risikogesellschaft* with that of *Unsicherheitglobalschaft* ... our dangers differ from those which the category of 'risk' strove to have captured and brought to light by being unnamed before striking, unpredictable and incalculable. And the setting within which our dangers are born and from which they emerge is no longer framed by the *Gesellschaft* – unless the '*Gesellschaft*' is coterminous with the population of the planet.

Institutional disparity

I've already mentioned the progressive separation leaning uncomfortably close towards a divorce between power and politics – the two seemingly inseparable partners residing for the last two centuries, or believed and postulated to reside, inside the territorial nation state. That separation has resulted in the mismatch between institutions of power and those of politics. Power has evaporated from the level of nation state into the politics-free 'space of flows' (to borrow Manuel Castells' expression), leaving the politics ensconced as before in the previously shared abode, now degraded to the 'space of places'.

The growing volume of power that matters (that is, the power having if not the final say, then at least the major, and in the end decisive, influence on the setting of options open to the agents' choice) has already turned global; politics has remained however as local as before. Accordingly, the presently most relevant powers stay beyond the reach of extant political institutions, whereas the frame for maneouvre in the inner-state politics continues to shrink. The planetary state of affairs is now buffeted by ad hoc assemblies of discordant powers unconstrained by political control due to the increasing powerlessness of the extant political institutions. The latter are thereby forced to severely limit their ambitions and to 'hive off', 'outsource' or 'contract out' the growing number of functions traditionally entrusted to the governance of national governments to the non-political agencies. The emaciation of the political sphere (in its institutionalized orthodox meaning) is self-propelling, as the loss of relevance of the successive segments of national politics rebounds in the erosion of the citizens' interest in institutionalized politics, and in the widespread tendency to replacing it with the drive to experiment with 'free floating', electronically mediated quasi- or inchoate/incipient politics – eminent for its expeditiousness, but also for its ad hocness, short-termism, one-issuesness, fragility and staunch resistance, or perhaps even immunity, to institutionalization (all those qualities mutually dependent and reinforcing).

To sum up: facing the triune challenge, and finding an exit from the state of interregnum and chronic as well as unredeemable uncertainty, would require *the restoration of the commensurability of power and politics*. The present-day uncertainty being rooted in the global space, that task can be performed solely at the global level, and solely by (alas not as yet existing) global law-making, executive and juridical institutions. This challenge translates as the postulate to complement the heretofore almost wholly 'negative' globalization (that is, globalization of forces intrinsically hostile to institutionalized politics – as capitals, finances, commodity trade, information, criminality, drug-and-arms traffic etc.) by its 'positive' counterpart (as, for instance, globalization of political representation, law and jurisdiction) which has not yet started in earnest.

Notes

1. *Quaderni del carcere*; here quoted after Antonio Gramsci, *Selections from the Prison Notebooks*, ed. and trans. Quintin Hoare and Geoffrey Nowell-Smith, London: Lawrence & Wishart 1971, p. 276.
2. See Keith Tester, 'Pleasure, Reality, the Novel and Pathology', in *Journal of Anthropological Psychology*, no.21, 2009, pp. 23–6.
3. John Gray, *Gray's Anatomy: Selected Writings*, Allen Lane 2009, p. 231.
4. Ulrich Beck, *Weltrisikogesellshaft*, Suhrkamp 2007. Here quoted after Ciaran Cronin's translation *World at Risk*, Polity Press 2009, pp. 4–6.
5. *Gray's Anatomy*, p. 236.
6. *Gray's Anatomy*, p. 223.

References

Agamben, G. (2003), *Lo stato di eccezione*, trans. by K. Attell (2005), *The State of Exception*. Chicago: University of Chicago Press.

Beck, U. (2007), *Weltrisikogesellshaft*, trans. by C. Cronin (2009), *World at Risk*. Cambridge: Polity Press.

Gramsci, A. (1971), *Selections from the Prison Notebooks*, ed. and trans. Q. Hoare and G. Nowell-Smith. London: Lawrence & Wishart.

Gray, J. (2009), *Gray's Anatomy: Selected Writings*. London: Allen Lane.

Tester, K. (2009), 'Pleasure, Reality, the Novel and Pathology'. *Journal of Anthropological Psychology*, 21, 23–6.

Index